T0285029

REVENUE
OPERATIONS

STEPHEN G. DIORIO
CHRIS K. HUMMEL

REVENUE
OPERATIONS

A NEW WAY TO
ALIGN SALES & MARKETING,
MONETIZE DATA,
AND IGNITE GROWTH

WILEY

Published by John Wiley & Sons, Inc., Hoboken, New Jersey.
Published simultaneously in Canada.

For general information on our other products and services or for technical support, please contact our Customer Care Department within the United States at (800) 762-2974, outside the United States at (317) 572-3993 or fax (317) 572-4002.

Wiley also publishes its books in a variety of electronic formats. Some content that appears in print may not be available in electronic formats. For more information about Wiley products, visit our web site at www.wiley.com.

Library of Congress Cataloging-in-Publication Data:

Names: Diorio, Stephen G., author. | Hummel, Chris K., author.
Title: Revenue operations : a new way to align sales & marketing, monetize data, and ignite growth / Stephen G. Diorio, Chris K. Hummel.
Description: Hoboken, New Jersey : Wiley, [2022] | Includes bibliographical references and index.
Identifiers: LCCN 2021062097 (print) | LCCN 2021062098 (ebook) | ISBN 9781119871118 (cloth) | ISBN 9781119871132 (adobe pdf) | ISBN 9781119871125 (epub)
Subjects: LCSH: Revenue. | Selling.
Classification: LCC HJ2305 .D56 2022 (print) | LCC HJ2305 (ebook) | DDC 336.02—dc23/eng/20220118
LC record available at https://lccn.loc.gov/2021062097
LC ebook record available at https://lccn.loc.gov/2021062098

Cover Images: Courtesy of Chris K. Hummel; © koosen/Shutterstock; © Ollustrator/Getty Images
Cover Design: Wiley

SKY10032386_030422

Contents

ACKNOWLEDGMENTS ix
INTRODUCTION xi

Part I Revenue Operations, A System for Growth 1

1 Take Control of the Revenue Cycle 3
   Introducing Revenue Operations, a New Way to Create Sustainable, Scalable Growth 3
   The Financial Link Between Firm Value and Growth 7
   The Challenges of Growth in the Twenty-First Century: Customers, Disruptions, and Fragmentation 15
2 Create Value and Impact from Revenue Operations 27
   How Revenue Operations Creates Value 28
   The Change Management Hurdle 32

Part II The Management System to Align Your Revenue Teams 35

3 Understand Six Pillars of the Management System 37
   Commercial Leadership That Unifies Marketing, Sales, and Service 41
   Commercial Operations That Support All Growth-Related Functions 44
   Commercial Architecture That Maximizes the Return on Selling Assets 47
   Commercial Insights Built on Customer Engagement and Seller Activity Data 50
   Commercial Enablement Capabilities That Turn Your Technology into a "Force Multiplier" 54
   Commercial Practices That Maximize Return from Customer Data, Technology, Content, and Intellectual Property Assets 56
4 Lead a Modern Business That Aligns Marketing, Sales, and Service 61
   Growth Levers Across Executive Functions 61
   A New Generation of Growth Leader Emerges 67
5 Use One of Three Leadership Models: The Tsar, the Federation, and the Chief of Staff 73
   The Tsar: Putting a "CXO" in Charge of Revenue Teams 74
   The Federation: An Alliance Among Leadership Functions 77
   The Chief of Staff: A Revenue Operations "Rock Star" 83
   Case Study: Enhancing Value Across the Company at GHX 84

Part III An Operating System for Conecting Technology, Data, Processes, and Teams 87

6 **Assemble the Nine Building Blocks of Revenue Operations 89**
   What Does an Operating System for Business Look Like? **90**
   The Building Blocks of the Revenue Operating System **92**
   The Team That Connects the Most Dots Wins **94**

7 **Connect Your Data, Technology, and Channel Assets to Acquire More Customers 99**
   The Importance of Strategically Managing the Return on Commercial
       Assets **99**
   Building Block #1: Revenue Enablement – CRM, Content, and Learning
       Technologies That Support Selling **103**
   Building Block #2: Channel Optimization – Selling Channels That Maximize
       Effective and Efficient Interactions **110**
   Building Block #3: Customer-Facing Technology – The Owned Digital Selling
       Infrastructure That Manages Customer Touchpoints **123**

8 **Blend Data into Insights That Inform Selling Actions, Conversations, and Decisions in Real Time 131**
   Unlocking the Potential of Analytics to Ignite Growth **131**
   Building Block #4: Revenue Intelligence – Manage and Measure Financial
       Value **135**
   Building Block #5: Engagement Data Hub – Leverage Advanced Analytics
       to Connect Growth Assets to Value **143**
   Building Block #6: Customer Intelligence – Use Customer Data to Inform
       Decisions, Actions, and Conversations **147**

9 **Extract More Revenue and Margins from Your Teams and Resources 155**
   Building Block #7: Talent Development – Attract, Develop, and Retain
       Commercial Talent **157**
   Building Block #8: Revenue Optimization – Allocate People, Time, and Effort
       Against Opportunities **165**
   Building Block #9: Revenue Enhancement – Increase Revenue Yield
       with Better Packaging, Pricing, and Personalizing Offers **171**

10 **Tune the Revenue Operating System to Get Maximum Performance 177**
   Digitize Planning Processes to Improve Agility in Deploying Your
       Resources **179**
   Use Analytics to Make Better Predictions, Forecasts, and Investment
       Decisions **181**
   Adopt Advanced Modeling Techniques to Evaluate More Scenarios and Build
       Consensus **185**

The Power of Simulations to "War Game" Scenarios, Pressure Test Plans, and Building a Common Purpose   **189**

The Power of Models to Algorithmically Balance and Tune Your Revenue Engine   **191**

Part IV   How to Get Started and Drive Impact   193

11   Deliver Growth with Six Smart Actions   195

Deliver Growth with Smart Actions   **196**

Six Proven Smart Actions That Work   **197**

Get Better Visibility into the Revenue Cycle   **198**

Simplify the Selling Workflow   **200**

Share Marketing Insights with Frontline Sellers   **201**

Develop and Retain High-Performing Selling Talent   **204**

Make Selling Channels More Effective   **205**

Streamline and Personalize the Selling Content Supply Chain   **208**

12   Tailor Revenue Operations to Work for Your Business, Big or Small   211

How Revenue Operations Can Grow Revenues, Profits, and Value in *Your* Business   **211**

Transforming the Large Enterprise   **212**

Actions Enterprise Leaders Should Be Prioritizing   **213**

Achieving Hyper-Growth for Small Companies   **217**

Actions Hyper-Growth Leaders Should Be Prioritizing   **218**

13   Make the Business Case for Your Growth System, from Activity to Impact   223

Prioritize Actions That Will Generate Short- and Long-Term Value   **223**

A Financially Valid Framework for Connecting Smart Actions to Firm Value: The Revenue Value Chain   **226**

How to Apply the Financial Framework to Create Budget, Buy-In, and Action   **228**

14   Practical Tools to Take Control of Your Revenue Cycle   233

GLOSSARY   243

REFERENCES   255

INDEX   265

Acknowledgments

We are grateful to the many people who took the time to share their thoughts and experiences with us. So many people helped us along the way who have our heartfelt thanks, and that list inevitably goes far beyond the people listed here. The leading minds in the science of growth from business, academia, consulting, technology, and association worlds participated in and supported this work.

That starts with all the executives and CXOs who graciously provided such detailed insight, anecdotes, and stories. Your real-world experience is the backbone of Revenue Operations. This includes the ongoing advice and real-world perspective from our network of executives who have led Fortune 500 sales and marketing organizations, including: Toni-Clayton Hine (EY), David Edelman (Aetna), Peter Horst (Hershey), Denise Karkos (Sirius XM), Shannon LaPierre (Stanley), David Master (Janus Henderson), Mike Marcellin (Juniper Networks), Jaime Punishill (Lionbridge), Steve Shannon (Kia Motors), and Connie Weaver (The Equitable). A big "thank you" to the hundreds of other executives we spoke with who are out there fighting to add science to the art of growth. This book is anchored by research, lessons, and insights from leaders of Analytics@Wharton at the Wharton School of Business, including Professors Eric Bradlow, Kartik Hosanagar, Raghu Iyengar, Leonard Lodish, David Reibstein, and Abraham Wyner.

We loved learning from several leading academics in the science of growth over the last five years. We are grateful to receive insights, research, and education from Neil Bendle (Terry College of Business), Bobby Calder (Kellogg School of Business), Paul Farris (Darden School of Business), Dominique Hanssens (UCLA Anderson School of Business), Peter Howard (Questrom School of Business), Purush Papatla (Northwest Mutual Life Big Data Institute), Don Sexton (Columbia Business School), Dave Stewart (Loyola Marymount University), and Kimberly Whitler (Darden School of Business).

Our research would have been impossible without access to experts who have helped hundreds of businesses become more data driven, accountable, and productive, including Howard Brown, Cam Tipping, and Neil Hoyne. This also includes key friends like Ian Lowles, Bill Wohl, Rick Devine, Rob Halsey, and Anthony Johndrow and others who provided counsel on the ideas and models we built.

We drew heavily from the Marketing Accountability Standards Board (MASB), and in particular their leaders Frank Findley and Tony Pace, who are doing the hard work of proving the financial contribution of growth assets and investments.

We learned critical lessons on breaking silos, aligning revenue teams, and creating a common purpose across the organization from General Stanley McChrystal and Victor Bilgen of the McChrystal Group.

We also received generous perspective and advice from the leading analysts in the sales and marketing technology sphere, including Brent Adamson of the Gartner Group and Rich Eldh, the Founder of Sirius Decisions

This research leaned very heavily on the decades of experience from the leadership of Blue Ridge Partners, an elite go-to-market consultancy. We relied heavily on the experience, judgment, and research of Jim Corey, Carter Hinkley, Marten Leijon, Allen Merrill, Jim Quallen, Michael Smith, and Corey Torrence.

We received tremendous support and access to research and executives' perspectives from the leading associations and professional organizations in the field of growth, notably: Bob Liodice of the Association of National Advertisers, Bob Kelly of the Sales Management Association, and Earl Taylor of the Marketing Science Institute.

We are indebted to the team that sponsored and guided the production of this book, including Richard Narramore, our editor at John Wiley and Sons, and his crack editorial, production, and marketing team that kept us on task and on time, including Jessica Filippo, Deborah Schindlar, and Donna J. Weinson.

Researching a book takes a tremendous amount of analysis and digging. Heartfelt thanks to our research team that analyzed thousands of technology solutions, including Blake Brown, Robert Diorio, Jeff McKittrick, and Greg Munster.

We needed the painful and valuable contribution of our crack editing team, including Ingrid Wenzler, Adam Sirgony, and Matthew Schmitd, plus special contribution from my brilliant daughter Anna Diorio, who added elegance to our visuals and storytelling.

Of course, none of this could have happened without the personal support and encouragement of our families. They were strong enough to push us when challenges seemed insurmountable and were gracious enough to give us the space we needed when we hit our stride. We are blessed to have our spouses, Lyn and Tatiana, who provided the support, motivation, food, and "air cover" to make this book possible. Our children, Anna and Robert and Angelina, Dante, Chris Jr, and Arabella, should all take credit in this, too, for the inspiration they provide us every day.

Introduction

Growth is good. Really good.

Growth elevates short-term performance. Growth has a disproportionate effect on valuation. Growth – especially organic growth – generates intangible goodwill and positive momentum among customers, influencers, analysts, and employees.

Here's the challenge: organizations too often treat growth like a disconnected, functionally driven art form rather than the interdisciplinary, data-driven science it should be.

The core revenue-facing functions – Marketing, Sales, and Service – all operate in silos. Each function is trying to do its individual job and maximize the impact of its activities on customers and revenue. Managers optimize the parts – brand, demand generation, pipeline conversion, retention rates, etc. – while coordination between the three is episodic, temporary, and heavily influenced by the personalities involved. They allocate resources as a cascade along organizational lines using historical precedents as the primary guide.

Even when this approach works, managers generally celebrate only the fact that growth happened, since they usually cannot explain why. Teams assume that someone else will take responsibility for the whole. When cross-functional collaboration happens, it requires Herculean efforts to marshal the collective troops and achieve one-time, almost artisanal objectives.

Who is ultimately responsible for coordination of key growth assets and initiatives in the business? That often falls on one person: the CEO. Because no other c-level officer typically controls more than 40% of the identified 18 levers of growth, CEOs get dragged into the nitty-gritty of optimizing all variables that cross organizational boundaries. There are a lot of these. Organizations may be built around functions, but real-world opportunities and challenges ignore those artificial boundaries.

So, we have functional experts trying to manage an interdisciplinary, multifaceted problem. This gap between the importance of growth to firm value and the limited understanding of how to achieve it creates heated discussions in boardrooms, management meetings, and planning sessions everywhere. What are we all missing?

Today we lack a system for growth.

Such systems for the back office and supply chain have already been developed over decades. It's time that we brought similar discipline, rigor, and methodology to the process of expanding our revenues. The three teams involved work hard and do their best, but somehow things just aren't clicking. The front office needs standardization and repeatability, too.

To understand how a systems-based approach to growth might work, let's look at what's happening inside each of the revenue-centric functions. To start, here are some common problems all functions are faced with:

- The financial criteria for allocating growth resources, OPEX, and CapEx across these disparate functions differs wildly.
- Change is everywhere. Not only does change scare people, but it raises questions about whether the benefits of transformation are worth the pain.
- Real-world problems are interdependent and interdisciplinary. Regardless of what its org chart looks like, any business needs to manage the entire revenue cycle as an integrated whole before, during, and after the transaction.
- The digital selling infrastructure, including the customer experience and data it generates, has become one of the biggest growth assets, even if ownership is unclear.
- Investors, owners, and boards need more predictable and forward-looking forecasts.
- Consistency, repeatability, and automation could help ensure that good performance is sustainable over time and scalable.

Marketing: Increasing Ambiguity

Telling the company story, getting the offer in market, and orchestrating the customer experience. These are valuable activities that all contribute to demand generation and firm value. In a digital world where innovation, trust, and customer experience matter more, the perceived value of marketing activities has increased, yet budgets are shrinking, and the scope of the function is fluctuating.

A relatively recent invention of the twentieth century, the Chief Marketing Officer (CMO) role has changed dramatically over the course of its short span of existence by shifting from managing media and building brands and demand in the last century to curating the customer experience in digital channels and managing customer analytics in the modern era.

At its best, Marketing should be a commercial function that delivers significant, tangible impact on the business performance of a company, affecting both revenue and valuation. Whether you're the CMO, a brand manager, or a creative specialist, the role can be exhilarating, frustrating, intellectual, administrative, strategic, creative, scientific, powerless, and game-changing – usually all of these and often simultaneously. Transformation is happening, and many fronts are moving. Ambiguity is a marketer's constant companion. Why?

- **The skill sets in marketing are in flux.** Technology, data overload, market noise, and fluctuating channels combine with massive variation in budgets, metrics, decision rights, organizational structure and incentives to present existential challenges.
- **The marketing toolset has democratized.** Other departments and functions can now execute "marketing" activities on their own, blurring areas of collaboration.
- **The marketing mix has changed.** Digital marketing technology infrastructure and the people data analytics and content required to support them now command the bulk of marketing budgets. Also, the budget allocated on "owned marketing" – where the company controls the message 100% – now exceeds paid media.
- **Marketing doesn't fully control the digital channels needed to do their job.** Most customer engagement now happens in digital and contactless channels, but in most cases marketing does not own or manage the systems, data assets, and blueprint for these increasingly important systems.
- **We all lost control of the buyer's journey.** While the idea of a linear demand funnel is archaic, marketers can still influence the buyer's journey having an engagement model for wherever the customer wants to go.
- **Organizational "flashpoints" are increasing in breadth and depth.** The tussle over marketing's intersections with product, digital, sales, and service teams challenges management structures.
- **Every marketing organization has a customized, unique structure.** Collaboration with peers can suffer when the size, scope, activities, and mandate of every marketing organization fluctuate constantly. Culture evolves organizations that are as unique as a fingerprint.

Marketing leaders need to recognize that these ambiguities weigh on marketing personnel and their peers across the company. At its most impactful, marketing orchestrates – engaging with all other parts of the company, providing holistic views of the customer perspective, and amplifying the best of the organization to create a whole that is greater than the sum of the individual parts. Otherwise, like a decaying satellite, the marketing function will continue to appear quite sophisticated and even cool from the outside as it inexorably heads toward its own demise.

Sales: Rising Complexity

Sales teams are tasked with converting interested prospects into transacting customers, increasing revenue per account, and managing relationships to increase loyalty and trust. These activities exist at the center of any drive to expand revenues.

Sales is a powerful function. The skill sets of sales reps, account managers, and other sales personnel can vary widely, though, and often depend on the sales model, product sophistication, and buying cycle. Because sales manages the pipeline of business, it has unparalleled visibility of the upcoming revenue streams. It also represents the "last touch" before the transaction with the customer. Sales leaders leverage that control point to exercise authority in many areas beyond their official remit. The surety of that dominant position, however, is now starting to fade as sales confronts transformation in its own area.

- **Selling has become more capital intensive.** More buying happens within digital channels, and sales people rely on analytics and automation to engage customers with the speed and personalization they demand. Sales leaders now hold two responsibilities: managing both sellers (the people) and selling (the system).

- **Selling has become a complex team sport.** No single organization controls all of the revenue growth levers, so the ability to move information quickly between functions helps get marketing, sales, and service silos working as one revenue team with a single common purpose.

- **Selling teams are more distributed, digital, data driven, and dynamic.** The role of sales has evolved to rely more on digital channels and collaboration technologies and less on planes, trains, and automobiles over time. The recent pandemic has only accelerated the move to sell bigger and more complicated products through digital channels. It has also created a skill gap for sales leaders and people who did not grow up with the skills to be effective in this environment.

- **More business models create more revenue streams going through more channels.** New approaches like subscriptions open up alternative and derivative products that can be monetized more and more through owned digital infrastructure outside of and in parallel with any traditional sales channels.

- **We lost visibility of what the customer is doing.** The volume of data we now collect on customer interactions dwarfs what we've been using to analyze transactions, but the fragmentation of that engagement data actually creates gaps in visibility for the sales teams that frustrate their efforts for a 360-degree understanding of their customers.

- **The old-school "art of selling" is struggling against the new school analytics.** Like the battles in Major League Baseball between grizzled old scouts and the new crop of data-driven analysts, the utility of many historical traits once considered critical for performance in sales are now being questioned as the selling process becomes more engineered.

- **Selling now requires less human interaction to enhance relationships.** The increasing automation of customer engagement, when used effectively, should unburden sales people from many administrative or low-value activities. Sellers now need to balance the volume, content, and frequency of digital interactions with person-to-person outreach to find the optimal revenue yield.

Even where sales leaders recognize the value of other functions in driving more and/or bigger transactions, they struggle with a lack of access to full information on all the touchpoints with customers. Technology needs to be seen as more of an asset than a tool. At its peak value, sales can act as a true customer advocate, serving as the bridge between customer and company and using its performance-driven culture to push accountability across all functions to serve the customer's needs. If not, sales may find itself stranded as the king of an increasingly less relevant hill.

Service: Progressive Emergence

In the context we use for this book, service drives the customer's consumption of your product or service. This function covers activities like onboarding, activation, implementation, support, adoption, change orders, upgrades, maintenance, and many more. In most cases, these responsibilities are distributed across multiple organizations with many labels such as customer care or field service. Occasionally, the role is so important that a company will bundle many of these responsibilities into a branded, differentiated service offering like Apple's Genius Bar and BestBuy's Geek Squad.

"Service" isn't really one function but rather an amalgamation of roles from a variety of other organizations. This minimizes the institutional authority of service, even though the product consumption experience has become one of the most important factors in growing lifetime customer value. Cloud software companies do often have a function called "Customer Success" that handles much of the adoption process for complex offerings, and this function is starting to pop up in other industries that have complex implementation requirements.

The role of service has been elevated as it now commands a rising share of the customer interactions in the business, play a bigger role in revenue growth and relationship expansion, and have more direct control over the primary objectives of the business: namely, growing customer relations' lifetime value and net recurring revenue.

- **The "service" function doesn't exist as one entity.** The product consumption experience is rarely managed inside one internal organization but is rather fragmented across regional, product, sales, marketing, and other teams with little rhyme or reason.

- **Service rarely has a seat at the executive table.** Since service usually doesn't exist as a single organizational entity, it lacks institutional authority as a "constituency" and feels the absence of a c-level leader to advocate for and allocate resources to improving the customer ownership experience.

- **Driving product adoption has become more important to revenue expansion.** Customer loyalty is critical to revenue expansion. First, customers are more focused on time to value and want faster returns on their assets and investments, so they buy in smaller, bite-size, iterative chunks. Second, subscription models also simplify the customer's ability to cancel the service, so the selling of value never stops.

- **Subscription business models are becoming the norm.** Subscription models where the customer pays a scheduled usage fee per agreed-on period have become very popular. Such annuity revenue streams are very attractive and have penetrated many sectors as either rental- or performance-based fee models. How to transform one's portfolio into a subscription model is one of the core questions we hear from many companies.

- **The customer success function is moving beyond software as a service (SaaS) companies as people recognize its value add.** Cloud companies natively understand the value of the customer ownership experience and have been pioneers in setting up "customer success" teams that manage the onboarding, activation, and training of new customers. That concept of a customer success function has migrated into many other industrial and technology businesses as a best practice.

Service leaders come from many different backgrounds – often project management – and hold many different titles. Yet the access to customer intelligence in this "function" rivals and maybe even beats marketing's data sets. This is a new, emerging space on the org chart that is worth watching.

The three teams work hard and do their best, but somehow things just aren't clicking.

Stepping back into the CEO shoes, there are common observations from all the functions.

- Change is everywhere: Not only does change scare people, but it raises questions about whether the benefits of transformation are worth the pain.
- Real-world problems are interdependent and interdisciplinary: Regardless of what its org chart looks like, any business needs to manage the entire revenue cycle as an integrated whole before, during, and after the transaction.
- A systems-based approach is required: Consistency, repeatability, and automation help ensure that good performance is sustainable over time and scalable.

About Our Research

This book combines primary and proprietary research, a deep analysis of existing academic and corporate material in the field, consultations with world-class experts and thought leaders, and finally our own decades of personal experience as practitioners and analysts in the business world. As only teaming up an authority on go-to-market transformation and an operational executive can do, we argued over big-picture and minute details. In the end, we both agreed on what the real issue is and what needed to be done.

The foundation of the book is our primary research. This includes thousands of surveys with executives, managers, and performance professionals who manage growth in large and small businesses across many industries. When we reference our surveys, we will cite the actual survey and source document in a citation.

We also conducted in-depth interviews with over 110 growth leaders. These generally included the most senior executive responsible for growth in the business. In many cases it was the President, CEO, or Chief Operating Officer because that was the only individual who managed all the growth functions – marketing, sales, and service. In other cases, we met with executives that had been given an expanded remit to align revenue teams and resources around the customer. These executives had titles like Chief Growth Officer and Chief Revenue Officer. In some other cases we interviewed the functional leaders of marketing, sales, and services. Sometimes these executives insisted on being interviewed together because they regarded themselves as a team, not a manager. We will reference these interviews in statistics and direct quotes and will use the material for case studies about their challenges, best practices, and accomplishments.

In addition to this primary research, we made an exhaustive analysis of academic research and commercial research on the subject, which are also cited in the text. Our team comprehensively analyzed the most meaningful and relevant academic and commercial research on the science of growth. Here we were lucky enough to have the support of the leaders of the Marketing Sciences Institute, The Marketing Accountability Standards Board, The Sales Management Association, Analytics@Wharton, the Association of National Advertisers (ANA), and many associations and partners. These studies and academic papers are cited directly with links to the complete research reports and publications provided in the citations at the end of the book.

Finally, this research initiative drew heavily on the experiences and expertise of the world-class practitioners, academics, and experts of the Revenue Enablement Institute. These world-class experts include sales and marketing executives like Jeff McKittrick, Michael Smith, Greg Munster, Bruce Rogers, and David Edelman. They also include leading academics like Professor David Reibstein and Raghu Iyengar from the Wharton School of Business. We also were able to tap into decades of experience from experts in the science of growth including Cam Tipping, Bob Kelly, Corey Torrence, Bruce Rogers, Michael Smith, Doug Laney, and Howard Brown. All of these experts are quoted directly in the body of the book.

Our analysis of the commercial technology ecosystem was based on a comprehensive analysis of over 4,000 technologies that support sales and marketing over the past 18 months. Using the Revenue Operating System that you'll learn about in the book as a filter, we arrived at an initial list of the top 100 that we believe are transforming the commercial model and enabling the emergence of Revenue Operations, a system for growth. While this list is dynamic and will evolve over time, these initial 100 innovators are mentioned in context in the body of the book, and a full list is available on a website and research report listed in the citations.

Finally, it's important to mention that we, the authors, have obviously colored this analysis with our own background and experience. Thankfully, that experience includes senior leadership and c-level roles at growth businesses and innovators like Oracle, SAP, Schneider Electric, United Rentals, Siemens, GE, and Citigroup. Ideally, this personal history helped us synthesize our research with a more practical perspective and amplified the solutions we outline with conviction of people who have been there. We've sat in the board rooms and management meetings trying to push growth agendas. We've made the hard decisions on where and how much capital to invest in different initiatives. And most importantly, we've lived with the consequences of those decisions.

The Bottom Line

Executives and managers today are using outdated twentieth-century tools to govern and manage twenty-first-century businesses. These archaic twentieth-century management tools were built around a functional structure that sought a balance between the responsiveness of a strong local presence and the efficiency of centralized, global-scale operations. Today's reality is different, and personalized offerings delivered with the efficiency of global scale are expected. We're fighting a different battle between fragmentation and alignment. To connect the dots and layer in the science of growth, data, insight, and knowledge must be shared throughout the organization to provide them the EQ, the IQ, and the bias for actions that deliver results.

That's what this book is all about: Revenue Operations, a bold system to steadily drive growth in the twenty-first century. We'll take you through three core sections. Part I defines Revenue Operations and its impact. Part II articulates the key pillars that make up the management system and helps you decide which leadership model works best for you. Part III lays out the building blocks of the operating system for your business. Here we focus on improving the return on your technology, data, process, and team investments and on giving you a good sense of the priority capital investments you need to make. In Part IV we bring it all together with the concept of Smart Actions and provide you tools to best implement Revenue Operations for your own company.

This book will help owners, CEOs, and the heads of the marketing, sales, and service functions – the growth leaders that we will refer to as "CXOs." This work will also help revenue-centric employees on the front line take a more systemic approach to growing their business. Furthermore, the lessons and insights inside will help large enterprises and small companies looking to accelerate growth.

We sincerely hope you enjoy *Revenue Operations*.

REVENUE
OPERATIONS

PART I

Revenue Operations, A System for Growth

CHAPTER 1

Take Control of the Revenue Cycle

Introducing Revenue Operations, a New Way to Create Sustainable, Scalable Growth

Revenue growth – the increase in a company's sales over time – is the primary basis for creating business value. The more sustainable and scalable that growth is, the more valuable your business becomes. Despite this importance, the "science of growth" is not well understood. Most businesses approach growth as a disjointed, episodic activity.

Why? The core reason is that many business owners, CEOs, and leaders lack a practical and proven system for growing their business. Every other primary function in a business – from the procurement, manufacturing, and shipping of products to the management of financial and human resources – has an established system. Purchasing, manufacturing, HR, and finance leaders have spent decades standardizing and automating those systems. Despite that, few of the executives we spoke with could clearly describe any kind of connected approach, system, or model they use to generate the revenue and profit growth they forecast to their investors.

They gave us some pragmatic reasons for this. First, go-to-market processes have proven hard to manage, measure, and systematize because they are more "art" than science. Second, customers and markets change too often and too quickly to create stable, repeatable processes. Third, they lack the customer feedback data needed to anticipate customer needs, measure performance, and manage the channels, investments, and actions aimed at meeting those needs.

These arguments had some validity in the twentieth century. Not so today. A revolution in data analytics and the emergence of digital selling technology has given managers unprecedented visibility into and control over the full revenue cycle. Analytics improve measurement of customer engagement and account health. They also help to manage selling teams and predict sales pipeline performance.

Our conversations uncovered a more fundamental reason. Namely, growing a business is an interdisciplinary endeavor with many moving parts that don't reinforce one another:

- It's challenging to create a "go-to-market" approach that has dozens of functions to manage and many more disciplines to master – particularly when 80% of CEOs lack direct operating experience in most of these disciplines.
- It's hard to align customer-facing employees who work in segregated marketing, sales, and service organizations.
- It's difficult to connect technologies that are deployed in silos of automation.

In other words, it's impossible to deliver a superior customer experience when your revenue cycle consists of disconnected processes, policies, procedures, and machines.

No established commercial model exists to get these different pieces of the growth equation working together. Business leaders lack a management framework for coordinating their growth teams, functions, and disciplines. They lack an operating system for managing their growth assets, technologies, data, and processes.

Until these fundamental issues are addressed, efforts to accelerate or sustain profitable growth will be defeated.

The solution to this problem is clear. A new system for growth is urgently needed. One that aligns revenue teams with the infrastructure, operations, and processes that support them across the entire revenue cycle. One that generates more growth from the expensive data, technology, and channel assets that are the foundation of modern selling.

Our goal in writing this book is to better define that system for growth. We call it Revenue Operations.

Revenue Operations represents a bold new commercial model for the twenty-first century. Its goal is to create sustainable and scalable business growth. As we define it, Revenue Operations comprises two components. First, the management system – our EQ – aligns the people in your revenue teams. Second, the operating system – our IQ – combines technology, processes, and data assets to generate more sustainable and scalable growth. Revenue Operations weaves these two together to grow revenues, profits, and firm value.

Throughout this book we strive to articulate what Revenue Operations is and to show you examples of how to make it work. This book will help every person who cares about growth – from the business owner to customer-facing employees on the front line – to take steps that can generate more consistent and scalable growth. Because everyone has a role in the growth equation.

The book will specifically help business owners, CEOs, and leaders of the marketing, sales, and service functions to better allocate growth resources, make more profitable growth investments, take intelligent risks, and create a common purpose across revenue teams. It provides operations leaders and performance improvement professionals a blueprint for knitting together the systems, processes, and operations that support revenue growth in ways that generate scalable and consistent growth. This work will also help customer-facing employees on the front line to better leverage the systems, information, and tools available to them and work together as one revenue team.

In addition, this book provides a career road map for any professional who seeks to advance their career and ultimately lead a business. It provides essential knowledge to any student who seeks a career in any growth discipline – marketing, sales, service, operations, or analytics.

Furthermore, the lessons and insights inside will help any business, from large enterprises to small companies, looking to accelerate growth.

How Is Revenue Operations a System for Growth?

At the simplest level, a system is a combination of *things* that *work together* as a *united whole* to achieve a *common purpose*.

Exactly what those "things" are, how they "work together," the nature of the "united whole," and the "common purpose" all define how any given system works. Systems can do many things: run a computer; educate people; manufacture and distribute products; and even manage money.

The "things" within a system can include a wide variety of ingredients – ranging from people and organizations to technology, devices, or software code to principles and procedures. The way they combine to "work together" can take the form of a machine (a computer), operation (manufacturing), a network (railroad), or a biologic process (digestion).

Businesses have established systems for most of their operations including: manufacturing, distribution, supply chain management, and finance. These systems are generally well organized, automated, managed, and measured in a mature organization.

The conversation changes when you start to talk about a system for growth. In most businesses, fragmented groups of customer-facing employees, silos of automation, and a lot of disconnected processes, policies, and technologies don't work well together. Nor do they work with a common purpose toward a common goal. There is no system to generate consistent, scalable, and profitable growth.

Revenue Operations changes that. It introduces new elements and shows how they work together. It offers a systems-based approach to growth across the entire revenue cycle: awareness, demand, purchase, and consumption (see Figure 1.1). Companies of all sizes and profiles can use it without having to rip the current business apart.

(continued)

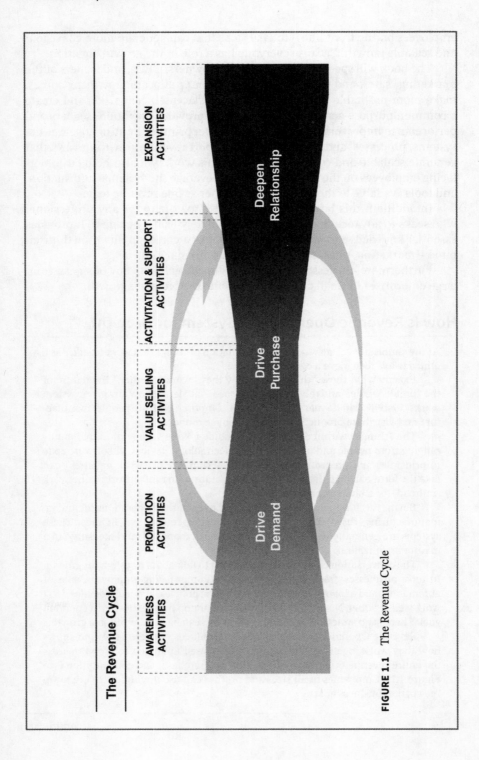

FIGURE 1.1 The Revenue Cycle

The Financial Link Between Firm Value and Growth

An organization's ability to grow revenues has become more and more tied to firm value than at any time in our business lives.

This relationship can be seen in the high valuations awarded to businesses that can deliver predictable, scalable, and profitable growth. For example, the marketplace values firms with hyper growth (e.g. annual growth over 40%) and predictable revenues (e.g. Net Annual Recurring Revenues of over 100%) disproportionately. That is why a hyper-growth business like HubSpot commands price/earnings ratios in the hundreds while not yet showing a profit. It also explains why a SaaS business like Salesforce.com with double-digit growth rates and recurring revenue streams will have a valuation in excess of 60 times its earnings – more than triple the S&P 500 average.[60]

An analysis of total shareholder return of the S&P 500 over a 20-year span found that 58% of value creation is attributed to organic growth (see Figure 1.2). That means the ability to grow revenues organically has created more firm value than all efforts to reduce costs, expand earnings multiples, and improve free cash flow combined.[101]

The capital markets value growth. Generating more consistent growth is a formula every business can use to create value. Private investors need growth to justify the historically high prices they are paying for businesses. Growth attracts talented employees, and buyers view it as a sign of innovation, quality, and validation.

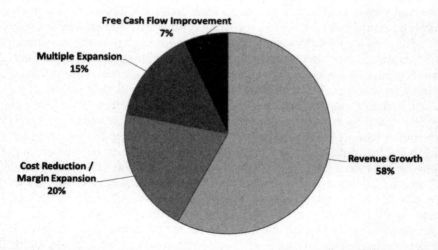

FIGURE 1.2   Sources of Shareholder Return. *Source: Data from E. Olsen, F. Plaschke, D. Stelter, "Threading the Needle: Value Creation in a Low Growth Economy"*

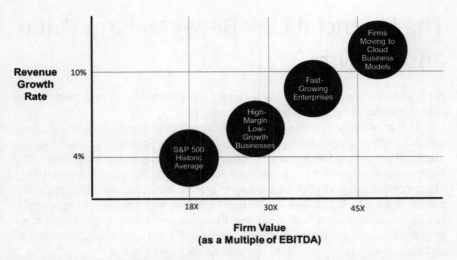

FIGURE 1.3 Revenue Growth and Firm Value. *Source: Blue Ridge Partners, Pitchbook, Blossom Street Ventures, Dow Jones, Refinitive 2021, Inc 500, NASDAQ*

Today the average business in the S&P 500 is growing top-line revenues at 4% annually and is valued at 18 times earnings (see Figure 1.3).[52] A firm that grows at double that pace is worth almost twice as much. Businesses that master scalable growth – by creating systems for growing revenues faster than the resources needed to generate those revenues – are even more valuable. For example, businesses that grow fast and have recurring revenue models are worth over forty times their profits. Companies like Google, Salesforce.com, or Citrix that have mastered the ability to scale revenues faster than costs are even more valuable. This is why so many private equity firms push their portfolio companies to move to a recurring revenue or cloud business model.

The growing importance of Revenue Operations as a practical way to create firm value is not lost on the owners and boards of high-growth businesses. Average purchase price multiples are at historic highs. PE investors are now paying in excess of 13 times EBITDA (which are **e**arnings **b**efore **i**nterest, **t**axes, **d**epreciation, and **a**mortization) to acquire businesses. Most PE firms believe financial engineering will not be enough to justify such high prices and deliver their LPs the returns they expect.[60] As evidence of this, over two-thirds (68.1%) of private equity firms are pushing their portfolio companies to grow at faster than 10% a year[58] to justify the price premiums they have paid.[59] Several private equity firms like Rockbridge Growth Equity, Morgan Stanley Private Equity, Tengram Partners, and Vista Equity Partners have created a growth culture, operating model, and infrastructure to support accelerated growth at scale across their portfolio. These growth-oriented investors have created centers of excellence in demand generation, call centers, and digital marketing channels. For example, Rockbridge is the private equity (PE) arm of the Quicken Loans group. They have been able to leverage their highly sophisticated marketing capability and focus on customer experiences that Quicken Loans used to become the #1 mortgage provider and launch Rocket Mortgage as a major brand across the other firms in the portfolio. Jim Howland, an Operating Partner at Morgan Stanley Private Equity, sees the role of the private equity investor evolving from pure financial engineering toward enabling faster revenue growth in the last few years. "What you do with an asset is as or more important as getting that asset at the right price," reports Howland. "The reality is that if you want to attract good deals and make a return in today's PE world, you need to have a plan for how you will add value over the entire ownership period and build it into the price you pay for the asset. And a big part of that value plan is built around marketing and growth capabilities."[103]

Investment banker Ben Howe, CEO of AGC Partners, reinforces reports that Private Equity owners are increasingly creating value using a "buy, grow, and build" model of governance and enablement. "The top tech buyout funds including Vista, Thoma Bravo, and Insight are relentless in their programmatic efforts to build organically and apply operational best practices to enhance organic growth via ongoing technology, go-to-market initiatives and product improvements across the organization" reports Howe. "Stories like Vista taking Marketo private for $1.8 billion with ample leverage, growing it at 66% and then selling it to Adobe for $4.8 billion generating a multi-billion dollar return in just 2 years tends to get LP's attention."[103]

Unfortunately, many people still perceive growth as a form of "art" and fail to understand the science of growth. These people often see business functions through a very narrow lens: marketing is a creative discipline with little or no connection to financial outcomes; selling is about personal relationships, not method; and superstar sellers are treated as kings and queens – despite being hard to manage and even harder to replicate.

Also, executives cannot agree on the causal chain of events that leads to revenue growth and future cash flow, the keys that underlie firm value. This leaves executives without a financially valid way to make growth bets, weigh trade-offs, and optimally allocate resources across growth alternatives. It also makes it difficult to build a business case and management consensus on the capabilities that can create the greatest value to the firm. For example, most business leaders pay lip service to the notion of being data driven, digital, agile, and customer focused as a basis for competitive advantage. They understand these things are strategically important, but in most cases, they don't have a basis for evaluating these strategic value drivers and lack a tangible set of corporate initiatives to exploit them in the marketplace. Academic research proves, however, that these are the primary causal factors that determine the financial value of the enterprise.

Corporate executives struggle with the long-term growth formula. They can rarely agree on the big questions underlying their growth strategy such as the measurement, value, and importance of growth assets. "With all the focus on advanced analytics and data-driven marketing, not much progress has been made on understanding the fundamental math of growth in a business," reports Professor Dominique Hanssens of the UCLA Anderson School of Management and author of the book *Long-Term Impact of Marketing*. "In my experience, executive teams that make the big growth bets often lack consensus and alignment on fundamentals like the true cost of customer acquisition, the right balance of customer acquisition relative to customer retention, and the financial contribution of the brand to the business."[104]

Real-World Problems Cross Organizational Boundaries

Growing a business is an interdisciplinary endeavor. A team sport. Any "go-to-market" strategy has dozens of functions to manage and many more disciplines to master. These functions include traditional growth disciplines like marketing, sales, and customer service. They also include brand management, product development, and the "4Ps" of pricing, promotion, product packaging, and placement. New disciplines like sales enablement, customer analytics, earned media management, and content management have emerged as these budgets have grown to command 15% or more of business-to-business (B2B) growth budgets.

There are job descriptions for all of these individual disciplines. There are millions of experienced managers and experts in these functional disciplines. Universities offer master's degrees and PhDs in most of these disciplines. Individually.

Organic growth requires all these disciplines to work together in unison toward a common end – consistent, profitable, and scalable growth. There is no curriculum for that. Few CEOs have direct experience in these disciplines. Less than 20% of CEOs have direct experience in sales. Few marketers become CEOs.

This is the underlying reason why few managers have been able to master the science of growth. "The root cause of this problem is that historically academic and business institutions have taught and managed the science of growth as a set of individual disciplines – branding, product management, marketing and analytics," says Professor David Reibstein of the Wharton School of Business. "But the real-world problem of growing a business is interdisciplinary in nature. We as teachers need to do a better job of creating skills, structures, and leaders who can manage, coordinate, and align all these disciplines coherently around the customer. Being the captain that coordinates and leads all those functions in a business is a very big job. But an essential one."

Academic and commercial research overwhelmingly supports the concepts that growth is a "team sport" and that there is a causal relationship between organizational competence in analytics, marketing, information sharing, agility, and cross-functional collaboration with enterprise value. This research shows that a 10% increase in organizational competence will drive on average a 5.5% increase in stock price.[7] An analysis of 380 CMOs by Forbes found that organizations investing in data-driven measurement processes, competencies and systems were achieving significantly higher levels of marketing effectiveness and business outcomes – achieving 5% better returns on marketing investments and more than 7% higher levels of growth performance.[105] The analysis revealed that these high-performing marketers – who were exceeding growth goals by over 25% – were significantly more data-driven in their approach to measuring, optimizing, and reallocating their offline and online sales and marketing investments.

The Role of Insight in Value Creation

Investments in customer insights and organizational agility do create firm value. How fast and effectively an organization analyzes, leverages, and shares information and customer data can increase tactical marketing returns but also generate long-term enterprise value.[63] Academic research has proven there is a significant relationship between how fast your organization shares data and customer insights across revenue teams and share price.[8] A comprehensive analysis of 114 academic research studies by the Marketing Science Institute (MSI) has demonstrated that the ability of an organization to generate, disseminate, and respond to market intelligence – called Organizational Knowledge Sharing – has a quantifiable positive effect on firm value and financial performance in terms of profits, sales, and market share.[6]

Managers need to recognize and prioritize the importance of sharing knowledge across the business. Modern selling systems produce customer data that allows revenue teams to identify trigger events that signal buying intent, flag inquiries from important influencers within accounts, and make decisions about next best actions based on past customer behavior. The window of time an organization has to act on that data is small, however – and is gated by customer time, attention, and expectations for response. This makes hastening data and decisions about an opportunity from the source (e.g. a website, an algorithm in marketing) to a customer-facing employee who can act on it (e.g. a relationship manager or customer service rep) a critical value driver.

Similarly, customer relationships, go-to-market effectiveness, organizational information sharing, customer experience, and the quality of products, people, and innovations have all been empirically proven to drive increases in firm value by academics.[6]

In particular, the push to focus the organization on customer lifetime value as the primary objective of the revenue team has a financial basis. Customer equity is a significant driver of share price. According to academic research, the value elasticity of customer equity is 0.72.[8] This means a 10% increase in the value of customer assets will drive a 7.2% increase in stock price because higher levels of customer satisfaction, trust, and online service innovations enhance long-term margins, sales growth, and enterprise value. Hence, lifetime value is being redefined as an economic model in a digitally driven economy. This is evidenced by the ability of businesses like Airbnb ($125B in firm value with no profits at the time of printing) and the GHX Global Healthcare Exchange to convert digitally enabled consumer and business networks into valuable assets.[108,60]

For example, Rockbridge pushes its portfolio companies to deploy advanced analytics and direct marketing competencies pioneered by another Rockbridge company, Quicken Loans, to accelerate revenues, profits, and firm value. One Rockbridge portfolio business that provides online postgraduate education, North Central University, was able to borrow demand generation practices developed by Quicken Loans to grow their enrolled student population from 5,000 to 9,000 over their six years of ownership. This led to rapid growth in revenues (from $31M to $114M) and EBITDA (from $6M to $29M) and a highly successful exit.[103]

Intangible Assets as the Foundation for Growth

Any business can also unlock more growth and value by improving the return on their revenue-generating commercial assets – by which we mean your customer data, digital technology, digital channel infrastructure, and customer relationship equity. These assets make up most of the growth investment mix in B2B organizations, according to an analysis by the Marketing Accountability Standards Board.[1] (See Figure 1.4) They also make up a significant portion of your firm's balance sheet. Most CEOs could generate more revenue and profits from these commercial growth assets if they only treated them like financial assets. Which is what they are.

The problem is these business assets that support growth as inherently "intangible" whereas factories, inventory materials, and trucks are tangible. This makes growth assets difficult to value, hard to manage, and difficult to build.

That's a problem managers must solve if they want to grow a business in the twenty-first century. Fast. The capital stock of the economy has changed, and managers need to change with it. Although the economy might have

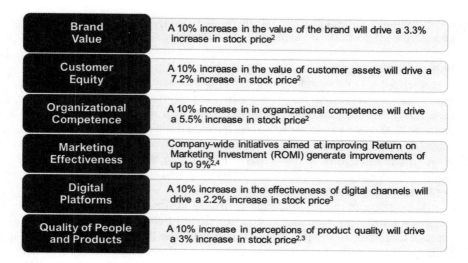

FIGURE 1.4   The Commercial Processes That Create Firm Value. *Source: 1) Brand Value as a Percentage of Marketing Capitalization. Applying the Brand Investment and Valuation Model. Analysis of Meier, Findley, Stewart. Marketing Accountability Standards Board. 2017; 2) Marketing's Impact on Firm Value: Generalizations from a Meta Analysis, AMA, Alexander Edeling and Marc Fischer, Journal of Marketing Research 2016; 3) Empirical Generalizations About Marketing Impact, Hanssens, Marketing Science Institute; 4) the Marketing Accountability Standards Board CIR Initiative, 2018.*

been built upon railroad tracks, canals, and factories in the past – today it is driven by intellectual property, software code, learning data sets, digital customer experiences, design, branding, and process know-how. Investment in "intangibles" exceeds investments in hard assets. They also explain over 80% of changes in firm value today. Far more (three times more) than they did in 1950, according to Jonathan Haskel and Stian Westlake in their book *Capitalism Without Capital*.[135]

For example, growth assets like brand preference, customer loyalty, and perceptions of innovation are valuable because they make customers choose your product more and pay higher prices to buy it. That is certainly the case for Apple, which values its brand at more than $250 billion at the time of publication.[108] But these business assets are hard to describe. They cannot be found on a financial ledger. There is no proven formula for creating, growing, protecting, and monetizing them. That's why most CEOs find it so difficult to fund smart long-term growth investments in many areas and don't understand how their marketing budgets create financial returns.

Growing a business involves managing a variety of commercial growth assets. Brand assets have traditionally been among the biggest growth assets. As buying has become more digital, data driven, and capital intensive over the last 30 years, an entire set of new assets have become critical cogs in the growth engine: customer data, advanced analytics, digital selling channels, and a growing portfolio of sales and marketing technologies.

The executives running marketing, sales, and service are the often unwitting caretakers of what may be their company's most valuable asset: its customer data. For example, customer data assets in the airline industry – which include revenue management, frequent flyer, and customer engagement databases – can account for 100% or more of an airline's profitability and value. Still, they do not show up on any balance sheet or management report. These databases are regarded as "intangibles" just like R&D, "process know-how," and brand equity. Accountants don't measure, report, or manage these as closely as such physical assets as inventory or real estate, even though they are far larger and more strategic.

As evidence of this, both United Airlines and American Airlines recently secured multibillion-dollar loans by collateralizing their MileagePlus and AAdvantage customer loyalty programs, respectively. The third-party appraisals of their data suggest that they are worth two to three times more than the market value of the companies themselves. United's customer data was valued at $20 billion, while its market cap at the time was about $9 billion.[62] Similarly, American's data was valued at a minimum of $19.5 billion and up to a jaw-dropping $31.5 billion, whereas its own market cap was hovering at less than $8 billion.[160] Unfortunately, most CEOs, CXOs, CIOs and their CFO counterparts don't put a financial value on their customer data because nobody is responsible for the assets and accounting regulations, and insurers say they don't have to, according to Doug Laney, author of the book *Infonomics*.

Unfortunately, most businesses don't curate, connect, manage, or monetize these growth assets very well. So for the majority of businesses, their largest business assets are underperforming.

Customer engagement data like this has become a key strategic asset in every business because it creates the foundation of future growth, profitability, and competitive advantage. This data grows firm value by optimizing pricing, conversion, account priorities, and the allocation of growth resources in every business. Managers must recognize, measure, and manage them as a real asset – including insisting on a financially viable return on asset (ROA).

The rising importance of intangible assets as the foundation for growth and firm value is a big change. Managers and accountants are very comfortable managing, measuring, and extracting value from tangible assets. Tangible assets are physical; they include cash, inventory, vehicles, equipment, machines, buildings, and investments. In 1975 these tangible assets made up over 80% of the value of a firm.[56]

It's not 1975 anymore. As the economy moved into the information age over the last half century, intangible assets have emerged as the leading asset class. Intangible assets do not exist in physical form. They include things like accounts receivable, prepaid expenses, patents, and goodwill. Increasingly, they are made up of assets like brands, customer equity, and customer data. These assets sound ethereal but have real financial value. A number of academic and industry research studies have documented that, when properly measured and accounted for, these intangible assets represent in excess of 80% of the value of a business.[7,55,56,57] The ability of revenue teams to deploy these assets to grow future revenues and profits by building customer preference, conversion, loyalty, and usage while commanding price premiums are the primary drivers of firm value. As evidence of this, over two-thirds (68.1%) of Private Equity firms are pushing their portfolio companies to grow at faster than 10% a year to justify the price premiums they have paid.[58]

This ambiguity and lack of stewardship applies to all the large and valuable growth assets in the business. In particular this applies to large capital investments in the sales and marketing technology portfolio and what we call the owned digital channel infrastructure (websites, digital marketing, mobile apps, and e-commerce). These are displacing paid media in the growth investment mix and have become essential to competitive differentiation in B2B selling.

The Challenges of Growth in the Twenty-First Century: Customers, Disruptions, and Fragmentation

Several factors have changed how we generate revenue growth in the past 30 years. Customer expectations have shifted as buyers have become more digital, better informed, and impatient. Traditional selling processes have been disrupted to become more capital intensive as more buying activity happens within the digital channel infrastructure and as sales personnel rely on analytics and automation to deliver against customers' demands. These challenges are being amplified by the growing appetite of owners, investors, and CEOs to replace episodic sales transactions and fragmented teams with reliable recurring revenues and aligned organizations (see Figure 1.5).

Here are some of the forces and megatrends that have changed the basis for generating revenue growth over the past 30 years:

- **Changing buyer behavior has elevated the customer experience and made it the primary goal.** Business-to-business buying behavior has passed the tipping point where "new school" digital buying behavior becomes pervasive and forces organizations to adapt traditional selling models to meet customer expectations for faster cadence, complete answers, digital channel engagement, and relevant content. It's well known that digitally enabled customers armed with better information are pushing sellers to deliver a superior customer experience in the

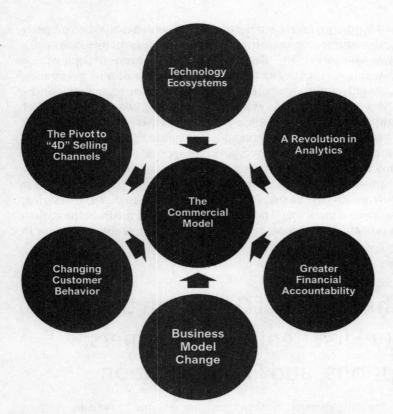

FIGURE 1.5   The Megatrends That Changed the Growth Formula

"moments that matter" across the entire revenue cycle. As buyers become more digital and demanding, those moments will ultimately become the only way to differentiate your business. Customers want more relevant information and complete answers faster. Recent research shows most buyers don't even want to talk to humans if they don't have to.

For decades, research and collaboration, and increasingly trans-actions have migrated to digital channels. Over 80% of customers now prefer to communicate via text, mobile, and online chat in service inter-actions according to the Salesforce.com "State of Service" report.[21] These changes in buyer behavior were accelerated by the impact that the recent pandemic had on customer engagement – which doubled the percentage of sales that occur in digital channels, according to research by the Duke Fuqua School of Business.[4]

Changing buyer demographics are also playing a big role in this change. About 10,000 baby boomers turn 65 every day, according to

Forbes.[39] Millennial buyers, on the other hand, were raised on Google search and digital channels and expect to do all or most of their buying 100% online; 83% of millennial B2B buyers expect e-commerce to keep them more informed about product choices than ever before.[40] Most (55%) of millennial B2B customers today would prefer to buy a complex solution without engaging a sales rep at all, according to Gartner.[17]

And when they do ask questions, they want fast and complete answers. "Today, half of the working population was born after 1977," says Jaime Punishill, CMO of Lionbridge. "That's important because the only information paradigm they've known is defined by Google – which is fundamentally an ask-response paradigm. They don't want to sort through big menus or wait for answers. They simply want to ask the question using Google, or voice search, or a human if need be."[33] This is forcing sellers to fundamentally shift the way content and websites are organized from a manual classification scheme to more data-driven response management paradigms based on how buyers search and ask questions. To adapt, sales enablement teams are shifting to a response management paradigm that uses AI to track and anticipate the questions customers ask and make it faster to provide a contextual answer by a sales rep, service rep, chatbot, or a voice-activated device.

But if the experience is bad, it can be fatal. Almost 60% would stop doing business with a B2B vendor based solely on a mobile experience that's difficult to use.[40] This has elevated the customer experience to the primary goal in selling. This primacy of the customer experience puts pressure on managers to better manage the end-to-end commercial process rather than a few parts or stages of it. Managers struggle to coordinate revenue teams, management systems, metrics, and platforms into a more unified customer experience. It puts a premium on systems and procedures and processes that improve speed and agility, as well as personalize customer experience and connect channels.

- **The speed and cadence of business is faster.** The cadence of customer communications has accelerated as conversations have moved from face-to-face to digital channels. There is less time to rest and regroup between calls. Sales velocity has become so fast that revenue teams and the executives who direct them require real-time customer intelligence and selling guidance. The managers and operations professionals we surveyed rated visibility of customers, seller effectiveness, account health, and pipeline health as the four top drivers of the performance of "4D" (distributed, diverse, digital, and dynamic) revenue teams.

- **Selling has become more capital intensive.** The executives we spoke to told us the key to leading a revenue team in the twenty-first century is more about managing selling systems and less about managing salespeople. As selling has become more digital, it has also become more capital intensive. The capital and operating components of the growth investment mix have both changed significantly in the past 30 years. For example, the commercial technology portfolio – or the sales and marketing technology stack – has grown to represent a large component of growth investment mix and sales and marketing operations overhead. Worldwide spending on customer experience (CX) and relationship management (CRM) software grew 15.6% last year as 81% of marketers say they will compete completely on the basis of CX, according to Gartner.[16] The Duke CMO Survey reports marketers are now investing more money in Customer Relationship Management than they are in Branding.[4] In all, the average enterprise now has invested in over 20 selling tools.[36] Smaller cloud-based businesses use over 30 on average to support selling.[26]

For the first time, as mass media declines in reach and privacy concerns make third-party media more untenable, at most firms more of the operating budget is being spent on "owned" digital channel infrastructure than on "paid" media (digital or otherwise).[161] As a by-product, businesses are investing over 10% of their marketing budgets on advanced analytics to find ways to monetize the valuable customer engagement, seller activity, and product telemetry data this digital selling infrastructure creates. These commercial systems need to be managed more like capital equipment than discretionary expenses if they are going to generate real revenue yields. All of this puts pressure on managers to rationalize, streamline, connect, and monetize the growth technology portfolio to generate greater financial returns from these assets and to better enable scalable and predictable growth. "Connecting the dots" across the increasingly complex and expensive technology ecosystems that support revenue has become a basis for competitive advantage.

- **Selling is more data driven.** A revolution in advanced sales analytics and Artificial Intelligence (AI) – fueled by rich new customer engagement, seller activity data, product usage data sources, and increased investment in analytics – is changing the way companies grow and create value. Advances in AI and a growing portfolio of AI-enabled selling tools are making data-driven selling possible. The benefits of this are faster information flow, better allocation of selling resources, and more visibility into pipeline, account, and opportunity potential. Advanced analytics are helping managers improve the performance of every aspect of the go-to-market system. Such tools will be the primary drivers of growth, competitive advantage, and value creation in the next 25 years. These changes amount to a Copernican revolution in selling, where every action and activity is centered around customer data.

- **The pivot to 4D selling has changed the economics and the architecture of selling.** The massive and continued shift to remote work, hybrid work, and work-from-anywhere practices by both buyers and sellers has made digital, data-driven, dynamic, and dispersed selling teams a primary channel to market. This has changed the economics of field sales by shifting dollars from travel and real estate to more scalable training and technology investments. It has also significantly altered long-standing assumptions about sales force emphasis, roles, workloads, selling costs, and the mix, nature, and cadence of engagement needed to convert prospects into customers. This has every organization rethinking geographic-based territory definitions, quota assignments based on face-to-face calling patterns, and labor-intensive coverage models. Readjusting the "architecture" of your commercial model to reflect these new dynamics can reduce selling costs and improve seller performance significantly with no additional investment.

- **Managing customer lifetime value has become a primary focus as businesses chase recurring revenues.** A business with recurring revenues is worth more than one that must sell their offerings to their customers one at a time repeatedly. So it's no surprise that most boards (53%) are pushing their CEOs to repackage their products and services as subscription pricing models, usage-based models, or cloud-based offerings, according to a report by CFO Magazine.[50] Almost every business (90%) that sells "on-premises" technology, equipment, or software is moving to a cloud model, according to Gartner.[17] Any business that can pull it off – including industrial firms like Honeywell, automotive firms like Audi, and infrastructure like Flexential – is trying to move to recurring revenues. Moving from selling products to selling subscriptions and SaaS solutions requires significant changes to the way you "go to market." It shifts the focus of selling from hunting for new customers to building more loyal customers and expanding relationships with them. It has increased the importance of growing customer equity and lifetime value as a driver of firm value. It has also forced organizations that engage customers – sales, marketing, customer experience, and support services – to find ways to work together collectively as one revenue team.

- **Growth has become a team sport.** There are 18 strategic levers that grow revenues, profits, and firm value, according to academic research compiled by the Marketing Accountability Standards Board.[7] These growth levers reside in different parts of your organization. They include the ability of IT to move information quickly, the ability of service teams to build customer equity, and the ability to deliver a superior digital channel experience. They also include the effectiveness of sales and marketing channels, the engagement of customer-facing employees, and the perceptions of innovation that your product team creates in the marketplace. No single organization or leader controls all 18 of these growth levers. Our analysis shows they are distributed across sales, marketing, customers success, product management, and sometimes information technology. When we add it up, none of these traditional job functions controlled more than a quarter of the levers of growth. And critical new pieces of the growth equation – such as customer analytics and managing digital channels – are being fought over by these executives. As a result, teamwork across functions has become fundamental to managing revenue growth. This is forcing managers to develop operating models, incentives, and platforms that help get marketing, sales, and service silos working as one revenue team with a single common purpose.

- **A growing focus on financial accountability has made it more difficult to fund smart growth investments.** Growth leaders – CMOs, CROs, and Chief Commercial Officers – are under growing pressure to prove the contribution of growth investments and assets to financial performance. This is a good thing. You can't manage what you cannot measure. Demanding to know the financial contribution of every growth action and investment to the business is essential to generating profitable growth. This focus on increased financial accountability is fundamentally changing how commercial resources and assets are allocated, organized, funded, measured, and deployed. But there's a problem. The way most organizations measure and calculate the performance of their growth investments is flawed. Simple revenue attribution measures favor short-term actions. Smart investments that connect sales to marketing and span budgets are hard to justify. Valuable capital investments like building the type of digital selling infrastructure that has made Amazon preferred by most shoppers don't fit into operating budgets. They also take too long to pay off for impatient CFOs. This has created unintended consequences that actually do more harm than good. For example, a bad short-term investment with clear attribution will take precedence over a profitable long-term investment that requires many different organizations to work together. This flawed approach to financial accountability has made it next to impossible for managers to create a business case for investments that can create scalable growth, such as one-to-one personalization, real-time coaching, response management, and account-based marketing.

The Challenge of Managing 4D Selling Systems

How Digitally Enabled, Data-Driven, Dynamic, and Geographically Dispersed Revenue Teams Are Changing the Way We Manage Selling Systems

A massive shift to work at home, hybrid work, and work from anywhere policies will act as a tipping point for sales transformation and dramatically alter the sales and marketing mix. Budgets are shifting to digital, data-driven, and measurable channels that accelerate the digital transformation of sales.

Remote selling is the "new normal" as the coronavirus pandemic forced over 4 billion consumers, customers, employees, and salespeople to work, sell, and buy from home. The dramatic displacement of revenue teams forced businesses to accelerate their transformation to a more digital selling model to adapt to remote selling and a new buying reality. Lost in the rush to enable remote selling is the fact that virtual selling channels offer growth-oriented companies the potential to transform sales performance and accelerate growth.

The shift to remote buying is having an even bigger impact as customers demand a faster cadence, more complete answers, and more personalized content at every stage of the customer journey – regardless of whether they are talking to an account rep, Business Development Reps (BDRs) product specialist, or customer service manager. "As B2B buyers' increasingly use digital channels and information in the customer journey, it is reshaping how B2B sellers engage with them," according to Brent Adamson, Distinguished VP, Advisory, Gartner.[160] "This presents a huge challenge to B2B revenue teams because our research tells us that most B2B buyers under the age of forty would prefer not to talk to sales and service reps at all, if it were possible, and they can see no difference in the digital buying experiences of most of the companies they try to buy from. It is going to be mission critical for reps to make the most of the moments that matter during this buying cycle." That means building buyer empathy, sharing more compelling content, asking smarter questions, and having conversations that build trust, communicate the financial value of their solutions, and reveal the nuanced differences between their competitors.

The shift has changed the ways businesses sell to customers by:

1. **Redefining field selling economics and capital investment.** From a sales perspective, sales executives have embraced the notion of remote selling channels as a way to sell more for less. Virtual reps offer the selling capabilities of a high-end field sales rep, but the visibility, coverage, cadence, and productivity of digital and direct channels. The shift to virtual channels will have a dramatic impact on the economics of selling in terms of big reductions in sales travel and real estate overhead and the increased use of technology and skills to leverage and enable sales reps in digital channels.

(continued)

2. **Creating a burning platform to redefine the customer experience.** From a marketing standpoint, over 80% of CMOs viewed the pandemic as a big opportunity to redefine the customer experience in digital and virtual channels and change the way they reach and engage customers (e.g. media mix, channels). This sentiment is being reflected in the way CMOs are reallocating their budgets in the recession. For example, 81% of traditional businesses are increasing investment in digital technologies to improve market coverage and client engagement.[5]

3. **Accelerating the adoption of advanced communications, enablement, and visualization technologies.** From a technology perspective, the pressure to adapt to this new buying reality is accelerating the adoption of existing but grossly underutilized technologies that offer the potential to multiply seller performance. These include algorithmic selling, sales enablement, 5G communications, direct-to-consumer (DTC) channels, and even augmented reality. Properly designed and equipped, virtual selling channels can dramatically improve the coverage, control, and cost-effectiveness of sales channels while offering buyers the speed of response and experiences they demand.

4. **Creating massive new customer and seller activity data sets.** "An explosion of sales engagement data has become available to analytics teams in the past 24 months," according to Len Ferrington, a managing director of Summit Partners. "This data is coming from first party systems, email, calendars, third party sources, recorded sales conversations (via Zoom, Teams or transcripts) and contactless selling platforms (like text and chatbots)."[159] The number of recorded sales calls has gone up thirty-fold since the start of the pandemic.

5. **Elevating the importance of analyzing customer sentiment and nonverbal cues.** "The rapid growth of virtual selling is creating a need for AI and analytics that inform the EQ of selling to help sales reps better understand customer sentiment, response, and relationships in the absence of face-to-face conversations," reports Professor Iyengar of Wharton.[18] "Businesses will need to find ways to use new data from customer transcription and digital engagement platforms like Zoom, Teams, or Cisco Webex to understand customer emotions and all the non-verbal elements of selling."

6. **Forcing sales operations to improve visibility and transparency.** Gaining access to real-time commercial insights into account health, opportunity potential, seller, and pipeline performance are now essential to managing the performance of digital, displaced, diverse, and dynamic revenue teams. These are regarded as the top drivers of remote sales productivity by sales managers and performance professionals.

Twentieth-Century Tools Are Obsolete

Each of these forces has disrupted the status quo in marketing, sales, and service. Collectively, they have made traditional notions of how to manage growth obsolete. Managers try to manage revenue teams and activities that require a far more advanced and digital selling model than the systems and tools developed in the twentieth century can provide.

Using an obsolete commercial model to manage a modern selling infrastructure has significant business consequences. Managing marketing, sales, and service resources as discreet functions is an obstacle to teamwork. The idea of a linear and orderly customer journey – with advertising in the front, selling in the middle, and service and support at the end – just doesn't work because customers don't buy that way. The historic reliance on traditional print advertising and in-person human selling as pillars of investment for marketing and sales sharply declines as the number of customers who prefer to buy online increases.

The financial consequences of relying on a commercial model developed in the last century to manage a twenty-first-century selling system are large. For example, the uncoordinated management of the revenue cycle leads to revenue and margin leaking through "air gaps" and handoffs in the customer journey. Organizations can leak 10 percentage points of EBITDA by failing to follow up on opportunities, enforce pricing discipline, respond to buying signals, or recognize when their biggest customers are about to take their business elsewhere. The disconnected management of the valuable technology, customer data, and digital infrastructure assets that support revenue growth can create even bigger financial problems. If you don't have a coherent system for curating and connecting these growth assets into selling outcomes that create value, the result will be lower than acceptable financial returns on investment and higher selling costs. Managing these valuable growth assets in many different functional silos is the equivalent of racing an expensive car that is not firing on all cylinders and needs a wheel alignment and a tune-up.

Management models have always evolved with economic and market change. The corporation, conglomerate, and business unit structures pioneered by Rockefeller (Standard Oil), Reginald Jones (GE), and Alfred Sloan (GM) respectively were all structural innovations that served their purpose in their time.

The world has changed. Dramatically. The "stovepipe" organization consisting of separate marketing, sales, and service functions is a vestige of another era when media had greater reach, digital channels were just emerging, and customers followed an orderly and linear buying process. The CMO role emerged when business could get by with a big media budget to drive demand. The VP of sales when managing "sellers" was the key to closing deals. Roles like sales operations, customer insights, and digital marketing did not even exist 25 years ago because digital technology and customer data were not key components of the selling formula.

The Role of Leadership

The leadership model for managing growth resources is similarly outdated. For example, the Chief Marketing Officer (CMO) is a job function built on big brands and TV budgets that has only existed for a few short decades. But those big media budgets have been in decline for years. This has left many CMOs struggling to find a seat at the table as their core budgets have eroded and fighting from being pigeonholed at the very front of the revenue cycle. Large field sales organizations like the famous IBM "Blue Suits" have been around a long time, but the selling function has evolved by adding multiple tele, social, web, and even contactless channels that don't necessarily need a field sales force to serve customers. Service has become far more elevated and strategic as product adoption and experience have become central to customer relationship building, revenue expansion, and customer lifetime value.

Today, the functional distinctions between marketing, sales, and service exist more because of cultural and operational inertia rather than market reality. The silos that manage these roles have become a political and operational necessity to keep the machine running and cash flowing in the short term. These silos have also led to dysfunction and waste. Strategically, the hard functional structures represent a boat anchor that holds back revenue growth in the twenty-first century by impeding horizontal information flow across the revenue cycle and by making it difficult to deploy technology as a force multiplier at scale.

The twentieth century commercial structure is collapsing under the twin pressures of changing customer behavior and shifting business models. "Organizations are going to need to rewire their commercial engines to better reflect the new buying reality where customers are channel agnostic and buyer behavior is non-linear," reports Brent Adamson, distinguished Vice President in Gartner's Sales practice.[129] "It's a big job. It's going to involve reworking the legacy commercial infrastructure, and creating new roles, processes and metrics."

Thus, it's no surprise that the vast majority of the senior growth leaders we spoke to in writing this book were taking steps to better align sales, marketing, and service teams to sustain and accelerate growth in light of the forces and dynamics we have outlined here. Over 90% were actively redefining the way they "architect" their selling channels and consolidating the operations that support selling and oversee customer data and technology assets. Eighty-five percent of CXOs were actively reconfiguring the roles and assignments on their revenue teams to improve the customer experience and grow the value of their accounts. And over 9,000 businesses have introduced "CXO" roles with a broader span of control over sales and marketing and a CEO mandate to lead commercial operations, systems, and processes across the entire business. Most significantly, almost all of them – regardless of company size or the industry they serve – believe fixing the commercial model in light of these market trends requires leadership from the CEO to succeed and a common purpose across every employee that touches the customer.

The CXOs we spoke with are also working to find ways to generate greater returns from the systems and technologies that support selling. Most feel their investments in CRM, digital selling infrastructure, sales enablement technology, and data assets are underperforming. They feel like they are working increasingly harder at the care and feeding of these tools, rather than the tools working harder for them. They feel their sales and marketing technology stacks have become too complicated. The majority tell us they are trying to rationalize, simplify, and better connect the many solutions in their sales technology stack. They are doing this to simplify the seller workflow, better leverage customer insights in day-to-day selling, and turn technology into a "force multiplier" to help them sell more for less.

This shift in focus is happening across businesses large and small, in every industry. Executives we spoke with agree on the importance of Revenue Operations, even if – until now – there has been little clarity on an exact definition or description of this still-maturing discipline. This book intends to change that.

CHAPTER 2

Create Value and Impact from Revenue Operations

We interviewed and surveyed hundreds of business leaders as part of our primary research. These included CEOs and leaders of growth-oriented businesses, large and small. In parallel we worked with the leading academics across the disciplines of marketing, sales, and service, as well as experts in areas like customer analytics, sales enablement, and marketing technology. Our research team evaluated thousands of technologies that are shaping and enabling the modern commercial model.

Most of the executives we interviewed described Revenue Operations as a system (or commercial model) for generating more sustainable and scalable business growth. The majority told us that Revenue Operations is an important if not existential business issue. They also felt that it was not fully developed as a business discipline, but it must become one because everyone will need to understand better if they expect to do their jobs, get promoted, and succeed in the marketplace.

Given the volume of online discussion traffic on the topic, it seems like many organizations are trying to deploy Revenue Operations in some form. Current research estimates project high levels of Revenue Operations adoption, particularly among smaller business-to-business organizations and technology businesses shifting to a recurring revenue model. For example, Forrester Research suggests over two-thirds of organizations have already deployed Revenue Operations – either partially (58%) or fully (an additional 10–15%).[127] Gartner forecasts that most (75%) of the highest-growth firms will have deployed a Revenue Operations model by 2025.[17]

In a broad sense, these forecasts are correct. The executives we spoke with intuitively know they must do more to align their teams and get technology working harder for them. Most of them are actively taking steps toward unifying marketing, sales, and service.

The leaders we interviewed regard these projections with a mix of urgency, optimism, and caution. These rosy adoption forecasts create a certain fear of missing out on a big thing and an urgency to act faster, yet they also give pragmatic executives pause. While most agree that Revenue Operations is a good thing, nobody has really defined it nor demonstrated the depth of how it can work. The how needs to be laid out, too.

More than 90% of the senior executives we spoke with were not clear on what exactly a Revenue Operations model meant – or how exactly it will pay off. This includes CEOs and executives who were actively taking steps toward unifying sales, marketing, and service.

This is not surprising because describing Revenue Operations is similar to describing great art, writing, or music. Most people agree it's a good thing, and everybody seems to know it when they see it, but few people can describe it. This ambiguity has allowed at least a dozen inconsistent definitions of Revenue Operations to flourish in written research, analyst reports, and software marketing and ads. These definitions range from a methodology to a strategy to a job function, software platform, and organization design.

This wide variety of inconsistent descriptions creates a practical challenge. If nobody agrees or understands what Revenue Operations is, how can analysts empirically prove that companies that deploy Revenue Operations are growing sales and creating value? If you cannot quantify the value of Revenue Operations, how can you size and sequence the effort involved in achieving it?

This book will lay out a clear execution blueprint for the individuals who must make Revenue Operations a reality – from the CEO to operations professionals to sellers engaging customers on the front line.

How Revenue Operations Creates Value

An analysis of the third-party research published by analysts, consultants, and solutions providers strongly supports the shift to Revenue Operations as a way to improve rep productivity and firm financial performance. Aligning the revenue-centric teams in marketing, sales, and service around a common workflow will also produce value in a variety of meaningful ways, including:

- Productivity: Rep productivity gains ranging from 10 to 60%.[26,47]
- Growth: Revenue growth improvements ranging from 19 to 31%.[45,17,26]

- Ramp: The speed of ramping new sales reps of up to 60%.[23]
- Churn: Reducing rep churn by 75% or more.[23]
- Quota attainment: Improvements in quota attainment.
- Value: Increases in firm value range of up to 71%.[21]

Although these are generalized business impact estimates, their collective bias suggests a significant and tangible opportunity. Until now, the current body of research has not yet answered the questions being asked by the senior executives our team interviewed. So far, research has failed to clearly define *what* a Revenue Operations model is, *how* those gains are being realized, and *who* specifically is achieving them. Broadly forecasting the financial benefits of moving to a Revenue Operations model in the absence of a concise definition of Revenue Operations or a few years of operating data is tricky.

This book tries to fill that gap by providing CEOs, CXOs, and their teams greater clarity on the financial contribution the Revenue Operations model makes to the business. We lay this contribution out in terms of the ability to meet or exceed top-line revenues targets while improving profits and growing firm value.

By working with hundreds of growth leaders and leading academics in the "science of growth," we and the rest of the faculty of the Revenue Enablement Institute were able to isolate the specific financial, operational, and management levers that CXOs need to pull to realize measurable benefits and put in place key leading and lagging indicators on what is going to be a multiyear transformation. According to the CXOs we interviewed, it is possible to achieve immediate financial gains and demonstrable signs of progress from taking specific and measured actions:

1. **Eliminate revenue leakage across the revenue cycle** by eliminating the handoffs and "air gaps" in the prospect-to-cash cycle to revenue and margin leakage with a single point of management of the customer journey across the enterprise. This revenue, margin, and price leakage can cost your company up to 5% of realized profits (EBITDA) on business you should already have, but fail to realize because of missed handoffs, lack of follow-up, and improper pricing. If you are a $100 million company, that translates to losses from $1 million to $5 million annually. Add in the opportunity cost of missing signals from new buyers, alerts from angry customers, and opportunities to expand accounts, and the impact is far bigger.

2. **Enable scalable technologies that multiply your efforts** by redeploying operations and analytics resources to create scalable and consistent growth including one-to-one personalization at scale, real-time training at scale, dynamic pricing, data-driven sales resource allocation, and account-based marketing. For example, using algorithms to enforce pricing discipline and dynamically match price to market demand can add

10 points of profit to your bottom line with no incremental resources or investment. A 1% increase in effective price with no commensurate volume loss will add 10% to your bottom-line profits, according to Professors Jagmohan Ragu and John Zhang at the Wharton School of Business.[102]

3. **Foster teamwork** by doubling the engagement, speed, and productivity of revenue teams by adjusting the way they architect and systematize their selling systems, so they can grow faster while reducing the associated cost of sales. "Organizations that have automated workflow processes are seeing efficiency gains of two to three times when compared to counterparts using manual or spreadsheet-driven processes," according to Michael Smith, a Managing Director of Blue Ridge Partners, who has helped over 300 B2B organizations unlock more growth from existing selling assets in the last decade.

4. **Improve the return on technology assets** by rationalizing the technology stack to reduce waste and sunset stranded or nonperforming assets. This will improve seller experience and adoption. Redeploying operations resources will streamline the administration of data, technology, and content. As we've discussed, these growth assets are expensive, valuable, and generate a significant portion of the financial value of your firm. In most firms they are underutilized and poorly managed. Putting these assets to work in ways that directly support scalable growth – such as better allocating resources and informing selling actions that yield higher prices, bigger deals, and better conversion rates – creates significant financial impact. For example, business-to-business selling organizations can get 50% higher engagement, speed of response and productivity from their sales reps at lower costs by incorporating virtual selling channels into their commercial model," according to Michael Smith.

5. **Use data to optimize selling and resource allocation** by generating more and better insights from customer engagement and seller activity assets. Any business can better focus their selling time, resources, priorities, and the way they treat customers to make more money. The emergence of digital channels and advanced analytics offer tremendous potential to improve the performance of selling teams and channels. Businesses can realize these efficiencies by sharpening segmentation, focusing account priorities, shifting engagement to digital channels, and fine-tuning the emphasis and priorities of their sellers. We call the optimization of all these selling system design variables "the commercial architecture." A properly designed and optimized commercial architecture that aligns selling roles, effort, and engagement with the right customers can contribute 5–10 points of profit contribution to the bottom line in the short term.

6. **Reallocate sales overhead** from real estate and travel to more scalable investments in training and enablement. The average organization spends over $10,000 a year on "selling overhead" on a per rep basis. Up until the mass adoption of work-at-home and work-from-anywhere policies, most of this overhead was associated with real estate, travel, and market development funds to take clients out to dinner. Very little – less than a third – was spent on scalable investments in training and technology to enable sellers. Replacing some or all of this overhead with technologies and training offers the potential to double visibility, speed, productivity, and engagement while still yielding a net reduction in cost of sell. Eighty-one percent of growth leaders surveyed by Wharton are actively optimizing that mix by increasing investment in digital technologies to improve market coverage and client engagement, while cutting travel and selling overhead budget to generate much higher sales at much lower costs.[5]

7. **Improve the economics of field selling** by improving the speed of ramping sales reps, raising the overall level of readiness and skill across the entire revenue team, and reducing churn to retain top talent that performs at a high level. A 5% increase in sales rep attrition across your sales team can increase selling costs 4–6% and reduce total revenue attainment by 2–3% overall.[137] For low-growth and low-margin companies, 10 points of salesforce attrition can wipe out revenue plans and margins if nobody picks up the slack. For instance, the difference between a 5% sales rep attrition rate and one of 25% means that your overall cost to sell increases by more than 50% and your revenue drops by 20%.

Eight Ways Revenue Operations Creates Financial Value

1. **Monetize commercial assets.** Putting your customer data, digital technology, and channel infrastructure assets to work in ways that create value – informing selling decisions, optimizing resource allocation, supporting higher prices, and better conversion rates – can grow revenues, profits, and firm value.

2. **Manage the economics of selling.** Simplifying the seller experience improves the economics of selling by streamlining and better supporting the day-to-day seller workflow. A less complex selling workflow will help you develop and retain talent, reduce selling costs, and improve the adoption of technology tools.

3. **Differentiate the customer experience.** Optimizing your commercial processes, portfolio of offerings, revenue team incentives, and enabling investments with a focus on differentiating the customer experience are

(continued)

fundamental to selling in a market where most buyers don't see a material difference between companies they buy from.

4. **Enable scalable growth technologies.** More centralized management and stewardship of enterprise data, technology, and content assets are essential to executing programs that multiply the efforts of every member of the revenue team, such as: one-to-one personalization, real-time coaching, response management, and account-based marketing capabilities.

5. **Support recurring revenues.** Creating a common purpose across the revenue team to grow customer lifetime value is essential to selling in a subscription, SaaS, and recurring revenue model.

6. **Improve visibility into selling performance.** Gaining access to real-time insights into account health, opportunity potential, and seller and pipeline performance is now essential to managing the performance of digital, displaced, diverse, and dynamic revenue teams.

7. **Motivate team selling.** All of the customer-facing employees across the sales, marketing, and customer-support teams need to be managed, measured, and incentivized as one revenue team focused on executing the corporate growth agenda and growing customer lifetime value.

8. **Turn technology assets into force multipliers.** Modern revenue teams have evolved to operate similar to an army that relies more on agile logistics and operational support infrastructure than individual heroics to be successful. One in four members of the revenue team are now in operations and enablement roles.

The Change Management Hurdle

A top concern among the executives we interviewed was whether the gains to be had are worth the pain. Will the growth and profits that result from deploying Revenue Operations justify the pain from organizational change and management time and attention?

The answer is yes. Deploying Revenue Operations will help your organization generate more growth, more consistently, and at lower cost. In fact, collectively and on paper, these economics suggest that current estimates of the impact Revenue Operations can have on firm value and financial performance are relatively low compared to what is achievable.

Moving to a Revenue Operations model may not be easy for many, yet the performance gains will make it worth the effort. The financial and business benefits of moving to a Revenue Operations model are clearly worth the pain of the change involved, especially by executing and stacking a series of small, incremental steps to achieve larger goals. Those improvements can also be sustained and scaled over time through rigorous, incremental process improvements.

Even greater gains await those who seek radical process improvement or full commercial transformation. Leaders from firms like Avaya, Konica Minolta, and Juniper Networks who have been willing to take on the political, cultural, and change management involved have successfully turned years of declining revenue into rapid growth. Growth leaders from hyper-growth firms like insightsoftware and Rev.com are also using these principles to scale their growth a hundredfold.

In the next chapter we will outline the discrete steps these organizations are taking to better align their revenue teams, operations, systems, and processes and to grow faster and at lower cost. At the end of this book (in the Appendix) we will provide tools you can use to systematically identify the three or four steps your organization can take today with the greatest short-term financial impact.

In the next section, we will detail the business practices underlying the Management System for Revenue Operations and provide examples of three leadership models you can choose from to deploy in your organization. We will rigorously discuss six specific pillars that span the people, process, and technology of revenue growth. These pillars provide executives and managers with a road map for aligning their revenue teams, commercial operations, automation, and processes to accelerate revenue growth and expand customer lifetime value.

PART II

The Management System to Align Your Revenue Teams

CHAPTER 3

Understand Six Pillars of the Management System

In Part I, we learned that Revenue Operations represents a bold new commercial model for the twenty-first century to create sustainable and scalable business growth. It has two components: a management system for aligning the people in your revenue teams, and an operating system for combining and connecting the technology, channels, processes, and data in your business to generate more consistent and scalable growth.

In next few chapters, we focus on the first component, the management system for Revenue Operations. We'll lay out six specific pillars related to the people, process, and technology of revenue growth and go into the detail behind each one (see Figure 3.1). We'll also look at some core leadership principles. And we will then present three alternatives on how to structure leadership of your revenue teams and the commercial operations that support them.

What does it mean to have a management system that aligns marketing, sales, and service to generate more consistent, scalable growth? The answer breaks down into six specific pillars for managing the people, process, and technology of revenue growth: commercial leadership, commercial architecture, commercial insights, commercial asset management, commercial enablement, and commercial operations.

1. **Commercial Leadership that unifies marketing, sales, and service:** Top-down leadership models to empower and endorse the transformation of the commercial model to unify sales, marketing, and service into one revenue team and become more accountable, data-driven, and customer focused.

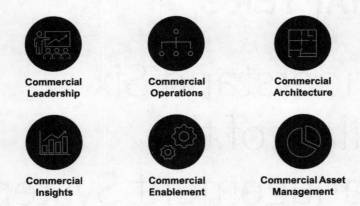

Commercial
Leadership

Commercial
Operations

Commercial
Architecture

Commercial
Insights

Commercial
Enablement

Commercial Asset
Management

FIGURE 3.1 The Six Pillars of a Management System for Revenue Operations

2. **Commercial Operations that consolidate and support all growth-related functions:** Ways you can reconfigure the operations that support growth to provide end-to-end coherent management of all sellers, customer-facing assets, enabling investments, and the customer journey.

3. **Commercial Architecture that maximizes the return on selling assets:** More systematic and data-driven ways you can design and optimize the many variables in the commercial architecture – from targeting and segmentation to selling channel design and incentives – to maximize return on selling assets in terms of speed, visibility, productivity, and engagement at a lower cost to sell.

4. **Commercial Insights that are built upon customer engagement and seller activity data:** The ways you can turn your customer engagement and seller activity data into commercial insights that create value and inform decisions, actions, and conversations at the key points of leverage in the revenue lifecycle.

5. **Commercial Enablement that turns your technology into a "force multiplier":** Smart ways you can deploy scalable enablement technologies that multiply the effect of your salespeople to generate more profitable revenue growth with fewer resources.

6. **Commercial Asset Management that leverages best practices for managing data, technology, content, and intellectual property assets:** The strategic management of the data, technology, content, and "selling IP" assets to maximize their utilization, impact, and contribution to revenue and profit growth outcomes.

These six pillars can be detailed even further. Our research identified 18 discrete steps that best-in-class, leading organizations are taking to better align commercial revenue teams, operations, data, and processes and to grow faster at lower cost. Individually, these actions can be piloted, sequenced, and measured to create economically viable, bite-size steps that move your organization through a transformation in ways that are politically, practically, and financially achievable. Collectively, these steps can yield transformational results.

Not every action will be equally important to every business. For example, the managers in slow-growth industries can generate higher valuations by focusing their revenue teams around a more precise set of high-opportunity clients, creating a culture of continuous improvement in the commercial process, and eliminating price, margin, and revenue leakage along their customer journeys. Faster-growing cloud companies can create exponential growth with high levels of net recurring revenues by unifying commercial operations, revenue teams, and assets around a single customer journey and by enabling ABM, personalization, guidance, and coaching in real time.

Here are some examples of how different organizations take different paths to build their management systems:

- CEOs in slow-growth industries can generate higher business valuations. You can create more value in several ways. One is by focusing your revenue teams around a more precise set of high-opportunity clients. Another is to create a culture of continuous improvement in the commercial process. Large and slow-growing businesses will also benefit greatly from redesigning their commercial architectures to improve the speed, engagement, and performance of their revenue teams. A fourth way to squeeze more growth out of your revenue team is by better managing the commercial process across the business. This involves assigning an individual accountable for finding ways to eliminate price, margin, and revenue leakage along your revenue lifecycle – which extends from awareness generation to account-building activities. For example, by establishing a single point of management across the entire revenue lifecycle it is possible to quickly eliminate the handoffs and "air gaps" in the prospect-to-cash cycle (a process that spans marketing prospecting and extends through purchase and payment). This will limit revenue and margin leakage.

- Executives leading large, complex enterprises can become more "agile." This will allow their teams to pivot more quickly to pursue emerging market opportunities and adapt to change. Some of the ways you can become more agile involve breaking down functional silos and using prescriptive commercial insights to improve the speed, engagement, and productivity of your selling teams. For example, you can likely unlock growth opportunities within your customer base quickly by using predictive insights to better focus account priorities based on potential, propensity to buy, and coverage difficulty. Managers trying to become nimbler in this way are demanding higher returns on their data, technology, and content assets. They are inventorying and evaluating the effectiveness of their growth technology portfolio, customer data, and content assets to identify ways to reduce overhead and increase speed. Most large companies will find immediate opportunities to rationalize the technology portfolio to eliminate waste, redundancy, or nonperforming assets. Once your portfolio of selling tools is pruned, you can create more value by connecting the elements of your selling systems to simplify and streamline the seller experience.

- Organizations undergoing business model transformation are trying to shift their selling approach from selling offerings like spare parts or "on-premises" software licenses one at time, to subscription-based services, or software as a service (SaaS), or "anything" as a service. Recurring revenue streams like these are more predictable and profitable. But they also require a different selling approach. If this is what your business is trying to do, you can accelerate the shift to a recurring revenue model by aligning sales, marketing, and customer teams around a common purpose of generating customer lifetime value and a superior customer experience.

- Hyper-growth cloud companies can create exponential growth in several ways. One is to unify their commercial operations (e.g. marketing operations, sales operations, advanced analytics, or training and development) and revenue teams (including success and service agents and marketing development, business development, account development reps) around a single customer journey. Another is to focus your enablement teams (like sales enablement, sales engineering, Revenue Operations) on finding ways to use technology as a force multiplier. These are company-wide programs that enable what we call "scalable" technology programs. These are systems that help you sell more without adding staff or budget. Examples of programs that can multiply the efforts and budgets include tools that help sellers personalize offers and proposals automatically. Managers often call this one-to-one personalization at scale because one machine helps hundreds of sellers personalize faster and better. Account-Based Marketing (ABM) programs are another "scalable" technology because it connects signals from marketing to account teams to help them develop accounts better. This allows your entire digital marketing and media budget to directly support frontline sellers. Using AI to provide real-time selling guidance can help sales managers to monitor, support, and coach many sellers at the most teachable moments. This is much more efficient than slogging through ride-alongs and coaching sessions in non-selling situations. This can multiply the efforts of managers, a very scarce resource. We will explain these smart and scalable actions in chapter 11 in more detail.

Later in the book we will provide a maturity assessment and financial framework to help you to systematically identify the current state of your capabilities, what actions you can take to get better, and what the financial impact of such actions would likely be.

Commercial Leadership That Unifies Marketing, Sales, and Service

Commercial transformation starts at the top because it requires change management and a commitment to culture change and teamwork. Moving to a Revenue Operations model requires top-down leadership, from the CEO on down. It takes leadership to empower managers and endorse the transformation of the commercial model because those things are risky, and managers are risk averse. Ultimately, only the CEO or chief operating officer can unify sales, marketing, and service into one revenue team because that is the only manager to whom these functions report.

In conjunction with the move to Revenue Operations, a new generation of growth leader has emerged, reporting to the CEO. This leader must have the span of control and remit to get sales, marketing, and service teams working together. They must have the skills, acumen, and credibility to push all the players on the revenue team to become more accountable, data driven, and customer focused. And they must find ways to get the people, process, and technology of growth in the business working more like a system toward a common purpose – growing customer and company value. We call this executive a CXO because it is a new role and one that has many titles. The "X" can change, but the mission does not. CXOs can be called chief customer officers, chief revenue officers, and chief growth officers and many other names. We will better define the CXO roles, and the three different leadership models that successful organizations are using to unify sales, marketing, and service.

Denise Karkos – the CMO of Sirius XM & Pandora and a former Division I soccer player – is a good example of a CXO. She understands the importance of working as one team toward one common goal. "In sports the scorecard for success is very clear – you win or lose as a team," points out Karkos.[105] "In business, each person has an individual definition of success. The opportunity in sales and marketing today is defining the win for the entire team. You can't delegate or outsource that job. As a leader, you can set the tone from the top."

Sales leaders at AT&T and Splunk have learned that team selling has proven to be more effective. This puts pressure on CXOs to establish organizations, systems, and incentives to get all of their customer-facing employees to operate as one revenue team focused on executing the corporate growth agenda and enhancing customer lifetime value.

Another area in which top-down leadership is important is ensuring that your company's investments in selling technologies and a digital sales infrastructure are getting results. According to Jeff McKittrick, Vice President of Sales Execution at WalkMe, top-down leadership is essential to using sales analytics and automation as a "force multiplier" to expand seller capacity and performance. "When it comes to generating financial returns from commercial assets," Jeff McKittrick observes, "leadership needs to demand, commit to, and support the goal of leveraging sales analytics and automation as 'force multipliers' to expand seller capacity and enable scalable growth with limited resources. When that happens, enablement investments generate much higher returns. In my experience, sales effectiveness and productivity can be increased twofold or even more by giving sales reps the right tools, information, and content at the right time, and giving managers the insights they need to make better resource allocation decisions and sales performance metrics. The trick has always been management's commitment to leveraging sales automation technology in the selling process by providing the right incentives, culture, and user experience to get salespeople to use these tools."

The top growth leader in the organization needs to focus on three areas to empower and endorse the transformation of the commercial model. This will help realize greater growth from existing resources. The incremental steps you can take to build these capabilities in your organization and the levels of sophistication within each competency include:

- **Demanding accountability from every revenue resource, program, and capital investment.** CXOs must demand full accountability for return on enterprise selling resources, assets, and investments by holding an individual accountable for the performance of the cross-functional commercial processes and for the financial return on selling assets and investments. For example, Lionbridge, a fast-growing translation and localization business, is establishing full accountability for financial outcomes for all growth teams, investment, and infrastructure assets. "Accountability is fundamental to scalable growth," says Jaime Punishill, CMO of Lionbridge.[113] "You have to hold marketing assets, investments, and front of the funnel marketing activity accountable for financial returns the same way you measure everything else in the business. That's fundamental to profitable growth because your job as the CMO is to get the CEO, CFO and CRO to understand and believe marketing is part of the growth equation. So we shifted our focus to understanding, measuring, and improving the contribution of the commercial assets we manage – digital technology, data, content, leads, and brainpower – to growth, profits, and firm financial performance. Over the past three years the percentage of revenues attributable to our marketing investment has grown from zero to 60%. Our return on selling content has grown significantly as we have become more scientific about what content to build, and why. We further leverage and reuse that content using systems that deploy it across digital marketing, website, sales, and service channels. Today we are driving five times the sales outcomes with thirty percent less marketing budget."

- **Assigning an owner of the enterprise commercial process, assets, investments.** CXOs need to establish a single point of decision making for the entire enterprise commercial process – from prospecting to customer expansion – as well as the assets, investments, and systems that support it. You can do this by giving an individual decision-making authority over the cross-functional commercial processes, digital selling assets, and sales and marketing support operations. For example, fast-growing organizations like Splunk and Rev.com with investor expectations for organic growth expectations in excess of 50% have taken steps to consolidate the operations that support marketing, sales, and customer success under a single operational leader. A wave of larger enterprises – including Cisco, Honeywell, GHX, and Pentair – have all taken steps to centralize all operations supporting growth by establishing "CXO" roles with a broader scope and a remit to better manage commercial assets, the operations and enablement infrastructure, and the customer journey across the enterprise. For example, Cisco established a vice president– level Chief Customer and Partner Officer role that is responsible for worldwide sales and marketing, field operations, and partnerships across the globe. Their goal is to align the sales and marketing organizations around the company's go-to-market strategy and growth opportunity while still overseeing Cisco's brand asset (which represents over 15% of their firm value according to Interbrand).[113] Smaller businesses are also consolidating their leadership of these core growth functions. For example, over 9,000 smaller organizations have put in place Chief Revenue Officer titles in the year leading up to the publication of this book, according to an analysis of job postings on LinkedIn.[112]

- **Leading change management from the top down.** Growth leaders must provide top-down leadership to enable the organization to transform the commercial model. They can do this by empowering top-down CXO leadership, which promotes a culture of growth, focusing on customer and common purpose across the entire revenue team. For example, Jim Chirico, the CEO of Avaya, established a common purpose across their entire revenue team by creating shared goals and incentives for all customer-facing employees. "We want our entire revenue team aligned around common goals, regardless of whether they are quota carrying, non-quota carrying or leadership," says Chirico.[132] "Our quota carrying reps are obviously [incentivized] by revenue. For the non-quota carrying employees in both sales and marketing we have a bonus structure that is built on the same revenue and profit metrics. And I am paid on the same incentives as the employees. We are all in it together. One revenue team. And I think that level of common purpose is extremely important, and it is a rallying cry for all of us."

Commercial Operations That Support All Growth-Related Functions

Marketing, sales, and service functions in organizational silos are vestiges of a twentieth-century commercial model, which is based on a lockstep sales funnel heavy on face-to-face selling and paid media. In the twenty-first century, the customer experience has become the basis of competitive advantage, and the growth investment mix is dominated by owned digital channel infrastructure and the content, data, teams, and technologies that support them. To succeed in this new market reality, growth leaders will need to reconfigure the operations that support salespeople and provide end-to-end coherent management of all customer-facing assets, investments, and the customer journey. "The CEO may give lip-service to 'customer centricity,' but who in the C-suite actually owns the cross-functional authority, budget, and process engine to implement the growth technology portfolio, set up the teams that will track and act on the data, and propose the bigger breakthrough innovations that cut across typical silos?" asks David Edelman of the Revenue Enablement Institute.[162] Managing cross-functional commercial assets, processes, and teams requires air cover and funding from their Chief Operating Officer, or from a newly created Chief Customer Officer, Chief Experience Officer, or other C-suite leader who has the authority to address tough issues that cut across the typical functional hierarchy of most large companies.

The operations and enablement teams that support frontline sellers must also better coordinate and unify their efforts to support one selling motion and one selling team. That "selling team" should include marketing and service operations, too, as both those functions play a bigger and bigger role as selling becomes more capital intensive, data driven, and digital. "Today one in four members of the revenue team are now in operations and enablement roles that don't directly face the customer," according to Corey Torrence, Managing Director of Blue Ridge Partners, a consultancy that has studied and optimized the commercial operations of hundreds of B2B organizations. "This makes financial sense because an incremental investment in enablement has a huge multiplier effect. It makes dozens or hundreds of sellers more effective in terms of revenue per hour of effort. Unfortunately, most organizations fail to realize these economies because they deploy these critical operational capabilities across four to sometimes eight different organizations. This fragmented and piecemeal management of critical commercial assets like customer data, content, and the tools in the growth technology portfolio is a real reason most organizations have failed to unlock the full growth potential of analytics and enablement technology."

Like the preceding commercial transformation, leaders have three key focus areas to reconfigure the operations that support growth and enable sales-people to provide coherent, end-to-end management of all customer-facing employees, assets, infrastructure, investments, and the customer journey. You can use these incremental steps to build these capabilities in your organization are outlined below and summarized in a maturity assessment later.

- **Make common purpose an operational reality.** A key to building and enabling a Revenue Operations model is to establish a common purpose across sales, marketing, and customer success teams by reconfiguring the operations to align the goals, objectives, incentives, and KPIs to create a common purpose and facilitate teamwork across all customer-facing employees on the revenue team. For example, Frank Jules, President of AT&T, created Total Billed Revenue (TBR) as a common measure of account and pipeline health for all customer-facing employees. "Total Billed Revenue is our biggest incentive because it looks at the whole picture and helps us grow our accounts," reports Jules.[120] "As a comprehensive metric, it gives our reps the flexibility and incentive to manage accelerating product life cycles, new product introductions, product expansions, and product sunsets – all while retaining the business we have. At the end of the day, we expect our reps to figure out a way to grow. TBR is the measurement that best guides them. This also fits with our strategic focus on NPS (Net Promoter Score) as a critical driver of revenue, EBITDA, and EPS (Earnings Per Share) growth. It motivates our revenue teams to focus on customer lifetime value. Most of our revenue is under contracts. So, every year you have contracts up for renewal. Our customers can choose to change out their networks, mobility suppliers, and wireline suppliers. So, without strong customer satisfaction, we're not going to achieve our revenue goals."

- **Establish more cross-functional commercial organizations.** A key to building and enabling a Revenue Operations model is to establish cross-functional organizational structures by reconfiguring the operations that support sellers across sales, marketing, and service functions including operations, and the management of data, tools, and analytics. For example, large companies like Ciena Network and hypergrowth businesses like Rev.com are taking steps to more fully integrate all Revenue Operations, enablement, and analytics functions with solid line reporting to a central operations function. "A really important step was putting in place a single Revenue Operations team with really solid, strong technical people from sales and marketing operations who can help us better leverage analytics to grow, reports Wade Burgess, the Chief Revenue Officer of Rev.com.[114] "We used to have a sales ops person and a marketing operations team. Both of those were separate before. When I came on board and sales and marketing were both under me and I really wanted one person responsible for the operational tools, processes and systems that we use for monetization. It's a roll up of sales, Revenue Operations, and also sales effectiveness is in there and we're adding an insights person to that team. It's essentially all of the non-customer-facing roles."

- **Establish a single, multidisciplinary, commercial process across the enterprise.** Reconfiguring the operations that support salespeople to better support a cross-functional commercial process that spans sales, marketing, and service functions, go-to-market channels and maps to the complete customer journey. For example, Pentair established a Commercial Excellence program that identified a number of ways to improve the "prospect-to-cash" process. These included customer segmentation, generating deep "voice of the customer" insights, and improving the product launch processes, to name a few. These are all potential areas to accelerate business with our sales and channel partners. "From a digital technology perspective, we've focused on the channel enablement process to provide our channel partners the information, insights, training, and visibility they need to realize more opportunities in their markets and share our performance end to end," according to John Jacko, the Chief Growth Officer. "We have also initiated a more robust Voice of the Customer program to get much more granular and actionable customer feedback. It drives our segmentation, priorities, and plans, and changed how we believed customers behaved." Like most of the executives we interviewed, Pentair has initiatives planned or under way to use AI to improve their customer journeys, revolutionize how they interact with customers, and deliver them more compelling experiences. For example, gaining visibility into the end-to-end commercial process is the key for Jacko. "Visibility is a big priority to our organization as we seek to digitize the end-to-end process and use technology as a force multiplier to make our sales teams and partners more productive. My view is visibility into granular sales activity and voice of the customer data is critical to getting sales, marketing, and channel partner teams working together. This includes improving the effectiveness of our partners, improving the visibility and ease of doing business with Pentair, and allocating resources to the best product, market, and client opportunities with a high degree of precision, all in the name of growth."[122]

Commercial Architecture That Maximizes the Return on Selling Assets

Growth leaders are reconfiguring their go-to-market strategies, sales force design, and territory and quota plans to reflect changes in customer behavior and response, the impact of enablement technologies, and the need to focus on customer lifetime value.

Such changes can add up to significant improvements in short-term efficiencies and long-term growth. To realize these gains, all aspects of the commercial architecture need to be updated to optimize coverage, control, cost to sell, and the customer experience and to reflect the productivity, engagement, and speed that enablement technologies and remote selling create. This involves redesigning the commercial architecture to maximize return on selling assets by improving the speed, visibility, productivity, and engagement of frontline selling teams and reducing cost to sell.

According to Corey Torrence, who has led a dozen Revenue Operations transformations in the past year, "A properly designed and optimized commercial architecture can contribute five to ten points of profit contribution to the bottom line in the short term, or if reinvested, can improve long-term growth prospects much more in the long term." A good example of this comes from Avaya, a digital communications company with a OneCloud ecosystem model. Their CEO Jim Chirico and his team reconfigured all aspects of the commercial architecture, including refocusing commercial operations on growing customer lifetime value, and aligning goals and incentives with the subscription model in order to accelerate the business model transformation at Avaya from an on-premises business to a growing cloud business.

John Jacko, from Pentair, views more precise algorithmic models of customer demand and opportunity potential and the attainability of markets as a big advantage. "Our segmentation exercise brought the customer, their insights, and their journeys right into the room with us," he reflects. That exercise disrupted individuals' personal, sometimes off-base, interpretations of customer experience. "Data wins and this was a real cultural shift," Jacko concludes.[122]

Redesigning the commercial architecture must focus on maximizing return on selling assets by improving the speed, visibility, productivity, and engagement of frontline selling teams while reducing cost to sell. Here are incremental steps you can take to make this happen:

- **Redesign the go-to-market approach to improve performance and engagement.** CXOs must redesign the go-to-market architecture to improve performance and engagement by restructuring market coverage, account targets, and segmentation to realize more opportunity with existing selling resources and assets. For example, the growth leadership at Pitney Bowes had to make some dramatic changes to their go-to-market architecture and a major shift in sales force focus, emphasis, and roles to accelerate sales of new solutions. Bill Borrelle, the CMO of Pitney Bowes, partnered with his peers in field sales and inside sales to refocus their go-to-market resource on new products, transaction types, and stages of the customer journey to ensure the business was creating channel efficiency and allocating the best-selling resource to the biggest opportunity. "We've focused salespeople on more complex and valuable transactions because the simpler transactions – a client buying supplies, a single piece of equipment that they will install themselves, or a lease renewal – can happen online," reports Borrelle.[121] "We need our valuable sales team working on complex transactions like an enterprise client that spans many locations. From an execution standpoint, segmentation and market sizing helped to understand the opportunity, and where to focus. For example, shipping clients will have more complex workflows, a greater mix of inbound and outbound volumes and bigger packages. We had to get more precise, and data driven to identify opportunities. We're starting to use data and analytics to create a new type of 'selling book.' We're also using IoT data from our equipment to look at usage, volume, size of package, and industry to better value, segment, and align selling messages and channel assignments."
- **Adapt the sales force design to improve speed, visibility, and engagement at lower cost**. Growth leaders must adjust the sales force design to improve performance, engagement, and costs. This involves reconfiguring sales force segmentation (the roles within the sales team), sales force emphasis (what products they sell), seller compensation, and

sales rep training and development strategy. Doing this well can significantly improve the level of customer engagement, speed of response, productivity, and sales outcomes that your sellers create. For example, over 85% of the CXOs interviewed in this analysis were redefining the segmentation of their revenue teams to adapt to these mega trends. They are adding development reps (SDRs, BDRs, MDRs, and ADRs) to manage engagement at scale at the front of the funnel, specialists to add value in the middle, and customer success managers (CSM) at the end to manage retention, usage, and upsell.

For example, businesses like Flexential, Rev.com, Honeywell, and ChowNow are actively redesigning their sales force segmentation to clarify roles of their revenue teams across the entire revenue cycle. They are adding lead generation resources at the front to better tap into market demand. Product specialists to promote new product innovations and cross-sell new products to existing customers. They are also elevating the role of customer success to support an increased emphasis on growing customer lifetime value.

- **Reconfiguring selling channels.** Tamara Adams, the SVP of Sales and Marketing at Honeywell, had to redesign the sales force segmentation, roles, and incentives to find ways to shrink the sales cycle in order to compete in the SaaS market. "When I joined, standalone SaaS software was a new business to Honeywell," reports Adams.[123] "We had to redesign our selling channels from the ground up. A key part of this was to enhance the role of our Customer Success Managers (CSMs) as a key part of the model to manage renewals and client engagement, at a lower cost of sales. We've also had to define the role of our Key Account Management and Project Management Operations as the other big pillars of our lead-to-cash process."

Chris Downie, the CEO of Flexential, also had to adapt the coverage model by adding specialists who can better sell the full value of the Flexential platform. "The new product platform has evolved into two distinct solution sets – cloud managed services and co-located data center services," reports Downie.[128] "Each of these product segments behave very differently in terms of how customers use them and the value they can deliver. We have folks on our sales team that can be good at selling one, but not as good at selling the other. We created a specialist overlay function to make sure that reps that were not as comfortable selling cloud and managed solutions have the ability to engage with the customers in their territories effectively to realize the full revenue and margin potential of our product portfolio and better communicate the unique value of concepts like Backup-as-a Service (BaaS) and hyper-scaling cloud management services."

- **Deploy sales performance management models and tools to better align with the opportunities.** Growth leaders are using advanced analytics to help them reconfigure their territory definitions, quota assignments, incentives, and account priorities to better align selling actions, effort, and investments with revenue and profit outcomes. Digitizing the process of planning, managing, and optimizing territory boundaries, seller targets, and quota assignments has many benefits. It will (1) make the process faster and less expensive; (2) speed up the process of making mid-period adjustments and plan reviews; and (3) make their planning process more data driven, accountable, and collaborative. Such changes have the added benefit of providing managers more visibility into seller performance against goals. For instance, Frank Jules, President of AT&T Business, embraces using analytics to adapt his coverage and territories to changing customer demand and market response. "We're shifting to a more science-based territory definition within the vertical structure," according to Jules.[120] "We have a sales operations team that runs analytics on things like the cost to serve an average client, what coverage models perform best, how quotas should be constructed by industry, and ultimately how we should compensate. This ties to our vertical focus because we're constantly rebalancing our allocation of resources and effort based on industry data. Is the healthcare, manufacturing, or hospitality vertical up or down? With Covid, our coverage and quotas have been disrupted. Transportation, hospitality, and airlines are struggling. At the same time, we knew that certain industries – like public sector and healthcare – were set to explode. Being data driven lets us set fair quotas based on competitive analysis and trends. This helped us turn on a dime early-on and figure out where we should double-down on resources and where we could lighten up on industries that were having a tough-go."

Commercial Insights Built on Customer Engagement and Seller Activity Data

The emergence of advanced analytics, AI, and Machine Learning (ML) – and the massive new sales engagement data sets to support them – represents the most significant opportunity to accelerate sales growth since the scale adoption of call centers (40 years ago), Customer Relationship Management or CRM (30 years ago), and digital channels (20 years ago) in sales. The ability to capture and unify customer data and convert it into commercial insights is critical to support sales, marketing, and service conversations. Insights that improve decision making, prioritization, actions, and workflows fundamentally drive growth and value creation. This value increases when the insights inform decisions, actions, and conversations at the moments that matter in the selling process. Kirsten Paust, the VP of Fortive Business Systems, reinforces the growing importance of advanced analytics in the commercial process. "More and more of our core commercialization processes are being supported by AI, insights and technology that [enable] our teams to get to insight and action faster," she observes.[130] Raghu Iyengar, Professor of Marketing at the Wharton School of Business at the University of Pennsylvania, echoes the importance of aggregating, orchestrating, and delivering actionable insights as the focus of Revenue Operations. "Having an automated way of analyzing such audio calls capturing the interactions with customers is critical to help answer operational questions, e.g. 'who are our best live agents' and 'why are customers calling us?'"[32] Professor Iyengar warns that many dashboards of commercial performance are improperly designed because they get the fundamental unit of analysis – customer health and lifetime value – wrong. "Many AI initiatives fail to get traction because their unit of analysis is mismatched with the engrained Key Performance Indicators (KPI) and incentives managers use to run business," according to Professor Iyengar. "For example, AI models are excellent at analyzing data about customer characteristics, responses, and behaviors to refine scalable ways to improve customer lifetime value through improved acquisition costs, churn, pricing, usage, and cross-sell. But most of the data sets in the business are organized around products, geographies, and business units."

Certain core capabilities enable the transformation of customer engagement and seller activity data into these valuable commercial insights. To improve performance and realize greater growth from existing resources, organizations should:

- **Convert revenue data into prescriptive and actionable commercial insights.** Convert revenue data into prescriptive revenue intelligence that informs day-to-day decisions, conversations, and priorities in real time. Better analytics support data-driven selling by better aligning selling resources and assets with opportunities. This also more intelligently routes insights to frontline sellers in real time to support their decision making, actions, and conversations. AI-enabled real-time guidance helps development reps, account reps, and customer success managers execute selling motions, playbooks, and value selling methodologies much more effectively. Sales leaders need to increase the speed of communication by providing real-time training and guidance to help frontline sellers respond immediately and completely to "new school" buyers and follow-up on signals of buyer intent or attribution while they still have time to affect the outcome. For example, Wade Burgess, the CRO of Rev.com, sees real-time customer analytics as a way to change the company's historic focus on new customers to cross-selling and upselling existing customers into enterprise accounts. "Analytics can also help us retain and expand those enterprise relationships," says Burgess.[114] "If an account has X amount of revenue forecasted for the year, but they're tracking above that number, a person on our team needs to be triggered to reach out and have a conversation with them to ensure they have the resources they need to be successful. This typically results in an add-on, upsell, or cross-sell opportunity. On the other hand, if utilization is way behind and we're three months into an annual contract, I want customer success reaching out right away to help them get back on track. This type of proactive engagement can significantly minimize churn. There's a gold mine of data opportunities for us to tap into."

- **Focus on KPIs, common objectives, and goals.** CXOs need to establish fact-based reporting analytics, KPIs, and dashboards of commercial performance. Key metrics and indicators align sales, marketing, and service around common objectives, goals, KPIs, priorities, and incentives and provide visibility into buyer engagement, seller activity, account health, and pipeline potential. Sales and marketing leaders need to push their analytics teams to use advanced analytics and AI to turn their sales engagement data into a common set of measurements and financial incentives that get sales, marketing, and service working as a team toward the goals of growing firm value, customer lifetime value, and profits. Without these unified and harmonized customer and engagement data sets, managers lack the facts to agree on the best allocation of people, coverage, selling effort, and technology investments to realize the greatest opportunity and growth. For example, the CEOs of Avaya, Mphasis, and iCIMS are aligning incentives across sales, marketing, and customer experience functions to ensure they are focused on corporate growth priorities and growing customer lifetime value. "An important aspect of getting sales, marketing, services, and customer success to work as one revenue team was to align incentives around a common set of strategic growth goals, reports Jim Chirico, of Avaya. "Aligning our incentives and KPIs with our overall objectives is extremely important to achieving our growth goals, especially as we move from a product company to a SaaS / cloud company," says Chirico.[132] "It is important to make sure that those incentives are driving the right outcomes and behaviors and drive accountability through the process as well. So, for the last four years we have spent a lot of time on incentive management as a senior leadership team. Every month the top 40 executives in the company review our incentives in excruciating detail."

Steve Lucas, the CEO of iCIMS, is focusing his revenue team on customer lifetime value by pushing his team to clearly define and quantify what a good client relationship looks like empirically on a scale of one to ten. He kept the bar high on engagement quality. Any account team with a customer engagement score of less than 9 had to take a series of actions to improve customer health. In parallel, he created a tightly defined customer persona called an Ideal Customer Profile (ICP). He created a vocabulary, criteria, reporting, and most importantly financial incentives for his go-to-market teams to develop relationships with these "ideal customers." To enforce this discipline of delivering high-quality customer engagement to the highest potential customers, his teams were paid 20% higher commissions when they engaged and developed ideal customers, as opposed to when they spent their energies on less than ideal prospects.

- **Develop predictive insights to improve account priorities and resource allocation.** Growth leaders need to use advanced analytics to create better predictions to inform their investment bets and evaluate more scenarios to optimize resource allocation decisions. AI-enabled algorithms and advanced modeling techniques can help you develop more accurate and predictive estimates of opportunity potential and your sales forecast. They can also teach you more about customers – who they respond to, whether they intend to buy, and how they fit with your sellers, products, and treatment types. In the absence of analytics that quantify account potential and propensity to close, most organizations chase too many low-quality clients and opportunities – those where they stand little chance of winning but want to feel like they are still in the game, according to Cam Tipping, who has led over 100 customer targeting workshops and even more simulations with sales teams over the last decade. "This behavior leads to bad outcomes – like bad service, high cost to sell, lower margins, and unsatisfied clients. It's a basic 80/20 problem. But a difficult one to solve. No business that I have seen is aware of this issue until they go through the analytics to understand it," continues Tipping. "Traditional CRM or financial systems are not set up to provide this type of information. It has to be understood through custom analysis and a review of client performance over multiple years. The data exists to create the facts that let us 'cut the tail.' And there are established tools like Deciling that can easily achieve consensus on the 80% of accounts not to call on." For example, Peter Ford, VP of Global Sales at iconectiv, a private equity–backed solutions business that connects networks, devices, and applications in the communications industry, was able to leverage analytics to "cut the tail" off the customer curve. He did this by becoming more scientific about prioritizing customers based on readiness and potential, and enabled different levels of customer treatment to manage cost to sell in smaller "tail" accounts. "We use analytics to create the curve of our customers," relates Ford.[117] "So, we treat a customer that generates less than $10,000 of revenue for us a year differently than a customer that generates in excess of $20 million a year. Understanding when to take a light touch approach versus hands-on sales or when an account should be more marketing driven is key."

Commercial Enablement Capabilities That Turn Your Technology into a "Force Multiplier"

Thousands of point solutions are built for the purpose of saving sellers time and making them more productive with customers.

One in four members of the revenue team is now dedicated to supporting frontline selling. To foster scalable and consistent growth, enablement and operations leaders need to focus these resources on achieving continuous improvement in performance and on finding ways to better support salespeople and maximize the contribution of selling assets and investments to revenue and profit growth. This cannot be done piecemeal across silos.

A unified capital expenditure and operating model is needed to execute scalable technologies that span budgets and organizations. These are programs that connect technologies from different parts of your business ecosystem in ways that make every customer-facing employee more effective. Some examples of these programs include initiatives that support personalization, coaching, and Account Based Marketing (ABM) at scale across the entire business. Another example is systems that help manage and measure the entire revenue cycle across many functions and systems.

These capabilities are critical to enabling human selling and maximizing the contribution of selling assets and investments to revenue and profit growth outcomes. Peter Ford reiterates the importance of focusing on ways to make continuous improvements to the commercial process as the path to transformation. "It's hard to pinpoint any one thing that was the key to fixing or transforming our sales organization, because it's really the sum of many different marginal gains," according to Ford.[117]

A common core of commercial capabilities will enable salespeople and maximize the contribution of selling assets and investments to revenue and profit growth outcomes. The following actions will create a "force multiplier" in your business:

- **Reconfigure enablement solutions to simplify day-to-day selling.** Reconfigure the commercial technology infrastructure to better support revenue teams by enabling frontline sellers with the intelligent insights, content, leverage, and guidance they need to focus on the customer, prioritize the best opportunities, and take the actions that will advance opportunities and grow customer lifetime value. CXOs are doing this by "knitting together" the various pieces of their sales technology portfolios to build digital selling platforms that automate, simplify, and speed up selling by addressing the major hot spots in the selling process, according to Jeff McKittrick, who has led sales enablement at Cisco, Hitachi and WalkMe over the past 15 years. "Organizations are eliminating points of failure, friction and manual labor in the day-to-day seller workflow by connecting these dots across CRM, sales enablement, sales readiness and digital asset management solutions – which are largely managed in silos in most B2B organizations." This can dramatically improve the productivity and experience of sales reps. For example, by reconfiguring the solutions that support the day-to-day selling motions of their sales development reps (SDRs), ChowNow, a leading online ordering platform for restaurants, was able to ramp up new sales reps to full productivity faster (in 60% less time), promote them sooner, and retain them longer (rep attrition dropped by 75%) because the seller experience was more automated and less stressful.

- **Reconfigure the readiness, training, and development technology portfolio.** CXOs need to do this to integrate learning and development tools into a closed-loop process that accelerates onboarding and ramping up of revenue teams, provides managers real-time visibility into seller activity and performance, and the ability to train sellers. For many, connecting these dots will represent a significant step forward as compared with the status quo. Equity Trust Company, a financial services company that enables individual investors, leveraged AI and conversational intelligence to coach at scale. The Sales Enablement team at Equity Trust combined sales readiness, engagement, and conversational AI into a closed-feedback loop that allowed managers to monitor more calls and provide real-time guidance and fixes to reps on calls. This allowed them to double the manager-to-rep ratio from 1:6 to 1:12 and improve conversion and rep satisfaction at the same time. "It would have taken 90 days for our sales team to audit calls on their own. With Conversation AI it took us a day to get the data we needed," according to Christopher Cases, Senior Manager Sales Enablement at Equity Trust.[69]

- **Focus the Revenue Enhancement technology portfolio to improve the lead to cash cycle and capture more revenue, margin, and price.** Growth leaders should do this in order to enhance the prospect-to-cash cycle and capture more revenue, margin, and price. You can do this by providing frontline revenue teams with configuration, pricing, and quotation (CPQ), order management, and fulfillment tools. These tools can help support the negotiation and closing phase of the revenue life-cycle. They help sellers optimize the pricing, personalization, and packaging of presentations, proposals, and solutions they present to clients. For example, Peter Ford at iconectiv views the transformation of a sales organization as about making 1% marginal gains in the prospect-to-cash cycle, eliminating little things that hold his sales team back, and eradicating revenue, price, and margin leakage. His Revenue Operations team is making a big cumulative impact by enhancing individual aspects of their core contracting, pricing, quoting, order management, and fulfillment processes – and retooling seemingly simple things like having NDAs signed, which took too long and created friction in the sales cycle. "I don't believe that there is a single thing that contributes to the transformation of a sales organization," says Ford.[117] "There are many important things to focus on as a sales leader. But it's about making those marginal gains in everything, whether that is the way we measure and compensate our people, or even something as simple as the process for agreeing and signing and executing an NDA with a customer – which took far too long in my opinion. All of these things contribute to friction in the sales cycle and points where you can either lose a sale or dissatisfy a customer."

Commercial Practices That Maximize Return from Customer Data, Technology, Content, and Intellectual Property Assets

Most organizations don't need more technology as much as they need higher returns on their commercial technology and customer data assets. Success in a twenty-first-century Commercial Model requires shared investment in commercial assets that enable revenue teams across the enterprise – including the sales and marketing technology portfolio, customer data, and owned digital selling channel infrastructure.

These commercial assets are among the most valuable but underperforming assets in a business. The strategic management and measurement of these data, technology, content, and IP assets can be used to maximize their utilization, impact, and financial return. Doing this is a critical component of a Revenue Operations model. "Without a business case for the capital expenditure required and operating model that looks at the revenue team and commercial process, it is extremely difficult to execute scalable technologies like one-to-one personalization, real-time coaching, and cross-functional customer journey management. You cannot manage, monetize, and scale these capabilities in a functional or piecemeal manner." advises Corey Torrence.

Growth leaders need to strategically manage their commercial data, technology, content, and IP assets to maximize utilization, impact, and return on investment. Here are some ways to accomplish this:

- **Establish common stewardship of customer data assets.** CXOs need to establish a common architecture and owner to strategically manage customer and engagement data assets and maximize their utilization, impact, and ROI. This is also important because it establishes a common fact base for data-driven selling and reporting. "A high priority for me [is] to get the right data infrastructure in place so that we can intelligently scale revenue growth," says Wade Burgess, the CRO of Rev.com.[114] "We're currently sitting on an amount of unstructured data that's not being used in an optimal way. I believe that access into customer insights and to be able to automate action against the opportunity they reveal is going to be a key for us to be able to scale. There is an enormous amount of unstructured customer engagement, behavior, and consumption data coming from our 170,000 customers who use our self-service engine. On top of that we have a whole bunch of people who interact with us on the top of the funnel that never convert." Wade Burgess consolidated Revenue Operations at Rev.com to establish consistent customer engagement and conversational intelligence data. "One reason Revenue Operations is important is because the revenue team uses the same data, and I didn't want multiple sources of truth," reports Burgess. "Many of the things we have to do involve being able to look inside of existing, transactional data to direct sales force actions like identifying cross-sell and upsell opportunities and targeting groups of customers who can be aggregated into enterprise accounts."

- **Centralize the management and operational administration of technology assets.** CXOs need to establish more centralized stewardship and a reconfiguration of the commercial technology portfolio across functions. By doing so, they can maximize utilization, impact, and return on investment as well as simplify and speed up selling activities. For example, Jeff McKittrick was able to improve seller performance and lower total costs by rationalizing and focusing the technology portfolio at Hitachi Vantara. He achieved these results by getting sales operations, sales enablement, and content operations teams to conduct a top-down assessment of the 20-plus tools in the sales technology portfolio. This identified and eliminated many tools that were redundant, not being used, or not supporting sales. They also started filling gaps in their commercial technology portfolio to support some key sales hot spots like opportunity prioritization and guided selling to salespeople. We profile how Jeff was able to do this in more detail in chapter 7.

- **Manage selling content as a strategic asset.** CXOs need to establish operational ownership over the organization and deployment of selling content across functions. You can do this by setting up a function to more strategically manage, organize, and deploy these content, knowledge, and "selling intellectual property" assets. These assets are severely underutilized in most organizations. Taking these steps will maximize their utilization, impact, and return on investment. This is important because selling content has emerged as the gasoline of modern selling systems. Today content can represent over a third of marketing budgets (according to HubSpot) and most organizations are increasing their investment in content and the systems that support its delivery. Unfortunately, the utilization of that content by sales remains extremely low, and it is hard to create customized content at scale.

  Meir Adler, Regional VP Sales Engineering at a fast-growing business, WalkMe, reinforces the importance of managing selling content as a strategic asset by using content reuse, templatization, and intelligence as ways to manage the growing cost and complexity of creating content to respond to increasingly demanding customers. "You quickly realize you can't afford to build content to spec," reports Adler.[34] "Reuse and templatization become critical. For us it started in bid management as we focused on simplifying and speeding up our RFP responses. In that process, we learned that 70–75% of the client questions are the same. This opens the door to templatization, libraries and reuse. Now we are looking to extend that capability to a wider range of more complex regional, local, and language scenarios. And find ways to deal with increased regulatory scrutiny."

As a summary, we have listed all 18 of the actions you can take in a table on the following page (see Figure 3.2).

As a reminder, not every one of these 18 actions will be equally important to every business. If you are working in a slow-growth industry, you may want

The Revenue Operations Management System

A Blueprint for Aligning Sales, Marketing, and Customer Success Teams and Optimizing the Performance of Commercial Processes, Operations, and Assets

DIMENSION	DEFINITION	CORE COMPETENCIES
	Establish a leadership model to empower and endorse the transformation of the commercial model to unify sales, marketing, and service into one revenue team and become more accountable, data driven, and customer focused.	**1.0 Accountability.** Demand full accountability for return on enterprise selling resources, assets, and investments.
		2.0 Ownership. Establish a single point of decision making for the enterprise revenue process, assets, and investments.
		3.0 Change Management. Provide top-down leadership to empower the organization to transform the commercial model.
	Reconfigure the operations that support growth and enable salespeople to provide coherent, end-to-end management of all customer-facing employees, assets, infrastructure, investments, and the customer journey.	**4.0 Common Purpose.** Establish a common purpose across sales, marketing, and customer success teams.
		5.0 Organization. Establish cross-functional organizational structures to support sales people across the enterprise.
		6.0 Commercial Process. Establish and manage a cross-functional commercial process across the enterprise.
	Redesign the commercial architecture to maximize return on selling assets by improving the speed, visibility, productivity, and engagement of frontline selling teams and reducing cost to sell.	**7.0 Go-to-Market Strategy.** Redesign the go-to-market architecture to improve performance and engagement.
		8.0 Channel Design. Adjust the sales force design to improve performance, engagements, and costs.
		9.0 Sales Performance Management. Modify assignments, territories, and incentives to align resources and opportunity.
	Turn customer engagement and seller activity data into commercial insights that create value and inform decisions, actions, and conversations at the moments that matter in the salespeople process.	**10.0 Data-Driven Selling.** Convert revenue data into prescriptive revenue intelligence that informs day-to-day decisions in real time.
		11.0 Key Performance Indicators. Establish fact-based reporting analytics, KPIs, and dashboards of commercial performance.
		12.0 Predictive Selling Insights. Use analytics to create better predictions, parameters, and scenarios to inform investment, allocation, and emphasis.
	Build a common core of commercial capabilities that enable salespeople and maximize the contribution of selling assets and investments to revenue and profit growth outcomes.	**13.0 Enablement and Engagement.** Reconfigure the commercial technology infrastructure to better support revenue team enablement.
		14.0 Readiness and Development. Reconfigure the commercial technology infrastructure to better support readiness, training, and development.
		15.0 Revenue Enhancement. Deploy technologies to enhance the prospect-to-cash cycle and capture more revenue, margin, and price realization.
	Strategically manage the commercial data, technology, content, and IP assets to maximize utilization, impact, and return on investment.	**16.0 Content Assets.** Establish operational ownership, organization, and deployment of selling content and IP across functions.
		17.0 Data Assets. Establish a common architecture and owner to monetize customer data assets.
		18.0 Technology Assets. Establish centralized stewardship and reconfiguration of the commercial technology portfolio across functions.

FIGURE 3.2   The Revenue Operations Management System

to prioritize actions that can generate higher valuations. This might include focusing their revenue teams around a more precise set of high-opportunity clients, creating a culture of continuous improvement in the commercial process, and eliminating price, margin, and revenue leakage.

If you work in a large, complex enterprise, you should likely focus on breaking down functional silos, leveraging prescriptive commercial insights to become more "agile," and improving the productivity of your selling teams.

If your organization is undergoing business model transformation, you may want to focus their short-term efforts on redefining incentives to focus revenue teams on customer lifetime value, retention, and annual recurring revenue. You will also benefit from establishing more quantifiable measures of opportunity potential, seller performance, account and pipeline health based on customer engagement and seller activity data.

If you work in a hyper-growth cloud company, you may choose to prioritize leadership by putting in place a single CXO (Chief Revenue Officer) to align commercial teams around the customer. You may also benefit to a greater degree from unifying their commercial operations to leverage customer insights and scalable technologies across the enterprise.

To help you start to build your system for growth, we will provide you some examples of how peer organizations have adopted Revenue Operations (in chapter 4). We also provide you some tools to systematically identify which steps your organization should prioritize to generate the greatest short-term financial impact (in chapter 14).

CHAPTER 4

Lead a Modern Business That Aligns Marketing, Sales, and Service

Growth Levers Across Executive Functions

Leadership must empower and endorse transformation of the commercial model. It's imperative that we unify marketing, sales, and service into one revenue team (though this does not automatically mean consolidation on the org chart, as we'll see in chapter 5). It's also integral to becoming more digital, data driven, and accountable.

"The two biggest headwinds for Revenue Operations are active championship from the CEO and creating cultural incentives to break down the organizational, budget and technology silos that divide people," according to Corey Torrence, a managing director of Blue Ridge Partners who has led over a dozen Revenue Operations transformations.

Other experts also stress the importance of top-down leadership to Revenue Operations success. Sales leaders must find ways to unlock the untapped value potential of critical but underperforming systems that support selling like CRM, according to Bob Kelly, the CEO of the Sales Management Associations. "Leadership must do their part to make this transformation happen. Right now, 95% of sales managers and practitioners cite the lack of management encouragement to adopt these technologies as a big part of the problem," warns Kelly.

Torrence's second headwind, the lack of cultural incentives to break down silos, reflects the failure of management to identify how so many organizations have failed to recognize the obvious: that growth is a team sport. As mentioned earlier, no single executive in a traditional functional management structure (other than the CEO) controls more than 40% of the growth drivers (please see Figure 4.1). This team really should include not only the obvious players like sales and marketing but also key leaders from the product group, IT, the regions, HR, and other key business units to do its best.

At the same time, much of the value sits at the intersection of the traditional functions. Responsibility and accountability for things like customer relationships, content, and even brand loyalty are at best shared – and at worst lost in the shuffle. Given that Customer Experience has become the primary competitive battleground in most markets, can any business afford any kind of ambiguity on responsibility and accountability there?

Experts like Kelly and Torrence point out the obvious: Revenue Operations requires change, yet senior leaders too often delegate the process of change to lower-level managers or professionals within the operations group. These managers, no matter how talented and motivated, usually lack the influence, authority, and risk tolerance to effect the change needed. Successful implementation of the management system for Revenue Operations will

FUNCTIONAL GROWTH DRIVERS	SALES	MARKETING	SERVICE
Compensation and incentive design	●		
Customer relationship	●		
Partner channel relationships	●		
Revenue enablement technology	●		
Sales Force design	●		
Sales Forecast	●		
Sales management	●		
Territory and quota planning	●		
Content	●	●	
Coverage model	●	●	
Customer data	●	●	
Owned digital infrastructure	●	●	
Sales events	●	●	
Segmentation	●	●	
Customer care			●
Service and support			●
Customer experience	●	●	●
Brand strategy		●	
Marketing communications		●	
Marketing strategy		●	
Media		●	
Promotions		●	
Pricing	●	●	

FIGURE 4.1 Distribution of Growth Levers Across Executive Functions

require a new generation of leaders with technical acumen and a mandate to harmonize sales, marketing, and service. We like to call them "CXOs" for simplicity, because the range of titles (denoted by the "X") can be confusing, but their mandate to systematize growth is clear. The continued need for growth – exacerbated by business model change, changing customer behavior, and investor expectations for data-driven growth – is forcing companies to create these CXO roles to lead the deeper structural and organizational changes required to move to a Revenue Operations model that aligns customer-centric functions like marketing, customer success, and support services.

Companies are faced with several critical business imperatives that challenge the existing leadership structure and accelerate the adoption of a new management system.

- **Addressing investor pressure to grow faster:** For many organizations, these leadership and organizational changes are in response to ongoing pressure from PE owners and investors for higher rates of growth and ever-improving performance. In order to maintain growth rates in excess of 50% at scale, Splunk brought in a new leader to integrate the operations that support the revenue teams and demanded higher returns on their investment in sales enablement and revenue intelligence. "We are trying to bring our operations team across customer success, marketing, and sales together," reports Christian Smith, the Chief Revenue Officer of Splunk. "To do this we brought in a new President and Chief Growth Officer, Teresa Carlson, and her job is to sit on top of the sales, marketing, and customer success organizations and get them to work better together."[163] Accelerating growth is a particularly big pressure for businesses transitioning to SaaS, cloud, or subscription business models, which rely on faster growth to transition from transactional to recurring revenue streams without a large short-term profit hit. For example, the pressure to accelerate annual recurring revenues to drive business model transformation at Avaya led their CEO, Jim Chirico, to move all their customer-facing functions away from the regional, geography-centric teams (sales regions) and consolidate their reporting structure to a single growth leader. "One of the things we did to make our revenue team more successful was to bring in a Chief Revenue Officer (CRO), Stephen Spears, to create a single point of authority over that entire go-to-market organization on a global scale. Stephen is the accountable party for marketing, sales, delivery, customer success, professional services, and all the channel partners that support our organization. These are hard line reports," says Chirico.[132]

- **Facilitating teamwork:** A big factor in the success of Revenue Operations is the growing mandate for teamwork. A primary goal for these leaders will be to force cross-functional collaboration across sales, marketing, and service teams to match buyer preferences, differentiate the customer experience, and grow customer lifetime value. This focus on teamwork across sales, marketing, and customer support is a primary growth driver, according to Frank Jules, President of AT&T Business. "I see three primary drivers of performance going forward – teamwork, vertical focus, and analytics," reports Jules.[120] "In terms of teamwork, our view is there's no problem we can't solve through teamwork. Our goal is to get the best of AT&T on a problem. When we do that, we win. As a growth leader, I can't be successful without my peers. The way it works at AT&T is we partner. I own sales, but at my staff meeting every Monday is my finance team, legal team, marketing team, product team, and all my sales leaders. There isn't a problem we can't solve when we come together to develop a solution. Without a doubt. The same applies to the sellers I manage. We've designed our selling architecture to foster teamwork. This includes tuning our incentives, quotas, territories and roles with collaboration and customer lifetime value in mind."

- **Adapting to customer behavior:** The commercial organization is becoming increasingly defined by the ways clients engage through a variety of human and digital touchpoints. Customers and end users now choose when, where, and how to engage with brands, forcing organizations to focus more on digital engagement and building customer lifetime value. For example, Pentair elevated John Jacko's role from Chief Marketing Officer to Chief Growth Officer, with a broader remit to support the digital customer and the shift to digital channels in the go-to-market model. "The change in role includes the addition of Corporate Communications, Enterprise Strategy, M&A and what we call the Digital Customer," Jacko reports.[122] "The shift to the Chief Growth Officer role has the benefit of providing more executive ownership of some key growth initiatives – notably our 360 view of our customer through responsible and secure data management, which our team is charged to bring together and govern. Given the importance of advanced analytics and personalization, the delivery of the right customer and product data provides the visibility our teams count on to optimize our growth formula. Forecast accuracy. Enabling digital channels. Arming dealers with leads and client insights. Creating more data driven incentives that map to customer lifetime value."

- **Taking on risk:** A very big but unspoken factor behind the failure of organizations to adopt enablement technologies and transform their organization and operations around the customer is risk. "Commercial transformation requires change management and with change comes a certain degree of personal and business risk," says Corey Torrence. "It's unrealistic to push the changes required to execute a Revenue Operations model deep down into the sales operations or enablement function as much of the literature around RevOps suggests. Operations directors and performance professionals lack the remit, currency, and influence to get peers in marketing, product, IT, and the geographies to change. To some degree they would be putting their jobs on the line to make the sweeping changes required. That type of leadership and change management has to come from the CEO on down to make an impact."

- **Improving speed and agility:** A higher scope of authority over customer data and commercial processes is necessary to speed information across the enterprise and ensure timely decisions that will affect results in the short and long term. The ability to share information quickly across the revenue team and support lightning-quick decision-making processes is a primary driver of firm value and competitive advantage in the Information Age. There are three keys to success in a SaaS model – speed, talent, and incentives – according to Tamara Adams, who was given the role of SVP of Sales and Marketing to accelerate business model change and revenue growth at Honeywell.[123] "We had to shrink the sales cycle dramatically to be effective."

Companies large and small are experimenting with new leadership models and organizational forms that seek to transform sales, marketing, and service in ways that accelerate growth and address the needs of digitally enabled customers. The executives we spoke with universally agree on one thing: the mandate for growth must come from the top, which ultimately means from the board and the CEO. However, they differ in terms of exactly how this leadership needs to manifest itself in different types of organizations.

The CEO Takes Control of Growth

Don Joos is the CEO of TPx, a privately held managed services provider that offers unified communications and managed IT services, continuity, and connectivity solutions to both large and small businesses. TPx is poised for exponential growth in the unified communications and collaboration market, which is expected to triple in size over the next several years (from $47B to $140B). The firm was acquired by Siris Capital 18 months ago with the goal of building on its industry-leading portfolio of award-winning products and large installed customer base to capture market share in communications, connectivity, and security solutions

Don Joos was brought in as CEO in July 2020 to lead a journey to transform TPx into a hyper-growth cloud business with the potential to realize increased market share within the large and rapidly expanding managed services market. "Our broader IT services portfolio is probably growing in the mid to upper

(continued)

single digits in aggregate," according to Joos.[134] "Newer segments like managed cybersecurity and communications are growing in the double digits. But, when you put it all together our recurring revenue from managed services, security, firewall, and backup services are growing 30% year over year. Part of the transformation is to accelerate these annual recurring revenues to offset the secular decline in the legacy businesses. We are not too far away from reaching that inflection point where the rapid growth in our cloud offerings will see us in a position of exceptional growth."

To realize the full revenue potential of the market for cloud-based unified communications and collaboration, Joos is leading the transformation of the commercial model at TPx to build a modern selling system. He is focusing his efforts on three foundational capabilities to accelerate cloud revenues: creating a channel strategy that covers the segments where demand is greatest, defining a scalable and repeatable process for acquiring and upselling their 25,000 customers, and building a demand generation engine to fuel them with opportunities.

"Revenue growth is a huge priority overall given the large and growing total addressable market we have before us," according to Joos. "But revenue growth itself is the output of building a foundation of capabilities and a ruthless focus on doing the things necessary to build a scalable and sustainable foundation to drive that growth. Do we have the right road map? Is my go-to-market model optimized? Am I retaining our existing customers? Are we expanding services to the base? And am I modernizing our systems and processes? Those things became the basis for our focus and revenue with speed and precision."

Transforming the business model into a high-growth cloud business requires a lot of change and complexity according to Joos, who is a three-time CEO with transformation experience. In parallel, the commercial model at TPx has become more complex with a lot of moving parts – a broader product portfolio, more complex channels, and more go-to-market motions. Joos believes that as CEO he is best positioned to see all those moving parts and affect the changes required to succeed. He views himself as the quarterback who pushes the Chief Revenue Officer, Chief Marketing Officer, and the Enterprise Program Management Office to transform the commercial model at TPx. "The heads of sales, marketing report directly to me and we all work as a team to drive growth," says Joos. "No one is motivated to operate on their own because we have the same short term and long term goals and alignment. We're all incented on the same objectives and tied to the same set of metrics, and we are all compensated the same way."

"This works for me because while marketing and sales are working closely on maximizing any demand generation investments, the CMO has a whole separate workstream establishing the TPx brand and positioning ourselves as an MSP in the marketplace, which is part of our transformation as the TPx brand was historically known as an access provider, not as a company focused on delivering managed services," he continues. "It also applies to change management. Another direct report leads our Enterprise Project Management Office who is driving a lot of these programs and alignment across the business with my team." Finding the optimal design for the sales team is an important issue as Joos pivots TPx to selling more specialized UCaaS, Managed IT, and Security cloud services. TPx leadership is actively rethinking their sales force design to balance sales generalists who represent the full product portfolio to customers with more specialists who fill key gaps in the commercial process, capability, and product knowledge. "Right now we are very horizontal in terms of covering the portfolio and the market segments we target," observes Joos. "We've discussed how that model can be optimized by having a generalist who carries the entire product portfolio but occasionally needs a specialist. As we move to a hybrid model with generalists and overlays, the cost to sell becomes an issue. We have to measure and manage our customer acquisition costs and balance the knowledge required to deliver on an experience with the profitability and growth of our company."

A New Generation of Growth Leader Emerges

More and more we see companies and boards struggling to match their existing management roles against twenty-first-century commercial requirements for serving customers and finding new sources to create value for stakeholders. They learned over time that it is difficult to manage and enable unified Revenue Operations. The traditional marketing, sales, and service leadership roles that delivered performance in the twentieth century have been rendered ineffective or even outdated in light of the trends outlined in chapter 1. Functional hierarchies create silos that are too slow and culturally toxic, and create bottlenecks. As revenue opportunities flow across the functions, too many failure points create leakage and underperformance.

The existence of silos in large enterprises is nothing new. It is one of the disadvantages of scale. But our research shows that the challenge of aligning marketing, sales, and service appears to be nearly universal within organizations of almost all sizes. You'd probably expect smaller companies to have advantages in connecting their teams, given the lower number of players and the higher frequency of individual leaders that combine multiple functions simultaneously. But we have worked with companies as small as $3 million in annual revenue that cite gaps in the revenue cycle and misalignment between functions as major obstacles to maximizing revenue. The common trigger that seems to cause these problems is when multiple revenue-facing functions are created under different leaders. This condition exists in businesses of every size.

That's why a new generation of growth leaders is emerging with an expanded mandate to unify sales, marketing, and service and to make the commercial model more data driven, digital, agile, and measurable. These leaders are bringing new skills and perspectives to the management of the entire revenue cycle by c-suite executives and buyers. "Today, growth-oriented boards and CEOs have started to recognize the lines across sales, marketing and customer success functions are blurring and new partnerships and 'CXO' roles are emerging," according to Giovanni Lamarca, partner at ZRG Associates, a leading executive recruiting firm that places boards, CEOs, and CXOs. "Boards, CEOs and HR leaders are rethinking their human capital strategy when it comes to growth leadership. There's a huge push right now for companies to rethink the role of growth leadership based on the ability to work cross-functionally with sales, marketing, product, and customer success, and to go beyond the traditional scope of CMO or SVP of Sales."

Based on our conversations with growth leaders across multiple industries, functions, and profiles, these emerging senior growth leaders must do five essential things:

1. **Provide direction on the allocation of growth capital and operating budgets.** Leadership must reallocate growth resources and investments to reflect the new economics of virtual selling, enable revenue teams to create more value in sales interactions, and maximize the returns on critical selling assets (data, content, and digital selling infrastructure).

2. **Create a common purpose across the organization.** Leadership must foster a culture that makes customer lifetime value the common purpose of every member of the leadership, management, and revenue teams, measurements, and hard financial incentives.

3. **Optimize the growth operating model.** Leadership must optimize the go-to-market architecture (e.g. expand market coverage, engagement model, territory boundaries, quota assignments, and controls) and sales force design (e.g. defining the roles, incentives, skills, and emphasis of the sales team) to maximize speed, engagement, productivity, and scalability of revenue teams and to better leverage digital channels and data-driven selling tools.

4. **Reimagine the growth technology portfolio from the top down.** Growth leaders need to reimagine their legacy growth technology portfolio from the top down to create highly productive ecosystems that eliminate the big points of friction in the sales process and simplify the seller experience. These reconfigured technology portfolios better leverage technology and training investments to drive scalable, consistent, and sustainable growth. They also dramatically improve the speed, quality, effectiveness, and transparency of customer engagement.

5. **Establish a growth culture and aggressive growth targets.** Only leadership can establish a culture that makes revenue growth the top priority of the organization by setting aggressive growth targets; measuring customer health, success, and value; and fostering teamwork and alignment across the six organizations that must work together: sales, product, marketing, customer success, HR, and finance.

These CXOs need to come from somewhere, though, so where do we find them?

Many of the CEOs we interviewed regard themselves as the top growth leader in their organizations. "I view my role as CEO as being the firm's Chief Engagement Officer," reports Steve Lucas, the CEO of ICIMS and author of *Engage to Win: A Blueprint for Success in the Engagement Economy*.[133] "My job is orchestrating the customer experience across many touchpoints and functions. This means developing a real-world strategy for customer engagement, which is something they don't teach in business schools yet because it is different from a traditional marketing or sales approach. Executing a customer engagement strategy involves creating a vocabulary, culture, measurement system and model for orchestrating the engagement of sales, marketing, and services with all the key customer stakeholders in ways that resonate and deliver a superior customer experience."

Several leading companies have redesigned such existing positions as head of sales or head of marketing to create CXO roles that have an expanded scope and mandate to accelerate revenues. The Chief Revenue Officer (CRO), for example, has become a popular title at growing cloud and technology companies in recent years. The number of CRO positions is growing at 28% a year according to LinkedIn job postings.[112] For example, Rev.com is a fast-growing speech-to-text service that is positioned for explosive growth as they move to a SaaS model and exploit a large and attractive market. Rev.com created a new growth leadership role, the Chief Revenue Officer, to help facilitate this transformation of the commercial model and accelerate revenue growth. "I'm not really into titles. I think titles like CRO, and COO can be misleading and different in every company," according to Wade Burgess, CRO of Rev.com.[114] "But it was important to create a new CXO type of role to take the business to the next level." CRO Burgess has a personal mandate to grow sales tenfold, from a hundred million to a billion in revenue over what is probably a five-year arc. He understands that getting there is going to take transformation of the entire go-to-market model – including reconfiguring the product portfolio and changing segmentation, channels, and linking top of the funnel market messaging and positioning to selling.

Other organizations are morphing the role of the Chief Marketing Officer (CMO), a transitory functional role first formally conceived in the 1990s at Coke and P&G, into new roles with broader remit and scope. The secular decline of large paid mass media budgets combined with increases in accountability, digitization, digital demand creation, and data-centric precision are forcing a pivot and a rethinking of the role, responsibilities, and structure of the CMO. Almost a third of organizations do not have a Chief Marketing Officer (CMO), according to Spencer Stuart.[64] Instead, organizations like J&J, Kimberly-Clark, Lyft, Pentair, and Uber are folding the marketing function into new "CXO" life forms – Chief (Growth, Revenue, Commercial, Experience, or Customer) Officers that have a mandate to unify and coordinate sales, marketing, and service organizations into a well-oiled growth machine. Seventy-one percent of the remaining organizations claim that their CMOs are highly integrated and cooperative with their partners in sales, according to the Duke CMO survey.[4]

Larger enterprises, such as Cisco, Honeywell, Splunk, and Pentair, are also introducing expanded CXO roles with titles like Chief Growth Officer, Chief Revenue Officer, Chief Commercial Officer, and Chief Customer Officer with broader scope and a remit to better manage commercial assets, the operations and enablement infrastructure, and the customer journey across the enterprise. For example, Cisco named Gerri Elliott its first ever executive vice president level Chief Customer and Partner Officer responsible for worldwide sales and marketing, field operations, and partnerships across the globe.[27] As the leader of both sales and marketing, Elliott will be aligning those organizations around the company's go-to-market strategy and growth opportunity while still overseeing Cisco's brand asset.

Some organizations are folding all Revenue Operations under one growth leader. GHX, a SaaS company that helps health care providers automate their supply chain processes, combined sales, customer success, and the operations that support them into a single function to support more sustainable and scalable growth. They appointed Scott Kelly as Senior Vice President of Sales, Customer Success, and Revenue Operations. His remit is to instill a culture of collaboration, continuous improvement, and ongoing learning to help revenue teams adapt to innovations in a dynamic market, and better enable the commercial process. As part of his job scope, he has created a Revenue Operations team that includes sales operations, training and development, and key enablement functions like the deal desk into a single organization to drive continuous improvement in the enterprise commercial process.

Ultimately, more wood behind fewer arrows makes the difference. "When sales and marketing work together it can be a force multiplier," reports Joe Cumello, the CMO of Ciena.[126] He works closely with his peers in sales to identify key points of leverage, shared talent, and the optimal mix of resources between sales and marketing in ways that create a multiplier effect between the two. This imperative to foster teamwork across sales, marketing, services, and customer lifetime value extends up to the CEO.

Regardless of the title, installing a primary growth leader to align sales, marketing, and service in accordance with the Revenue Operations model should accelerate growth. Titles, remits, and job scopes will vary from company to company. But the challenge of getting marketing, sales, and service working as one revenue team will not disappear based on nomenclature. A CXO title alone will not empower an executive to make the changes required for Revenue Operations to succeed, warns Corey Torrence. "Merely anointing an individual with a CXO title, e.g. Chief Transformation Officer, Chief Growth Officer without a strong mandate, clear scope, and measurable KPIs to transform commercial operations and a robust Revenue Operations function to drive execution in the field is a weak solution to a problem that is not going to drive desired results."

CHAPTER 5

Use One of Three Leadership Models: The Tsar, the Federation, and the Chief of Staff

As demonstrated in the prior chapter, organizations are experimenting with different leadership structures to find a better way to align revenue teams and unlock higher growth. The functional model that has grown dominant over the last half century provides a comforting familiarity with minimal disruption. Many organizations have become too comfortable in their current set up and find themselves burdened with outdated structures and frustrated staff. A few innovative leaders, however, have moved beyond the status quo and clustered around three new leadership models for Revenue Operations: the Tsar, the Federation, and the Chief of Staff. Like different political systems – autocracy, democracy, or monarchy – none of them is perfect, and there are certainly shades of gray between them. Still, these three archetypes represent new approaches to draw upon and potentially sources of competitive differentiation. In this chapter you will find a profile of each, including typical pros and cons, and examples of how leading firms have deployed these leadership models.

The Tsar: Putting a "CXO" in Charge of Revenue Teams

The first organizational model that emerged from our research and conversations with industry leaders is called the "Tsar."

The Tsar uses institutional authority to align all the revenue teams. In this approach, the company consolidates decision making and operational control for all revenue-related functions under one leader. In other words, this model creates structural change – whether for a temporary period of time or on a more permanent basis. The traditional functional organizations of marketing, sales, and service may still exist as separate entities, or they may begin to morph and blur lines between them. The big change is that they are all now beholden to one common leader (aside from the CEO). This leader holds all the typical management discretion and tools you would expect: hard reporting lines, budgetary oversight, incentive setting, etc. Here are a few examples that demonstrate how companies have deployed the Tsar approach.

Centralize All Operations Supporting Growth Under a CXO with a Broad Transformation Remit and Authority

A wave of B2B firms, including Avaya, Cisco, Honeywell, GHX, Splunk, and Pentair, have executives with "CXO" roles that have a broader scope and a remit to better manage commercial assets, the operations and enablement infrastructure, and the customer journey across the enterprise.

Often the CEO, President, COO, or business unit head will take on the role of the growth leader by becoming a point-person for all revenue-related functions, centralizing the allocation of all growth resources, and creating a common purpose for all customer-facing employees and functions. Alignment happens from the top down because a single leader, the "tsar," approves the growth strategy and allocates the resources to make it happen. Unfortunately, most leaders don't have a professional background or hands-on experience in each of the core functional areas and thus struggle to competently extract the best from all of them. Also, many organizations don't give these executives the span of control they need, or in the case of the CEO, put too much control in that one person's hands, creating a devastating bottleneck in the operation of the business. Nonetheless, naming one growth leader remains attractive to many for its clarity, and many organizations are adopting this approach.

Establish a CXO Executive to Lead Commercial Transformation and Coordinate All Revenue Team Functions

Avaya put sales, channels, customer success, and marketing under one CXO to create a culture of teamwork and a single point of accountability for all revenue teams. "One of the things we did to make our revenue team more successful was to bring in a Chief Revenue Officer (CRO) to create a single point of authority over that entire go-to-market organization on a global scale," says Jim Chirico, the CEO of Avaya.[132] "The CRO is the accountable party for marketing, sales, delivery, customer success, professional services, and all the channel partners that support our organization. These are hard line reports. Subsequently we brought on a global head of services, an SVP in charge of global channels, and a global head of strategic partnerships who are key to bringing new technologies to market – all reporting to our CRO. It is working out extremely well. The teams get along quite well, which has really reinforced our core cultural principles of teamwork and trust. It has also made things simpler – because this is a much simpler organization. It may sound complicated, but it is much simpler because there is a single point of accountability, and he makes sure our revenue teams are empowered and in control of their success. It is a matrix environment. The teams still work in the local theatres on a dotted line basis. And the theatres still manage the direct business."

Centralize All Decisions About Cross-Functional Resource Allocation, Infrastructure, and Commercial Architecture

Splunk centralized the management of their commercial operations, enablement systems, and insights that support the revenue cycle to drive double-digit growth at scale ($2.4B in revenues). To facilitate those changes, they brought in a new leader to integrate the operations that support the revenue teams across customer success, marketing, and sales, and demand higher returns on their investment in sales enablement and revenue intelligence. The company established a President and Chief Growth Officer function to sit on top of these growth functions to get them to work better together. This approach demands accountability from every revenue resource, program, and capital investment by defining financially valid criteria (SLA) to prioritize, size, allocate, and measure growth resources and capital investments.

Christian Smith, CRO of Splunk, understands the impact of holding every commercial function, including sales enablement, accountable for generating measurable growth outcomes and financially valid returns on investment. "One of the first things I did when I took on global sales was to measure the impact of enablement, which is controversial," says Smith.[163] "I wanted to know that what we were doing was actually working, and that's essential to unlocking more growth potential from data and technology. And that focus on ROI has really helped us optimize our enablement philosophy. It has led us to focus on high impact goals like enabling just-in-time learning and specializing our enablement investments to make them more role based and goal oriented," he continues. "Measuring the impact of enablement helps us understand if the productivity initiatives that we have are paying off. For example, we have actually gotten our productivity of ramping new hires to be 35% faster than a year ago. We also measure the impact of investments on the productivity of existing reps. It's part of our corporate metrics that we review at e-staff every week."

Creating a Common Purpose and Culture of Growth

Marc Lautenbach joined Pitney Bowes as CEO eight years ago on a mission to turn a business in secular decline into a growth business that offers market-leading mailing, shipping, e-commerce logistics, and financial services solutions. Lautenbach set corporate performance goals that defined success for all go-to-market functions and cascaded down to customer-facing teams. He provided the leadership the business needed to deliver more value to its clients and return the business to revenue growth – from launching digital channels, to championing the go-to-market transformation, to investing in product innovation in mailing, shipping, and logistics markets. Marc has the entire organization focused on accelerating profitable revenue growth going forward. Lautenbach laid out three clear go-to-market performance goals that define success for the revenue team – to build a digital sales and service channel for their new Sending Technology business, improve the customer experience, and reduce selling costs with better teamwork between marketing, field sales, and inside sales channels. By working together, his sales and marketing leadership were able to sell the majority of their simpler transactions directly on the web, halve inbound phone account servicing calls by migrating those transactions to a digital sales and service channel, while significantly improving the client experience with digital customer satisfaction scores above 80%. As a by-product of all this effort, the company was able to free up sales resources to focus on growth, higher-potential market segments, and most importantly, to deepen their client relationships.

The Federation: An Alliance Among Leadership Functions

The second organizational model that emerged from our research and conversations with industry leaders is called the Federation.

It uses processes outside the organizational structure to foster teamwork. In this approach, the company creates rules of engagement, steering committees, and service-level agreements among growth leaders to coordinate priorities, manage growth initiatives, and work together to remove obstacles. A matrix overlay emerges to establish joint accountability and common purpose without making any official changes in the reporting structure or organizational chart. This last point makes the Federation the least disruptive to the status quo of our three org models. This model emphasizes teamwork while still allowing the functions to build domain expertise. Such an arrangement relies on trust – which is notoriously absent in most corporate teams – and requires time, another precious and rare commodity, to build any real consensus. Here are a few examples that demonstrate how companies have deployed the Federation approach.

The Wonder Twins at insightsoftware

Joe Healey and Stacy West, the company's Chief Operating Officer and Chief Marketing Officer respectively, represent a new generation of growth leader with an expanded remit to drive organic growth and a mandate to align sales with customer success and professional services.[118] As the COO, Joe maintains direct control over sales, customer success, customer support, professional services, and a tight partnership with Stacy in marketing. Joe and Stacy work very closely on sales force design, go-to-market strategy, and the methods they deploy to manage the commercial teams, processes, systems, and operations that support revenue growth. "Joe and I refer to ourselves as the wonder twins," reports West.[118]

"We think alike, and we approach situations the same way so frequently that I find myself saying, get out of my brain. I don't think there's anything revolutionary about the need for sales and marketing to work closely together but making it a successful reality is another story. Joe and I share a mutual respect, and we feel equally responsible for maintaining strong lines of communication and working in lockstep to scale this business. Our past experiences leading previous sales and marketing teams is a real benefit, and it allows us to better understand the upstream and downstream impact of the decisions we are making. That's where I occasionally see other leaders 'shoot themselves in the foot.' Sometimes, sales will make a decision, and they don't understand, or consider, the impact it will have on marketing, or vice versa." Stacy and Joe collaborate very closely to aggressively penetrate and expand share of a growing market. Together they are building out and enabling a mix of direct and indirect channels, redefining the roles in those channels to improve front of the funnel business development, product expertise, and account management, and focusing these teams on tighter market segments and buyer personas.

To coordinate all moving parts, Stacy and Joe are using process overlays more than official changes to the organization. For example, they are moving toward a Revenue Operations framework for managing the people, processes, and systems responsible for revenue growth. They are actively synchronizing the two operations teams that support revenue: marketing operations (owned by Stacy) with sales and service operations (owned by Joe). "I've deployed Revenue Operations and integrated sales and marketing operations in past companies," says Healey. "Our path right now is to continue to have marketing ops and sales ops separate today but sharing information and working together to support the entire customer journey. For example, Stacy and her team make sure first party signals and intent data from ABM are fed to the BDR teams, Account Development Reps (ADR), and Client Development Reps (CDRs) in partnership with our sales and customer success operations teams."

By working together, West and Healey have been able to effectively share data and insights across sales and marketing to adapt to market opportunity and manage the end-to-end commercial process in a more unified and coordinated way. Stacy's marketing team designs go-to-market content that delivers a consistent value proposition, and Healey deploys all members of the revenue team to carry that message to their target markets. "Beyond sales and marketing, it's important to involve key customer support, technical support, and customer success team members in the customer journey," says West. "I think of it a little like lean manufacturing – you train people up and down the line to help bolster the teams' efforts and achieve desired outcomes. We are continuously improving this model within sales, marketing, customer success, and customer support. And we work hard to retain our top talent to build institutional knowledge and continue growing at this rapid pace."

Common Purpose and Culture of Teamwork at Ciena

Joe Cumello and Jason Phipps lead marketing and sales respectively for Ciena (CIEN), a networking systems, services, and software company.[126] Over the past four years they have forged a tight partnership that is rare in terms of trust, teamwork, and results – contributing to over $1 billion in new growth.

Though the "marriage" of sales and marketing challenges every organization, especially in the B2B technology sector, Joe and Jason have been able to build a highly effective working relationship. Their partnership has been tremendously successful when it comes to culture, teamwork, and revenue growth. Over the last five years, Ciena has grown revenue from $2.4 billion to $3.6 billion.

Joe and Jason have cracked the code on what is a huge problem for most enterprises – getting sales and marketing to work as one. "It all starts with an invitation by sales leadership to set the table in some ways, and a recognition of the value of marketing," says Joe Cumello, who leads marketing. "I've got to compliment Jason for setting up the arrangement because at the time I reported to him as SVP of sales. Jason invited me to be a strategic partner with a seat at the table for every strategic conversation about growth in the company because he understands when sales and marketing work together it can be a 'force multiplier.' That's certainly different from what I've experienced throughout my career, where marketing has traditionally been viewed as 'serving' sales."

"I'd start with the first conversation I had with Joe when we were considering bringing marketing and sales together under one umbrella a number of years back," says Phipps. "Just to be clear, today sales and marketing are two peers on the executive leadership team, reporting to the CEO. There are a few factors underlying our bringing the sales and marketing functions together. Leverage and talent. Sales plays a big role in our growth, and there was a fear that sales was going to take all the marketing money. But frankly, that had already happened, so I viewed this as actually a way to reallocate those resources more optimally by taking advantage of the 'multiplier effect' between sales and marketing. This was important because growth dollars are not unlimited, and at some point putting another body in front of the customer doesn't create the growth that putting that dollar into marketing will accomplish. I believe there is a lot more leverage putting the next growth dollar into marketing, particularly when you've reached critical mass."

"From a talent perspective, coupling sales and marketing allows us to have more interactions in terms of talent on both teams and opinions," according to Phipps. "One of the things Joe did was bring in new talent in terms of adding key people to the operations and product marketing teams who had sales backgrounds as well as marketing experience. These key managers brought immediate credibility and respect that made it easier to create leverage and synergies across our teams. Trust and teamwork are critical components of business in the twenty-first century, even if the results can be harder to quantify."

Phipps identified a key to their collaboration is that Ciena is a very metrics-driven business. "We both realized it's important to capture the more qualitative aspects of growth in terms of meaningful conversations with the customer and the number of times the sales team raised their hands," Phipps reports. "And we brought marketing – as well as the engineering and product teams – into the conversations with the customer, in quarterly business reviews, and other account development activities. These collaborations demonstrated we were building trust and that marketing was being viewed as an extension of the sales team. So, we've moved to more of a 'Quality of Engagement' (QOE) score to measure our account teams that reflects all of the actions, activity and engagement that contribute to account health and lifetime value."

"Traditional demand generation metrics – MQL, SQL – were not effective or relevant for us because we have very deep customer relationships and a long (nine months or more) sales cycle," adds Cumello. "So, we had to adapt our approach. What we really care about is moving the needle within an account – focusing on the next RFP or engaging more deeply with the key stakeholders – to open up different areas of the account or diversify the business strategy within the account. I want to be able to supply our sales team with data about how customers engage with us across all our materials and enablement, and then give that to Jason and say this is what a winning engagement model looks like when we win, and this is what happens when we lose."

"So, we've developed customer engagement reporting and Quality of Engagement (QOE) measurements that give us a more complete and real time picture of the breadth, depth, and frequency and impact we are having on our customers," he continues. "Our dashboard is like an 'EKG for selling' that gives us a dynamic and digital picture of what is going on in the account. Are we engaging the right levels in the organization? And are those stakeholders attending webinars, participating in 'Demo days,' or downloading materials?"

"Bringing it all together takes more than teamwork; it also requires that different functions share data," says Phipps. "A big part of that is rethinking how we organize our operations and enablement organizations. Operationally, we've had to coordinate and integrate marketing and sales operations. Joe and I have a common operations support team. Joe has Marketing operations on this team which creates the customer engagement dashboard, or what we've been calling the 'EKG.' The sales enablement and sales operations folks who are focused on QOE (Quality of Engagement) measurements are on my team. But they'll have a connection to Joe's marketing operations leader, because when he's looking at the customer engagement dashboard, or EKG, in the field, we know this is going to be correlated to the Quality of Engagement score. So, if we have a high QOE on a particular account, then it should have a better EKG."

This teamwork extends just beyond the two leaders and encompasses the entire business. "We've also worked with our partners in IT to better leverage data from across the organization," says Cumello. "A lot of companies, and ours is one of them, have data silos from operations to the finance function. This goes beyond what Jason and I have control over so that's a bigger discussion than just sales and marketing operations. So, we had to step back and have a bigger discussion amongst the leadership about what we want to do with data and analytics and AI and how we amalgamate and create value with the data. This will create a big opportunity."

The Demand Generation Board at Oracle and SAP

Globalization of functions – the consolidation of functional resources, people, and budgets from all parts of the company into one global organization – has become popular over the last few decades. This effort is usually intended to increase professionalization by consolidating domain expertise and to improve efficiency by reducing fragmentation. The consolidation of back-office functions is fairly commonplace, yet globalization of customer-facing functions like marketing and sales tends to generate more internal friction. For example, the creation of a global marketing function can also create greater separation and misalignment with other business functions, such as sales, which will resent the loss of control.

Oracle globalized its marketing function in 2000, moving all the budgets, headcount, and program prioritization from the regionally based teams to the CMO. To maintain connective tissue with sales, the field marketing leaders in Asia and Europe pioneered a new concept, the Demand Generation Board (DGB), to serve as a transparent planning, prioritization, and alignment process between sales and marketing. The DBG was, in essence, a quarterly meeting between the key heads of sales and marketing in the region to

1. review market, revenue, and customer data;
2. agree on the primary go-to-market plays that we wanted to make; and
3. prioritize the allocation of resources to generate sufficient demand for us to meet and exceed our revenue targets.

Enthusiasm for the process grew, and Charles Phillips, President of Oracle at the time, imported the process from the regions to set it up globally. That move extended the DGB up to corporate leadership and down to subregions. Once successful, the meetings added more functions to the roster, and eventually the DGB evolved to serve as a leadership meeting dedicated to go-to-market topics for the entire business.

A few years later, SAP adopted a similar practice to foster the successful alliance between sales and marketing work. This time the DGB used more analytics to measure the before and after results and to assess the revenue impact of marketing efforts. Using the DGB process, SAP generated 55% more pipeline opportunities and increased the combined value of those marketing-generated opportunities by 48% with roughly the same resources.

Collaborative Resource Allocation at Juniper

Mike Marcellin and Marcus Jewell are respectively the Chief Marketing Officer and Chief Revenue Officer of Juniper Networks, a leader in secure, AI-driven networks that connect the world. Over the past several years they have forged a tight partnership between sales and marketing that is rare in terms of teamwork and results – contributing to a surge in revenue growth and turning Juniper back into an agile growth company.

After a decade of profitable but relatively flat growth as their core telecommunications and infrastructure markets have matured, revenue growth has increased to 8% in the last sales quarter on a large base of almost $5 billion in revenues, with record levels of customer satisfaction and new logo sales. Their go-to-market team has expanded Juniper into new markets where they are growing much faster – including AI-driven enterprise solutions (28%), cloud-ready data center solutions (28%), and security (21%). This has moved Juniper from what Mike Marcellin describes as a "margin maximizer" to an "agile growth" enterprise with the ability to pivot faster and realize the potential of new and attractive growth markets.

"A few years ago we as a leadership team realized we would not achieve our growth objectives by just selling to the same customers we've sold to in the past," adds Marcellin.[116] "We made that decision collectively as a leadership team. That was a sales statement, a marketing statement, and a product build statement. Growth has become a team sport and all of those things together have now allowed us to expand successfully."

To go after those markets, Juniper has invested tens of millions of dollars more into sales and marketing over the last several years. And they are getting results. Because they work as a team, Marcellin and Jewell were able to balance how those growth funds were invested across the revenue cycle. They also were very thoughtful about the portion of funds that should go toward capital investments in technology versus adding the right skills to the revenue team.

"How we allocate that investment is interesting," says Marcus Jewell. "The emergence of low-touch and no-touch digital channels and the need to align sales, marketing, and customer success have really changed the way we think about budgets and resource allocation. Mike and I look at the increases in growth investment as a 'fungible budget' between ourselves in terms of where we spend it. We run a small steering committee to figure out where we should put this money to drive the greatest growth and realize the most opportunity across our markets. We set clear OKRs (Objectives and Key Results) about the outcomes we are looking to achieve and use that to agree on the best allocation. Ultimately, we don't really separate the sales and marketing budget when we look at our growth engines. We make sure that those investments are linked across our organizations, and we keep it flexible and dynamic."

"In my years of experience allocating marketing and product budgets, that's pretty unique," adds Marcellin. "Normally everyone gets their budget target, and you do what you can with that. But there's a limited ability to shift money around in real-time as we see opportunities pop up. I think you have to be more agile and be thinking about your entire go-to-market engine to compete in the rapidly evolving markets we operate in."

The Chief of Staff: A Revenue Operations "Rock Star"

In the Chief of Staff organizational model, sales operations, marketing operations, and other similar roles – like sales enablement, customer analytics, and training and development – merge into one unit that provides support for the marketing, sales, and service functions. Though closer to the field, such teams are still relatively new. The mix of institutional authority and indirect influence required creates an ambiguity that some organizations find challenging to balance. Still, this approach is gaining some traction. Fast-growing organizations like Splunk and Rev.com carry investor expectations for organic growth in excess of 50% and have taken steps to consolidate the operations that support marketing, sales, and customer success under a single leader. TPX Communications, Avaya, Sirius XM, and Rev.com have taken more formal steps to put one leader in charge of all revenue-centric operations functions with hard-line reporting relationships, including sales operations, marketing operations, and sales enablement of the deal desk.

This allows them to have one executive with the mandate to "connect the dots" across the systems that support marketing.

For example, this structure makes it much easier to collect first-party data from website and digital marketing campaigns (owned by marketing operations), match it to account structures and contacts in CRM (owned by sales operations), deliver it to frontline sellers (using tools owned by sales enablement), and report on account health (owned by customer analytics).

It also helps connect selling playbooks (that reside in sales operations) with training systems (owned by training and development) with systems that track, record, and analyze what actually happens in sellers' calls (owned by sales enablement).

It's helpful to have one executive pulling the lever on all the systems that support the revenue lifecycle. It's easier to have one "throat to choke" accountable for curating your customer engagement data, which lives in dozens of different systems.

In many ways this is the most visible change from the status quo, as a "new" function is created on the org chart, and that function changes the authority matrix at its lower but not its top levels. Not surprisingly, there is a growing trend to name this new function simply "Revenue Operations." Although such a step does move toward Revenue Operations, the material in this book presents a more comprehensive and proven approach.

Case Study: Enhancing Value Across the Company at GHX

In his role as the leader of Sales, Customer Success, and Revenue Operations, Scott Kelley's remit is to align GHX customer-facing revenue teams and the commercial operations that support them to deliver more sustainable and scalable growth and realize the full potential of this dynamic market.[127]

Over the past two decades, GHX has grown both inorganically through acquisition and organically through its customer relationships. The potential to create value across that ecosystem of trusted relationships has made accelerating organic growth a strategic organizational priority. "Organic growth has emerged as a top priority in our organization because we have such a big opportunity to create even more value across our customer network," shares Kelley. "Given our strong market penetration, we are largely focused on delivering even greater value to our existing customers – this often means partnering throughout our innovation process, deepening our understanding of their needs and connecting them with in-house experts."

As GHX has expanded its network and offerings, the complexity of its products, customers, organization, and go-to-market approach grew dramatically. "As we acquired businesses we've added complexity to our commercial model," says Kelley.

This growing complexity compelled leadership to transform their commercial model to align commercial teams, processes, and resources around expanding customer lifetime value and finding ways to simplify and streamline the cross-functional customer journey. "We realized that in order to support sustainable organic growth as our business grew more complex through acquisitions and innovations, we were going to have to evolve the organizations and operations that support growth to drive alignment across those individual customer segments that each of our businesses serve," reports Kelley.

Kelley believes that commercial transformation starts at the top, and leadership is by far the biggest factor in supporting current and future growth. "We believe that a strong culture can overcome a variety of growth obstacles," shares Kelley. "So our leadership has focused on building a culture of continuous improvement and collaboration."

Scott Kelley's scope of responsibilities includes the need to instill a culture of collaboration, continuous improvement, and ongoing learning to help align revenue teams to innovations in a dynamic market, and to better enable the commercial process. To empower Scott to make the changes needed to scale, GHX combined sales, customer success, and the operations that support them into a single, aligned structure to support more sustainable and scalable growth. To integrate these critical functions, Kelley has created a Revenue Operations team that includes sales operations, training, and development, and other key enablement functions, e.g. the deal desk, into a single organization to drive continuous improvement in the enterprise commercial process.

"It's all about alignment with our customers," reports Kelley. "Alignment – team alignment, technology alignment and, most importantly, cultural alignment – is critical to our ability to unlock greater value for our customers and, in turn, the growth potential of our offerings. My job is to make sure all our sales and customer success teams are aligned across each of our segments and that our customers see us as one GHX – a single organization focused on helping them solve problems, unlock value and drive cost out of healthcare. To do that we need to have our finger on the pulse of what our customers are going through and what they need to achieve their goals. And one of the best sources for voice of customer are the sales team."

Optimizing the commercial architecture has become increasingly important as GHX has evolved as a SaaS business. This has shifted the emphasis of the sales organization to maximizing customer lifetime value and the penetration of its full suite of supply chain, compliance, clinical and financial offerings. Kelley is constantly monitoring changes in customer behavior and revisiting historical assumptions about sales performance to optimize the commercial architecture to better cover the market and allocate resources. To accomplish this, Scott's team has refocused account priorities, buyer personas and calling points within accounts. Kelley has also introduced new specialist roles in the sales force and placed a greater emphasis on customer success.

"The single biggest thing that keeps me up at night is how effectively we are engaging with our customers," shares Kelley. "As a SaaS business, if we are not engaging in a manner that aligns with client goals then we're not successful. We need to constantly evaluate questions like do our front-line sellers know the most important customers and calling points in every account? Are they in regular and meaningful contact with them? Is our customer success team engaging in a way that's not only fixing a problem but being proactive and helping customers get the most out of our solutions? Do we have technology in place that provides us visibility to when our customers are or are not using our tools – and will our customer success team rally quickly to engage with that customer? Will we find the right balance between videoconferencing and face-to-face engagement as we come out of the pandemic?"

Kelley is extremely data driven and metrics oriented. He uses pipeline health, customer engagement, and seller performance data to optimize resource allocation and seller performance. He does this by testing the assumptions underlying sales territory definitions and quota plans to find the optimal balance between realizing the most market opportunity and sales rep quota attainment, capacity, capabilities, and stress. "As an operating executive, I look at the sales team as the most important customer touch point in an organization that needs to be carefully modeled to effectively engage with customers while not overly stressing sellers and customers," shares Kelley. "I also want to know the math behind plans to generate a specific amount of sales. We use that information as the underpinning of the performance metrics we track to align our salespeople to their territories, quotas, and incentives. The historic data – the average time to close a deal, the cadence of sales calls made by reps, and the historical performance of a rep (in a given role) – to guide us."

Another key to success has been to establish and enable a culture of continuous learning and process improvement. "Continuous learning is critical to keeping up with the rapid evolution of our products, network, and market innovations," reports Kelley. "Going back early in my career with GE and Fuji Medical, I really learned to treat training as a continuous process, similar to other highly skilled professions."

An Operating System for Conecting Technology, Data, Processes, and Teams

PART III

CHAPTER 6

Assemble the Nine Building Blocks of Revenue Operations

In Part I of this book, we established that organic growth is the primary driver of firm value. That growth formula keeps changing, however, as buyer behavior changes, as digital technology becomes critical to selling, and as our organizations deal with the fragmentation of growth functions. To solve these challenges, companies need to balance the art and science of growth by adopting a systems-based commercial model. That model is Revenue Operations.

In Part II of the book, we introduced a management system for aligning your revenue teams. That management system has six specific pillars that embed several core leadership principles. Based on our research and interviews, we presented three alternatives on how to structure the leadership and operations of your revenue teams.

In this section of the book, we introduce the second component system of Revenue Operations, an operating system. This operating system combines technology, data, processes, and teams to help you generate consistent and scalable growth.

Consistency may be boring, but it represents a manageable path to value creation. Businesses like Toyota and GE created hundreds of billions of dollars of firm value by applying continuous process improvement to their operations and supply chains. For this they used principles like Lean Manufacturing, Kaizen, Six Sigma, And Total Quality Management. Why not take a similar approach to the customer-facing part of the business? Consistent, repeatable revenue growth earns a lot of benefits: sellers execute the assigned selling motion and playbook better; programs generate predictable outcomes; analytics make more accurate predictions about who to call and what to do; and more sellers make quota.

Scalability is even more attractive to investors. Digital technology – especially advanced analytics and AI – offers enormous potential to improve the productivity, engagement, speed, and visibility of sales teams. At their best, data, infrastructure, and processes interact within a technology ecosystem to accelerate sales growth, multiply the return on selling assets, and increase firm value. Although sales and marketing technology investments may have generated returns in narrow or isolated situations, the technology has rarely fulfilled anything close to its immense promise.

This operating system creates value in three ways: revenue expansion, cost reduction, and improved customer experience. Individual actions can realize continuous improvements in revenue, cost, or customer experience. If you find ways to improve two of those elements at the same time, that's what the late Professor Sumantra Ghoshal would call *radical* business performance improvement in his book *Radical Change*.[107]

How about delivering all three at once? That used to be considered impossible. But it's not! Building on our research and conversations with so many CXOs, targeting improvements in all three areas simultaneously is not only possible but also essential. Such transformation can only happen by adopting a systems-based approach. That's Revenue Operations. Whether you want small wins, big wins, or even commercial transformation, it offers the best path to get there.

What Does an Operating System for Business Look Like?

Connected data, technology, automation, and processes serve as a bridge between the nine building blocks that make up the foundation of the operating system that enables Revenue Operations to take hold. To make this less of a mouthful, we simply call this the Revenue Operating System (ROS) Technology infrastructure. At its heart, the Revenue Operating System uses commercial insights to connect your growth assets and value drivers in ways that generate growth and create firm value (see Figure 6.1).

Growth assets include the physical and increasingly important intangible assets you use to acquire, develop, and expand customer relationships. People, data, technology, brand preference, selling methods, customer relationship equity, channels, and mindshare represent just a few of these.

FIGURE 6.1 The Revenue Operating System: Introduction

The people in your marketing, sales, and service teams are often the biggest resource in the selling system, though the shift to digital channels and selling infrastructure have made selling more capital intensive. Over 90% of the CEOs and leaders we spoke with told us, in one way or another, that "our people are our biggest growth assets." Collectively, these growth assets represent large financial investments in your business with an operating budget that generally ranges from 15 to 50% of overall revenues, depending on company size and scale.

Commercial insights inform actions, conversations, and decisions. To us, commercial insights are the intelligence that informs management decisions, selling actions, and resource allocation. Not data alone. Insights act as the mechanism that allows you to connect your growth assets to the value drivers. Advanced analytics delivers intelligence about customer demand, buyer preference, opportunities, seller productivity, and customer response. Intelligence about seller skills, activities, and performance improves skill training, content, resource allocation, and effectiveness. Using top-down and bottom-up insights, leaders gain visibility into account health, pipeline health, seller performance, and dynamic changes in the market.

Value drivers are capabilities that generate more revenue and margins from your teams and resources. Talent management, innovation, pricing, promotions, and process automation help optimally allocate resources against opportunities, maximize the yield from every selling interaction, and unlock the full potential of your selling talent. For example, B2B selling organizations can get higher engagement, speed of response, and productivity from their sales reps at lower costs by migrating more customer interactions to low-touch digital channels and by using enabling technologies to enhance the value of personal interactions.

Most organizations have historically managed their growth assets and capabilities in fragmented and tactical ways. For example, three decades after the advent of CRM, 67% of enterprise CRM implementations still generate lower than acceptable return on investment, less than satisfactory user adoption, and an unfortunate amount of unrealized potential, according to research by the Sales Management Association.[2]

To be clear, the problem is not CRM technology. Salesforce.com is integrated into most of the leading sales enablement, engagement, and analytics tools in our list of the top 100 technologies that are transforming the commercial model.[25] The failure to make CRM part of a simplified seller workflow and system of record for all customer engagement data, however, is the problem. It's a systems problem – not a technology problem.

The Building Blocks of the Revenue Operating System

According to our research, the Revenue Operating System can be broken down into nine discrete building blocks. Three growth assets include the selling technology stack, the customer-facing technology stack, and the channels your organization uses to engage and sell to customers. Commercial insights include data around customer engagement, data around seller behavior, and an advanced analytics hub that consolidates and examines all revenue-related data for patterns, insights, and triggers. Three value drivers also identify the capabilities to find and develop talent, optimally deploy resources, and deliver revenue enhancements like pricing, packaging, and promotions.

Here is a list of the nine elements (see Figure 6.2):

1. **Revenue Enablement:** The commercial technology assets, capabilities, and systems that support sellers. These include CRM and sales enablement, engagement, content management, and readiness systems. Also, they encompass a wide range of specialized tools and solutions that support the day-to-day selling workflow.

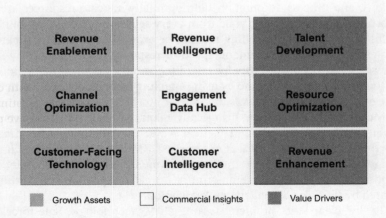

FIGURE 6.2 The Revenue Operating System: Building Blocks

2. **Channel Optimization:** The systems, processes, and capabilities that improve the engagement, productivity, cadence, intersection, and coverage of selling channels – both digital and analog (human).

3. **Customer-Facing Technology:** Your "owned" digital selling infrastructure, including websites, blogs, mobile apps, and e-commerce platforms. It also includes your marketing automation, contactless selling, and social media solutions you use to attract and engage customers digitally.

4. **Revenue Intelligence:** The analytics and information technologies that extract insights from your selling and transaction data sources to help growth leaders manage and measure the financial return on growth strategies, investments, and programs. Such intelligence includes measurements, dashboards, and analytic capabilities that your organization uses to assess the financial return on growth strategies, investments, and programs.

5. **Engagement Data Hub:** The technology and capabilities that aggregate, transform, and monetize all customer, revenue, and seller activity data from first-party systems and third-party data sources.

6. **Customer Intelligence:** The software applications, capabilities, and processes that convert customer data into actionable insights and help customer-facing teams to make better decisions, optimize campaigns, recommend actions, answer questions, and set selling priorities.

7. **Talent Development:** All the technology, processes, assets, and capabilities that you use to attract, develop, and retain selling talent across all functions. This includes training methodologies, selling playbooks, learning management systems, sales readiness and development software, and learning and development programs.

8. **Resource Optimization:** The technology, processes, and capabilities your organization uses to optimally allocate people, time, and effort against customers and markets. It includes applications and analytics that help you define territories, set quotas, prioritize accounts, and direct demand management activities.

9. **Revenue Enhancement:** The technology and processes that help sellers generate more margin, revenue, and value in their interactions with customers. These include tools, capabilities, and solutions that help optimize and enforce pricing, personalize offerings, and create more effective presentations and proposals.

Every organization must develop each of these building blocks, even if the deployment and execution vary slightly with the competitive differentiation of every company. Some will involve tangible software platforms and organizations, such as CRM or a sales enablement function. Others will be "intangible" elements that exist between the ears of your team members as belief systems, selling expertise, or operating assumptions. For example, most territory and quota plans allocate resources based on historical performance data and institutional predispositions that are not documented, widely shared, or periodically retested against dynamic market conditions.[130]

These nine building blocks are universal to any modern selling system. Managers from different organizations, perspectives, and backgrounds can understand them. Importantly, the standardization of the nomenclature provides a common vocabulary that allows different players to identify, agree upon, and communicate around collaborative efforts that accelerate revenue growth, reduce costs, and improve the customer experience.

These building blocks serve as centers of gravity within your organization without taking away what makes you who you are. Historical organizational structures and legacy technology investments can certainly create barriers to growth, but the operating system here creates a resilience and an always-on focus that most businesses don't have.

The Team That Connects the Most Dots Wins

Revenue Operations requires real alignment and integration across traditionally compartmentalized divisions of your revenue team to be successful. This operating system looks for ways you can use insights to connect all the pieces in meaningful, differentiated, and value-creating ways.

The team that connects the most dots wins.

Finding the connective tissue between building blocks amplifies results and creates inherent value from better channel performance, optimized resource allocation, more effective offerings, and of course, more engaged employees.

Here are some of the top ways the executives we interviewed connect the dots to create value:

- Eliminate margin, price, and opportunity leakage by getting greater control over the entire revenue cycle (demand, transaction, and consumption).
- Increase the speed, visibility, and performance of your customer-facing employees by simplifying day-to-day seller interactions.
- Turn your technology into a force multiplier that increases your return on growth assets, resources, and investments.
- Attract, recruit, ramp up, and retain higher-performing sales talent that stays at your company longer.
- Balance resource allocation to support more quota-achieving sales reps and capture more market opportunities.

Business leaders need to connect the dots across an increasingly large and complex technology ecosystem to generate more consistent and scalable growth. The choices for sales infrastructure and customer-facing technology solutions has exploded the range of point solutions, customer touch points, and data sources that we all have to sort out. "Marketers are dealing with an exploding possibility curve in terms of channels, investments, choices and change—it's difficult to set priorities when there are so many smart things to pursue," says David Edelman, former CMO of Aetna. In the past 20 years, this portfolio of technology investments now occupies a significant portion of the sales and marketing mix and balance sheet. Owned digital infrastructure and resources (i.e. content, data scientists, bloggers, and promotions) arguably fill two-thirds of the marketing mix, for example, according to an analysis by the Marketing Accountability Standards Board.[1] (See Figure 6.3.) Yet these critical growth assets are still managed tactically and in silos.

No single tool will solve every problem. It takes many steps to collect, transform, and deploy information from one source to the person or place where it can create value. Getting effective sales content to sellers at the moment they need it, for example, takes at least three steps and spans many systems. Data about customers is the same. Capturing, aggregating, analyzing, and deploying insights based on customer interaction data is also a multistep journey.

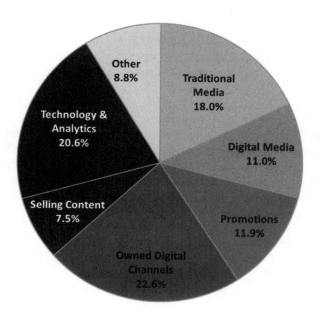

FIGURE 6.3   The Modern Growth Investment Mix. *Source: The Marketing Accountability Standards Board*

Historically, technology vendors would constantly redefine market categories in smaller and smaller terms to find a space where they could defensibly claim a #1 leadership position. A whole industry of analysts has grown up that reinforces this notion with an ever-expanding array of "magic quadrants" and vendor analyses that narrowly define solutions into smaller and tighter market segments. Where a technology provider exists in multiple categories, it too often has to prove its worth as a "platform" or be punished as disjointed and confusing.

Now, rethink this through the lens of the Revenue Operating System, and you'll find leading providers of revenue enablement solutions like Revenue.io, Highspot, 6sense, RFPIO, and Varicent span three or more established technology categories. These providers defy conventional categorization because they've found a better way. They assert that connecting the dots across multiple technology ecosystems is a *good* thing. In fact, every solution included on our rankings of the top 100 technologies that are transforming the commercial model connect at least three of the nine building blocks.[25] They don't see this integration as excess; rather, they promote the connection as a core tenet of their solution's value.

Robert Wahbe, CEO and Co-Founder of Highspot, a platform dedicated to connecting the sales and marketing technologies into more coherent selling workflows, reiterates the importance of having an "operating system" that supports sellers better. "There are thousands of technologies that can improve the performance of revenue teams in terms of generating more consistent revenue attainment, improving the customer experience and selling more value," says Wahbe.[71] "Organizations have invested in 20 on average. Some have 10. Some 40. What's important is not the number of tools, but your ability to connect the dots across the sales and marketing technology ecosystem. This looks complex. And from a product integration and data flow perspective it is. That's where we invest most of our money."

Viral Bajaria, the CTO and Founder of 6sense, reinforces the notion of connecting the commercial technology portfolio into an operating system for growth. He thinks about the sales and marketing technology ecosystem as a periodic table of elements that can help you grow. "You need a holistic system like this because that is how you improve the customer experience, create value and margin, and grow," he says.[70] "You need to orchestrate across the different silos of technology. That's how value gets created in modern selling."

Successful growth leaders like Juniper Networks and Hitachi are using an operating system structure to break down silos of automation and reconnect their sales and marketing technology ecosystems.

"Connecting these dots may sound complicated, but it doesn't have to be," says Jeff McKittrick of WalkMe, who has also led sales enablement at Cisco and Hitachi. "One thing I've learned in 15 years of building and implementing digital selling and sales enablement platforms at Cisco, Hitachi and now WalkMe is that when it comes to technology people tend to overthink things. In reality, knitting together a highly profitable and productive portfolio of selling technologies is not rocket science. It does require hard work, teamwork, and leadership. But there's definitely a cookbook – and the recipe for success is pretty straightforward."

Marcus Jewell, CRO of Juniper Networks, suggests that "the technology tools are useful, but they are really just ingredients to an operating system for growth. The real value," according to Jewell, "is in connecting the dots."[116] Jewell believes that leaders should be orchestrators of different technologies that augment seller activities and customer interactions in a manner consistent with your organization's uniqueness. "Every organization has its own unique 'operating system' for selling," Jewell continues. "So, it's a fallacy to think that there's going to be one platform to fit them all. And why would you abdicate such a strategic asset to an outside one size fits all tool?"

Mike Marcellin, CMO of Juniper Networks, adds: "It's particularly important to connect the dots between sales and marketing because selling is not a linear process. Both sales and marketing operations both have assets that can enable the complete revenue cycle. Sales may dip in and do some things. Marketing may engage in other parts of the revenue cycle. If one doesn't know what the other is doing you've lost, and the customer has a horrible experience."

Maximize and interconnect your building blocks to create significant growth upside because the current approach likely isn't working. Twenty-five years after the dawn of e-commerce, less than 25% of B2B sales are delivered through digital channels, despite a recent bump from the pandemic. A decade into the era of big data, the impact of analytics on decision-making and firm financial performance remains basically flat, according to research by the Duke Fuqua School of Business.[4] Sales leaders and practitioners are not leveraging the data they have to improve seller effectiveness or discern buyer intent. Adoption rates of other highly touted and ready-to-deploy technologies – 5G communications, augmented reality, and AI – remain less than 10%.[13] Like most selling initiatives, these technologies require effective leadership commitment and change management to realize their potential.

Ultimately, Revenue Operations will manifest itself in a complete rethinking of the full commercial technology stack (meaning all of your sales and marketing technology). The new generation of leaders distinguish themselves by how they get technologies to work together. For them, the building blocks weave together in technology ecosystems that generate higher returns on their selling assets and grow sales, profit, and firm value.

In the next several chapters, we will break down the nine building blocks of the Revenue Operating System into their component parts (see Figure 6.4). We define each of these for clarity in the glossary at the end of the book.

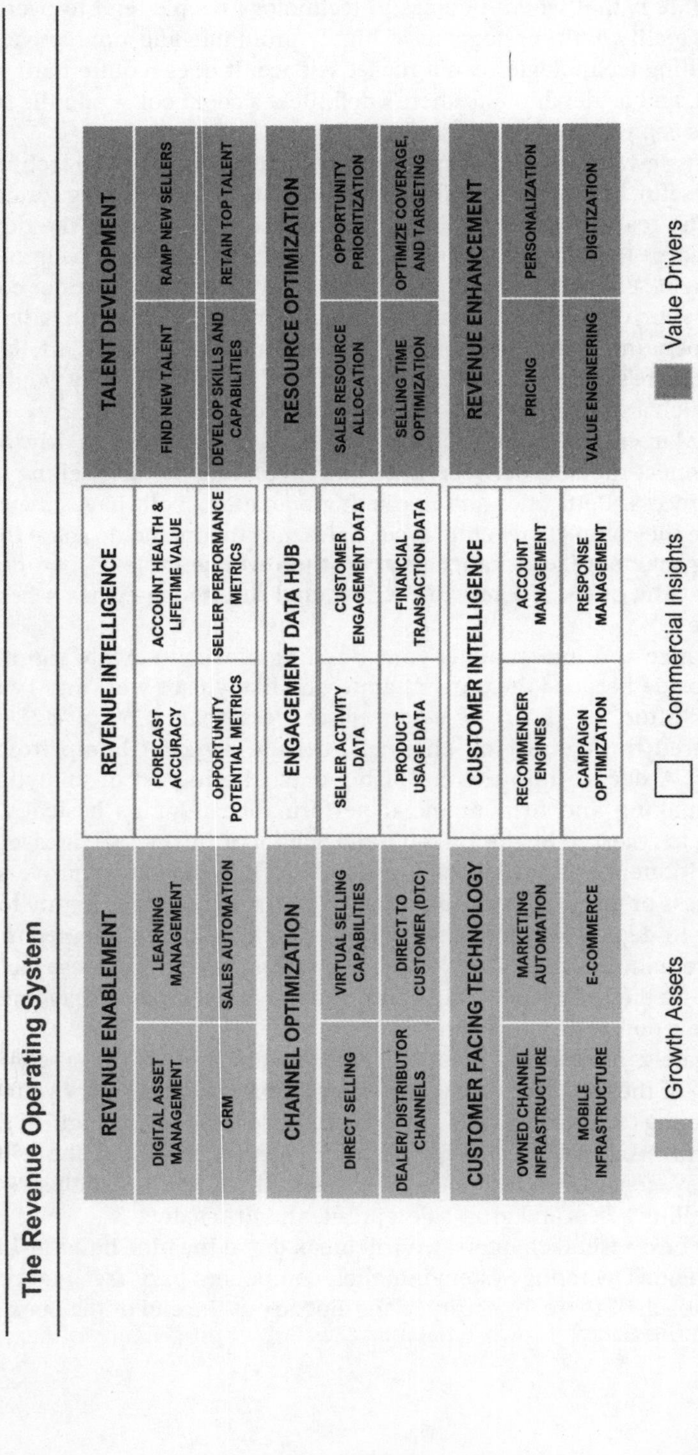

The Revenue Operating System

REVENUE ENABLEMENT		REVENUE INTELLIGENCE		TALENT DEVELOPMENT	
DIGITAL ASSET MANAGEMENT	LEARNING MANAGEMENT	FORECAST ACCURACY	ACCOUNT HEALTH & LIFETIME VALUE	FIND NEW TALENT	RAMP NEW SELLERS
CRM	SALES AUTOMATION	OPPORTUNITY POTENTIAL METRICS	SELLER PERFORMANCE METRICS	DEVELOP SKILLS AND CAPABILITIES	RETAIN TOP TALENT
CHANNEL OPTIMIZATION		ENGAGEMENT DATA HUB		RESOURCE OPTIMIZATION	
DIRECT SELLING	VIRTUAL SELLING CAPABILITIES	SELLER ACTIVITY DATA	CUSTOMER ENGAGEMENT DATA	SALES RESOURCE ALLOCATION	OPPORTUNITY PRIORITIZATION
DEALER/ DISTRIBUTOR CHANNELS	DIRECT TO CUSTOMER (DTC)	PRODUCT USAGE DATA	FINANCIAL TRANSACTION DATA	SELLING TIME OPTIMIZATION	OPTIMIZE COVERAGE, AND TARGETING
CUSTOMER FACING TECHNOLOGY		CUSTOMER INTELLIGENCE		REVENUE ENHANCEMENT	
OWNED CHANNEL INFRASTRUCTURE	MARKETING AUTOMATION	RECOMMENDER ENGINES	ACCOUNT MANAGEMENT	PRICING	PERSONALIZATION
MOBILE INFRASTRUCTURE	E-COMMERCE	CAMPAIGN OPTIMIZATION	RESPONSE MANAGEMENT	VALUE ENGINEERING	DIGITIZATION

■ Growth Assets   □ Commercial Insights   ■ Value Drivers

FIGURE 6.4 The Revenue Operating System

CHAPTER 7

Connect Your Data, Technology, and Channel Assets to Acquire More Customers

The Importance of Strategically Managing the Return on Commercial Assets

The assets that support growth – e.g. customer data, digital channels, sales content, product knowledge, and so on – are among the most financially valuable assets in your business. We like to call them commercial assets. Your operating system must give you the capability to strategically manage those assets.

We've gone from managing sellers to managing selling ecosystems. Humans are still critical, but money and budgets are shifting from human capital to the tools that make those humans more effective. As part of this change, the growth technology portfolio for selling has grown in scale, cost, and complexity.

To acquire new customers, the operating system must help sellers without overburdening them. It must rebalance channels appropriately to maximize revenue yields and turn an organization's owned digital infrastructure into a competitive weapon. Here are some examples of managing core growth assets:

1. **People:** Improve the return on investment from your customer-facing employees. Focus them on the right actions, clients, and conversations. Maximize time spent engaging buyers. Optimize your ability to onboard, ramp, coach, and reinforce the selling behaviors and activities that create customer value. "We focus a lot on our return on assets and the return we get on investment capital – which is north of 20% for us," reports Chris Downie, the CEO of Flexential.[128] "I think of our sales machine as a growth asset, and we invest in developing our sales and channel resources and training them is central to our go-to-market approach and delivering our value proposition to customers."

2. **Customer data:** Manage customer data like the asset that it is. Convert that data into insights that drive revenue and help reps in real time. Unify sales and marketing data sources, transforming and translating them into insights that inform tactical actions. "Business leaders who fail to measure the value of their customer data assets are ignoring the new business realities of the Data Economy and the economics of information in a 21st Century Commercial Model," according to Doug Laney, the author of the book *Infonomics*.[131] "Measuring a data asset's contribution to income streams and expense savings can justify budgets for its care and feeding and establish a minimum for the business value to substantiate data investments to maintain and to monetize that data."

3. **Digital selling technology infrastructure:** Reimagine technology portfolios as an interconnected ecosystem that combines all your existing tools – data, content, people, technology.

4. **Selling content:** Align all selling content, regardless of which organization creates it, around a consistent value story and go-to-market strategy. Consolidate, manage, and align selling content with the customer journey. Use playbooks, training, thought leadership, and validation material to support more relevant, compelling, and impactful interactions. "If data is the oxygen that runs the modern growth engine, content represents the gasoline required for combustion," reports Bruce Rogers, author of "Publish or Perish: A CMO Roadmap for Managing the Content Supply Chain."[67] "Content is a valuable commercial asset because modern selling is increasingly centered around owned digital selling channels that rely heavily on timely, targetable, personalized, and compliant content."

Maximizing the return on growth assets like salespeople, data, and content, which are severely and persistently underutilized, can unlock significant firm value. For example, sales reps still spend most of their time not talking to customers, data is not fully leveraged, marketing content is not utilized, and most CMOs don't believe technology is replacing their marketing staff any time soon.

After decades of digital innovation and investment, selling technologies have not yet lived up to their immense potential. Our interviewees expressed frustration with the persistently low levels of adoption and utilization of these technology assets. For example, most CRM implementations have lower than acceptable return on investment, less than satisfactory user adoption, and significant unrealized potential, according to research by the Sales Management Association (SMA).[22] Much like trying to drive a professional race car on local roads, most revenue-centric technology stacks have ample unused functionality, yet cannot even justify the current spend levels because of underperformance.

For sales, low levels of adoption by the customer-facing employees limit impact. Most sales personnel struggle to put new sales methodologies into daily practices, input data into CRM profiles, execute the right sales plays, and use expensive thought leadership content developed by marketing. For marketing, accountability and teamwork are challenging because most stakeholders – mainly CEOs, CFOs, and CROs – question the potential impact of marketing activities and suspect any justification of the investment. Measurable return on assets in both categories is low.

Most organizations are not data driven. For example, the majority of the 360 CMOs surveyed by Forbes report they don't support decision making or measure results with the first-party data within their CRM, Marketing Automation, and Digital Marketing platforms.[15] The same goes for sales. Most sales managers and performance professionals told us they cannot effectively use AI and advanced analytics to understand seller effectiveness or buyer intent.[9] (See Figure 7.1.)

The operations around the selling technology infrastructure don't work well either. Selling content is a big and growing component of the growth investment mix (41% of marketing budgets, according to HubSpot[52]). Eighty percent of CMOs report they are increasing their investment in content creation and delivery.[5] This includes things like guided selling, next-best-action guides, playbooks, recommendation engines, real-time scripting, and automated chatbots. Unfortunately, these do not scale in a modern selling model, making them very expensive. For example, localizing, targeting, and personalizing a branded content asset in five market segments is more than 20 times the cost of the original content asset, according to the Forbes Publish or Perish study. Add new digital channels and one-to-one segmentation at scale, and the cost curve accelerates dramatically.[67]

If you need a reasonable financial return on investments in analytics, digital selling technology, and content, you will need to change your approach to managing technology and data assets.

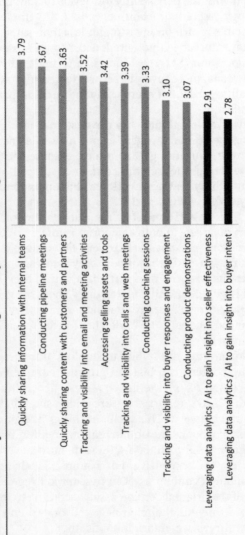

Rate how effective your team is at working remotely in the following areas

Quickly sharing information with internal teams — 3.79
Conducting pipeline meetings — 3.67
Quickly sharing content with customers and partners — 3.63
Tracking and visibility into email and meeting activities — 3.52
Accessing selling assets and tools — 3.42
Tracking and visibility into calls and web meetings — 3.39
Conducting coaching sessions — 3.33
Tracking and visibility into buyer responses and engagement — 3.10
Conducting product demonstrations — 3.07
Leveraging data analytics / AI to gain insight into seller effectiveness — 2.91
Leveraging data analytics / AI to gain insight into buyer intent — 2.78

FIGURE 7.1   The Effectiveness of Technology Infrastructure Supporting the Sales Team

Jennifer Mauldin, President and Chief Customer Officer of Inmar Intelligence, reinforces the importance of return on selling assets and supports long-term sustainable growth as a metric of success. "A key to making smart investments ahead of the curve has been the focus from the board on down to the C-suite on sustainable growth and the contribution of growth investment to firm value," says Mauldin.[125] "When we think of growth, we don't think of growth at all costs. Rather we look at prudent and sustainable growth. Put another way we look at growing firm value and the things that contribute to that – intellectual property, innovation, and people."

Developing the operating system offers the best way to improve productivity of salespeople, technology adoption, and return on selling assets. It will connect and coordinate your core selling CRM, sales enablement, training, and content management, and selling structures. That connection of growth assets will simplify the day-to-day selling workflow and generate more consistent and scalable growth.

With a systems-based approach, it becomes easier to establish clear strategic and financial criteria to help your enablement and operations teams to evolve your growth technology portfolio. We'll now detail three building blocks related to growth assets:

- **The CRM, sales enablement, content, and learning technologies that support selling**
- **The direct, field, and partner selling channels that engage customers in human interactions**
- **The owned digital selling infrastructure that engages customers digitally**

Building Block #1: Revenue Enablement – CRM, Content, and Learning Technologies That Support Selling

REVENUE ENABLEMENT	
DIGITAL ASSET MANAGEMENT	LEARNING MANAGEMENT
CRM	SALES AUTOMATION

Customer Relationship Management, digital asset management, and training tools and platforms represent a significant portfolio of assets on the balance sheet. Most organizations already have 20 or more of these tools in house with thousands more out there trying to get in.

These assets underperform relative to their capabilities and the expected financial impact, putting more pressure on growth leaders.

CRM platforms too often only serve as systems of record for the sales teams, yet sellers do want help actually *selling* – and try to ignore anything that feels like a burden. Interestingly, the key measures of sales productivity – time spent with customers (34% of rep time) and quota attainment (42% of all reps) – have not moved materially over the last few decades based on a survey of 2,900 reps.[20]

The enabling tools are no better. Digital asset management systems that house sales plays are disconnected from the training and development systems that teach them. Sales engagement and conversational intelligence solutions aimed at arming reps with better insights bypass CRM. The content, data, and IP in all of these systems are not widely distributed. "Today the selling assets are all there," reports Christian Smith, CRO of Splunk.[19] "But our team has to go and get them, which is optional, self-service, and manual to some degree. We need to do a better job of more effectively suggesting what you should do next, automatically. I think that is a big opportunity to drive that consistency and performance."

Fortunately, sales analytics and AI are accelerating the convergence of traditional sales enablement, readiness, and engagement software. This will make frontline selling faster, simpler, and more consistent. Individually, these solutions are automating and enabling critical aspects of the day-to-day customer workflow – from finding content, preparing for sales calls, and logging the results in CRM to responding to RFPs. Connecting them will revitalize legacy investments in CRM, sales enablement, digital asset management, training software, and customer data. As a result, they create selling outcomes that grow revenues, enterprise value, and profits.

In the past few years, there's been an explosion in accessible sales engagement data from first-party website, email, calendar, recorded sales conversations, contactless selling platforms, and third-party sources. AI is increasingly being used to mine all this data, which should help sales reps to make better decisions and managers to evaluate training needs, selling priorities, and seller performance. High-performing sales organizations are using a new generation of AI-enabled tools to augment, automate, and leverage their sales support infrastructure assets to generate better sales outcomes and higher levels of frontline sales productivity.

New systems have emerged that aggregate, orchestrate, and deploy all this customer engagement data even while using CRM as an administrative system of record. These business innovations must still overcome too many disconnected applications vying to be the "single pane of glass" and too much tool fatigue. "We have a lot of disparate systems in the commercial technology ecosystem," Greg Munster, VP of Global Sales Operations at Canonical. "It's making things complicated for the customers, for internal sellers, and the operations and enablement executives who manage those systems. It often feels like we are working for the selling tools rather than the tools working for us."

These developments are being amplified by continued changes in buyer behavior to change the vendor landscape, too. This has led to a wave of consolidation, mergers, and acquisitions in the sales and marketing technology sectors. For example, sales enablement (sales guidance), sales readiness (sales training), and sales engagement (data-driven selling) solutions are converging as the fragmentation of the day-to-day sales workflow and seller experience are no longer acceptable. Sales enablement firms rooted in managing selling content and digital assets like Highspot, BigTinCan, and Showpad have been developing, acquiring, and partnering with sales training and development solutions to combine sales readiness with traditional sales enablement. This overlap in capabilities has forced a rationalization of sales enablement and readiness players. This makes sense because:

- They support the same core day-to-day selling activities – target, prioritize, prepare, engage, follow up, report, and repeat.
- They use the same content – sales playbooks, training content, product content, and selling content – to prepare for meetings, practice the skills needed on the call, and communicate with the clients.
- They increasingly use the same data – customer engagement and seller activity data drawn from actual presentations and conversations as well as from call recordings or practice demo presentations.

This is just the beginning. There is still a long way to go. This represents a real opportunity to materially transform the economics of selling and radically improve the experience of sellers and customers. Big financial rewards await the sales leaders who can knit together end-to-end platforms that effectively use AI and advanced analytics to deliver speed, simplicity, and scalability.

How can you take advantage of this opportunity now? The executives we spoke to are using advanced analytics to connect stranded sales support assets in several ways:

1. **Rationalize the Revenue Enablement Stack.** Most companies have invested in too many selling tools – more than 20 on average – to automate and support the day-to-day selling workflow: how we train, coach, disseminate content, enhance customer relationships, and efficiently manage contracts. Many operations and enablement leaders are concerned about the growing complexity of this selling stack and the

negative impact this "technology mayhem" is having on selling costs, the seller experience, and even sales rep attrition. Spending the time to evaluate your sales technology portfolio and customer data assets will identify immediate ways to rationalize the technology stack. This will eliminate waste, redundancy, and stranded or nonperforming assets. It will streamline the seller experience, improve adoption, and increase productivity, sometimes by more than 50%. It's an opportunity to reduce duplication, disconnected apps, and underutilized assets while improving value, impact, and seller experience.

2. **Simplify the Day-to-Day Seller Workflow.** You should do this to enable salespeople and maximize the return on investments in sales enablement, CRM, and engagement technologies. Improving usability and adoption by frontline revenue teams pays off financially by reducing costs, improving return on assets, and generating more consistent growth. "Most organizations have not yet realized the immense promise of sales technology," notes Greg Munster of Canonical. "A big reason has been the lack of focus on the seller experience and the usability, utility, and adoption of the selling tools they deploy as a key strategic and operational goal of their selling technology deployments. The root cause of these problems has less to do with the features and functions of the tools you buy, and more to do with how easy they are to use and how well management supports them. This is particularly evident with CRM deployments but extends to every other class of tool designed to help revenue teams become smarter, faster, and more effective. As a consequence, the financial returns on most investments in salespeople, data, technology, and content fall well short of their potential by any financially valid measure – Return on Assets, Return on Investment, sales productivity, and quota attainment."

Some of this responsibility falls on sales teams. Sales leaders need to insist on making the simplified seller experience a primary goal of their sales enablement strategies. Some responsibility is on the vendors. Forward-thinking solutions providers like Highspot and Revenue.io are connecting the dots across the sales technology portfolio to converge around one pane of glass, one selling motion, one system of record. In any case, overall costs and the seller experience will improve in any organization by simplifying the day-to-day seller workflow and streamlining the administration of data, technology, and content in their business.

3. **Automatically Enrich, Update, and Augment CRM with Real-Time Customer Engagement and Behavior Data.** Most (61%) high-performing marketers are developing a single view of the customer to direct targeting and inform multichannel customer engagement

programs, according to an analysis by Forbes.[15] This is because common customer and account profiles fuel an array of event-triggered Account-Based Marketing (ABM), sales engagement, digital marketing, and media communications across marketing, sales, and service touchpoints. As the speed of modern selling increases to keep pace with customer expectations, these triggers and alerts are happening faster and faster, often in real time.

To create these profiles, sales enablement teams are unifying data from many touchpoints, channels, and media interactions into a system of record that stores a common customer profile rather than keeping data in independent fragmented applications. The best solutions automatically and immediately augment CRM systems, syncing customer engagement and seller activity data without data entry by reps – this ensures data integrity and process consistency. More and more business processes rely on the signals from this profile data, so any delay or inconsistency in updating profiles (say, uploading in 10-minute batches) can create interval problems in a mature revenue enablement model.

"Many sales engagement and conversational intelligence tools use single streams of digital engagement and conversation data to help sales reps with sequences, priorities, and outreach," states Howard Brown, CEO of Revenue.io, a business that has helped hundreds of organizations leverage insights to grow. "The real value is created by combining conversation data with other engagement data like marketing automation data, external intent data, and opportunity data in CRM to help optimize or prescribe who sellers should be contacting, what actions they should be taking to deliver the best results, and what skills they need to be developing."

4. **Align Sales Enablement, Digital Asset Management, and Sales Readiness into a Single Selling Motion.** Advances in analytics have pushed the sales enablement, readiness, and engagement software categories toward a single end-to-end platform. Sales operations, training, and enablement managers assemble these capabilities to create a closed-loop feedback system that integrates planning and prioritization (before the sale) with action and engagement of the buyer (during the call) with reinforcement and coaching (after the fact). They combine the core sales enablement capabilities of delivering the right content to the right seller at the right time in the right context with training and development capabilities. This improves sales readiness before calls and evaluation of skills based on actual performance. These insights target microlearning and reinforcement to address in-the-moment sales needs and long-term skill gaps.

Hitachi Vantara Connected the Dots to Simplify the Seller Experience

Hitachi Vantara provides a good example of how growth leaders can address major issues in the selling process by connecting pieces of their technology portfolios to automate, simplify, and speed up selling. Jeff McKittrick and Jim Blum, who led the sales operations team at Hitachi Vantara, focused their efforts on connecting and creating a Digital Selling Platform. For these efforts, they were recognized as the "Sales Operations Program of the Year" by Forrester/Sirius Decisions.[69]

"When it comes to technology, people tend to overthink things," shares Jeff McKittrick. "In reality, knitting together a highly profitable and productive portfolio of selling technologies is not rocket science. But it does require hard work, teamwork, and leadership. But there's definitely a cookbook – and the recipe for success is pretty straightforward."

"One key is to apply the '80/20 rule' and not let perfect get in the way of profitable," he continues. "Most B2B sales teams struggle with the same fundamental things. Research with sales operations executives consistently identify the same five or six problems or 'hot spots' in the sales process that hold salespeople back. These include finding the right product, solution, and selling content to meet customer expectations. Getting quick and easy access to competitive information and customer references to support the deal. And getting help finding and preparing proposals, pricing, and RFPs."

Delivering contextual training and readiness resources to sellers when they need it could reduce the time required to prepare for and prioritize sales calls.

"It's not easy to connect these dots across the day-to-day seller workflow and create results," says McKittrick. "Just straightforward. The most difficult part of stitching together the different pieces of the sales portfolio to create a sales experience that delivers the right tools, information, and resources at the right time are a) leadership, b) change management, and c) taking a team approach to tailoring it to your process."

According to McKittrick, there are five keys to connecting the dots across the revenue enablement technology portfolio to build a Digital Selling Platform that creates value:

1. **Take a top-down approach to technology.** Sales leadership needs to agree to take a top-down approach when evaluating the entire sales and marketing technology portfolio with value creation and capture in mind. Titles matter less here, but there should be an individual or team tasked with determining how all the pieces in the sales technology portfolio play together to create firm financial value.

2. **Identify the key points of leverage and failure in your sales process.** "Our Sales Operations, Sales Enablement, and Content Operations teams worked together to conduct a technology stack assessment and rationalization analysis," reports McKittrick. "First we conducted a sales activity analysis – a qualitative and quantitative survey of the entire revenue team. This allowed us to identify the top five to six 'hot spots' in the seller workflow

and focus our sales technology portfolio on the places we needed to better leverage, automate, enable, and support these specific hot spots."

3. **Rationalize and focus the technology portfolio.** To do this at Hitachi Vantara, McKittrick's team conducted a top-down assessment of the many tools in the technology portfolio to zero in on the places they needed to better leverage, automate, enable, and support these specific hot spots. "Our tech stack rationalization analysis identified many disconnected or duplicate capabilities and technologies that were not supporting sales because they were either not being used or were not useful," reports McKittrick. "This saved us a surprising amount of money when you added up all the cost of administering many redundant tools in many different functional silos."

4. **Fill critical gaps with best-in-class tools.** "In parallel, we conducted a gap analysis to prioritize capabilities and tools that needed to be upgraded to fill in the areas our technology was not effectively supporting the key sales hot spots," McKittrick continues. "For example, we added sales engagement tools to our roadmap to provide better opportunity prioritization and guided selling to salespeople because pre-call planning was taking up so much of their time."

5. **Leverage digital adoption solutions to multiply utilization.** "In the final step of our evolution to a digital selling platform, we focused on better utilizing the solutions we already had or getting rid of them," McKittrick says. "We measured user adoption by connecting all the critical tools and capabilities to a digital adoption software package that makes it easy and fast to discover and use all the tools available to them. This proved to be a simple and highly profitable exercise. We learned that while we had 'pockets of adoption' across the revenue team, no single sales rep or manager was aware of all of the tools we already had. More importantly, from a business case and value perspective we realized that a little adoption goes a long way when it comes to leveraging selling tools and resources. In our experience a two-fold increase in adoption will yield a five to ten-fold return on existing technology, content, and data assets."

"The only way to truly simplify and streamline the seller workflow is for every solution in your stack to connect with every tool or platform in the selling workflow," he continues. "But we have to partner and integrate with CRM and the other core platforms in this ecosystem like competitive intelligence and platforms that generate contracts, RFPs and selling documents. It's important to recognize that CRM is where sellers need to live and represents the foundational platform and system of record for sales teams. If a rep has to use ten panes of glass to do their job, that is not the best way to support, enable, and empower them. You have to simplify that so they are only using one or two panes of glass and can do most of what they need to do in CRM and the other platforms they actually use on a day-to-day basis like Outlook, Gmail or a tablet to access all these things." See Figure 7.2 to see how Jeff laid this all out.

(continued)

| Readiness and product understanding | Prioritizing leads and opportunities 7% of selling time | Call planning and content preparation 9% of selling time | Data entry and logging activities in CRM 8% of selling time | Competitive, customer, and product research 9% of selling time | Proposal, pricing, and presentation development |

FIGURE 7.2   Aligning the Technology Stack with the Most Common Points of Failure in the Day-to-Day Selling Workflow

"The elegance of assembling a Digital Selling Platform is that it provides sales operations executives a rare 'win-win-win' initiative that is popular with the sales force, politically practical, and financially sound. Assembling the various non-performing pieces of the sales technology stack into a Digital Selling Platform gave us quick wins in terms of advocacy from the sales team and success stories. We also got very high returns on investment because a small increase in adoption will yield a large return on growth assets. From a strategic perspective, the platform helped us address digital buying behavior and the increased cadence of virtual selling by enabling virtual, remote selling and 'new school' digital selling channels. Politically the program improves the impact and effectiveness of expensive legacy CRM infrastructure and reinforces its role as the system of record and single source of truth driving the sales process. Finally, the 'connect the dots' approach gave us a systematic way to generate ever increasing returns by continuously improving the consistency and performance of the selling system through a series of incremental gains and micro disruptions that avoid the change management issues typically associated with commercial transformation projects."

Building Block #2: Channel Optimization – Selling Channels That Maximize Effective and Efficient Interactions

CHANNEL OPTIMIZATION	
DIRECT SELLING	VIRTUAL SELLING CAPABILITIES
DEALER/ DISTRIBUTOR CHANNELS	DIRECT TO CUSTOMER (DTC)

The emergence of 4D selling channel systems – digitally enabled, displaced geographically, data-driven, and dynamic – has had a dramatic impact on the way organizations manage and optimize the performance of their selling channels.

The Keys to Improving the Economics of Selling Channels

The rapid shift to 4D selling has reconfigured the budgets and infrastructure that support selling. Partially in response to digital transformation, CFOs have cut or shifted funds that previously went to sales travel, real estate overhead, entertainment, and events and moved them into technology and training via digital channels. That shift has freed up more time for selling; accelerated adoption of digital selling – in 2020, over 99% of sales calls were digital due to the pandemic – and increased visibility and auditability, e.g. recording of most sales conversations. The compressed nature of these changes during the pandemic in 2020–2022 proved that selling via virtual channels without face-to-face engagement can work, even with complex, highly experiential solutions. "B2B selling organizations learned they can get 50% higher engagement, speed of response, and productivity from their sales reps at lower costs by incorporating virtual selling channels into their commercial model," said Michael Smith of Blue Ridge Partners.

Research from the Wharton School of Business reveals the response to the displacement of employees is leading to shifts in the go-to-market investment mix:

- 97% of organizations are changing their go-to-market strategies
- Over 80% have cut business travel and event budgets
- Most are making work at home or work from anywhere policies the status quo
- About half are cutting the size of their field sales forces
- 81% are increasing investment in digital technologies to improve market coverage and client engagement
- 88% agree the pandemic represents a big opportunity to change the way they reach and engage customers.[5]

This has had a profound impact on the economics of selling. The financial impact on 4D selling – combined with a revolution in sales technology and analytics – can exceed the mass adoption of direct and teleweb channels that led to a transformation in selling over the last two decades. In the 1990s channel innovators like Dell, IBM.com, GEICO, and Charles Schwab reduced the cost of selling more than twofold by migrating lower-value PC, software, insurance, and financial transactions from expensive field sales reps to less expensive direct channels.

Selling organizations can achieve similar or greater gains by fully embracing the potential of commercial transformation. AI-enabled service automation, virtual assistants, contactless selling, and conversational intelligence tools can significantly improve the cost, effectiveness, and experience in any sales channels, physical or digital. In the short term, these tools automate sales tasks, guide sales decisions, leverage agent time, and capture sales conversations for analysis, prioritization, and personalization. For those willing to harness readily available but not broadly applied technologies like AI, augmented reality, 5G communications, and haptics to truly transform the selling experience, 4D selling offers even greater untapped potential for financial gain and competitive differentiation.

Over time, AI tools, conversational commerce, and emotion processing will create even more value by helping virtual sales reps assess customer sentiment and build trust in the absence of nonverbal cues and body language, according to Prof. Raghu Iyengar of the Wharton School of Business. "Advances in Artificial Emotional Intelligence (AEI) are going to allow for more nuanced reactions to human emotions.[32] The market for these technologies is estimated to grow to $41 billion by 2022, and emotional inputs will create a shift from data-driven IQ-heavy interactions to deep EQ-guided experiences, giving brands the opportunity to connect to customers on a much deeper, more personal level," according to Iyengar. "Companies that carefully plan for how Perception AI, which covers the gamut of sensory inputs including voice, vision, smell, and touch, can complement their offerings will find a competitive edge."

Corey Torrence of Blue Ridge Partners reiterates the importance of providing frontline, customer-facing employees with real-time coaching and guidance at scale. "To make the greatest use of scarce time we must equip sellers with better information about where the buyer is positioned in the buying cycle and meet them there with the information, content, and plays the buyer needs much faster."

General Stanley McChrystal, author of the book *Team of Teams,* emphasizes the critical importance of speeding up communications in the face of rapidly changing market and customer buying behavior. "The speed and interconnected nature of the world in which we function have rendered traditional organizations with rigid functional structures and process hand-offs between members of the revenue team too stoic and slow to keep up with customer expectations and the accelerating pace of market and competitive change," reports General McChrystal.

Unfortunately, traditional organizations with rigid functional organizational structures and process hand-offs between teams have a hard time moving information that fast. "The organization as a rigidly reductionist mechanical beast is an endangered species," says McChrystal. "As the world grows faster and more interdependent, we need to figure out ways to scale the fluidity of teams across entire organizations: groups with thousands of members that span continents." To accelerate the flow and cadence of information sharing, he advises sales leaders to dramatically increase the cadence of communications to customer-facing employees. This means moving from making weekly updates to the field to daily updates and ultimately to real-time communication to ensure critical decision-making, coaching, and prioritization information cascades down quickly to sellers at the edge of the organizations who must make fast decisions and engage customers with the right messages and solutions at the right time.

As an illustration, McChrystal points to the success of the US armed forces as they adapted to the new challenges of fighting the war on terror. Under McChrystal's leadership, the US Joint Special Operations Task Force was forced to abandon the hierarchical, top-down command and control structures and linear planning processes that were the foundations of military command for centuries. To defeat new threats from highly adaptable and networked terrorist groups like Al Qaeda, they were forced to discard a century of conventional wisdom to find ways to become faster, flatter, and more flexible. They looked at best practices of their highest-performing teams of Navy Sales, CIA operatives, or Army Rangers – and found ways to extend them to thousands of people on three continents. They built a network of teams that functioned with extremely transparent communication and decentralized decision-making authority. They tore down walls between silos. Reversing years of "bottom up" information flow, the Task Force pushed "general and officer level" information and awareness throughout the ranks to give people on the front line the information, context, and understanding they needed to take initiative and make decisions quickly. To facilitate that information flow they built a "virtual" Situational Awareness Room (SAR) – an adaptive intelligence hub that provided real-time information critical to ongoing anti-terrorist operations. In practice, the SAR acted like a central nervous system where 7,000 team members spread across 70 locations globally would meet in daily operational and intelligence briefings.

The results were dramatic. "When we tried to do the same things tighter and faster under the constraints of the old system, we managed to increase the number of raids from 10 to 18," reported McChrystal. "Under the new system, this figure skyrocketed to 300. With minimal increases in personnel, we were running 17 times faster."

Sales travel, events, and offices are not going to disappear from the selling formula. But they will be significantly reduced and reallocated. "Every organization will refine its spending based on its own competitive situation, buyer preferences, and go-to-market model. But our experience tells us that

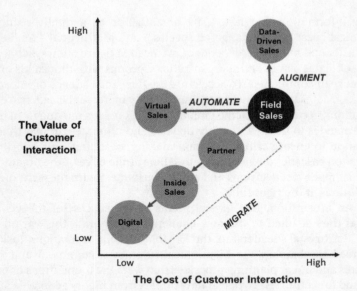

FIGURE 7.3 Three Ways Technology Can Enhance Selling Channels

a data-driven 4D selling channel system can generate sales productivity gains of over 50% with cost reductions of 10%, as compared with traditional field sales," according to Michael Smith, who has helped dozens of organizations reduce selling costs and improve engagement by adding "virtual account executives" to the coverage mix.

These performance gains will come from three primary sources (see Figure 7.3):

- **Migration** moves expensive selling interactions from high-cost field sales channels to lower-cost call center, digital, and contactless selling channels. For example, a fully loaded field sales visit can cost more than $1,000, whereas a call center interaction costs well under $100. It is possible to move less important interactions to lower-cost, low-touch, or even no-touch channels. Many customers even prefer it. AI-enabled contactless selling innovations like self-service chatbots, contactless selling platforms, and recommender engines offer continuous improvements in migrating interaction types to the optimal channel. Even firms that deal with heavy equipment like Ryder System and United Rentals have already migrated hundreds of millions of dollars of sales to low-touch and no-touch channels. Over the last several years, John Gleason, EVP of Sales at Ryder, has successfully adapted his commercial model by shifting sales coverage of smaller transactions and clients to a call center. "When I joined Ryder, we had zero inside salespeople," says Gleason.[119] "Now Ryder has 170 inside salespeople and they tackle one of the biggest issues – used vehicle sales. Ryder is the largest seller of used trucks in North America and most customers are small accounts with under three trucks. Today, 35% of all those vehicles are sold by our inside sales team with higher productivity, better customer satisfaction, and lower costs. When I gave small accounts (under three trucks) to inside sales, our customer retention rose from 50% to 72%, our CSI (Customer Satisfaction Index) went up 400 basis points, and our cost dropped in half."

- **Automation** removes low-value time investments for customer-facing employees and eliminates less productive tasks in the day-to-day selling workflow. There are challenges here. By nature, the sale process is non-linear, unstable, and constantly changing – realities that hinder automation efforts. Also, the human nature of sellers may mean that any time saved gets reallocated to other similarly nonproductive or nonbusiness activities. All that said, anything that provides for more seller time spent in front of the customer has revolutionary possibilities.

- **Augmentation** helps sellers add more value during customer touch-points and interactions. Sellers create more value by telling better stories, executing the proven selling motion, and focusing time on the most profitable opportunities. Arming, training, and coaching sellers with more effective value proposition content and/or delivery could reshape economic impact in terms of revenue per rep, deal size, price, margin realization, customer lifetime value, relationship equity, and differentiated customer experience. "The biggest opportunity for technology and systems to improve selling performance, by far, is enhancing the value of a sales interaction," according to Marcus Jewell of Juniper Networks.[116] "Augmentation rules everything. That's where we are seeing the biggest gains. We're still a belly-to-belly selling system – we sell deals up to $120 million – so you have to have human interaction. But there are many ways you can make those sellers better in ways that impact margins, total contract value, seller effectiveness, and can differentiate the buyer experience (which is our number one goal)."

Optimizing the Technology of Your Selling Channels

Technology has become central not only to the broader selling structures but more specifically to the channels through which you sell to your customers. Technology can optimize the cost, effectiveness, and experience of your channels, regardless of whether they are direct or indirect, physical or virtual. Here's how business leaders are taking advantage:

1. **Automating Direct Sales and Service Channels.** Service organizations struggle to keep up with changing customer preferences for speed, completeness of response, and relevant content, according to our survey of

sales managers and effectiveness professionals. Eighty-two percent of service executives believe they must transform their customer service operations to remain competitive in the face of growing volumes of customer engagement and service cases in direct channels, a continued shift to remote buying, and the evolution from products to SaaS and subscription services.[21] AI-enabled service automation, virtual assistants, contactless selling, and customer service automation tools can cost-effectively manage increased transaction volumes and deliver high-quality customer experiences. AI virtual assistants screen, qualify, adjudicate, coach, and even script conversations in real time. Cogito, Narrative Science, and SalesWhale use engagement data to provide in-call guidance and narration. Tact.ai, and Zoovu use a combination of conversational intelligence, chatbots, and automation to boost agent productivity and effectiveness. Customer Success Platforms like Gainsight and Totango help agents protect and grow customer relationships by connecting customer engagement and activity data sources and then actively monitoring customer health changes to head off problems and churn.

2. **Enabling Virtual 4D Sales Reps with Tools and Technology.** In 2020, field sales reps had to adopt virtual selling due to work at home and shelter in place mandates. Thus, the volume of sales interactions on videoconference platforms like Microsoft Teams and Zoom grew thirty-fold since the pandemic began. Most sales organizations weren't ready. The rapid change put everyone under pressure to develop virtual sales channels and digitize their go-to-market model. Sales teams use conversational intelligence tools like Chorus.io, Gong.io, and Revenue.io, as well as sales engagement platforms like SalesLoft, Xant.ai, and Outreach. io to simultaneously increase transparency into sales calls; create insights that improve decision making and customer engagement; and highlight opportunities to tune and improve selling skills.

3. **Optimizing Direct-to-Customer Channels.** The majority of customers prefer to engage in online channels for service, including chat (81%), text (78%), social media (71%), and mobile apps (82%).[21] Digital conversations are happening across touchpoints with interaction management platforms like Podium that connect webchat, text, and messaging into a seamless customer experience. Chatbots from providers like Ada, Conversica Drift, and HubSpot Sales Hub are being deployed to answer questions, share information, and book meetings without an agent getting involved. Given that fewer than a quarter of service agents are using AI assistants, guides, and chatbots like these in their day-to-day operations,[18] that leaves a lot of value out there to be had.

4. **Migrating Sales and Service Interactions and Transactions to Low-Touch and No-Touch Channels.** Migrating selling interactions from high-cost field sales channels to lower-cost telephonic and digital

channels is not new, but the economics remain compelling. For example, IBM migrated $8.6 billion in transactions from their vaunted "blue suit" direct sales channel to what they called a teleweb channel.[132] In doing so they reduced selling costs by 40%, saved $1.86 billion in hard dollar service costs, improved customer satisfaction, and grew sales by 50% while cutting thousands of "blue suit" field sales reps from their selling roster. Migration is a never-ending process as more customers move online, and new AI-enabled technologies create more transaction types. AI-enabled innovations like self-service chatbots, contactless selling platforms, and recommender engines allow more interactions. As more millennials and B2B buyers are asking for 100% no-touch buying experiences, channel migration is the gift that keeps on giving. The percentage of sales through digital channels has doubled from 2018 to 2021, according to research by the Duke Fuqua School of Business.[4]

5. **Augmenting and Enhancing Seller Performance by Providing Guidance and Coaching They Need "In the Moment."** Fueled by the explosion of accessible new customer engagement and seller activity data sets, the introduction of AI into the selling process provides unprecedented potential to augment the performance of frontline sellers. Sales reps that use AI in selling are almost five times more productive.[19] This twin development of data and analytic capability represents a significant opportunity to accelerate sales growth.

For the past three decades, most sales data was manually entered and then stored in CRM. Marketing data was locked in digital marketing systems and rarely shared. But in the past few years, there has been an explosion in customer engagement and seller activity data available to analytics teams. Much of this data comes from four core data sources: CRM, sales enablement, recorded conversations, and exchange data (which includes email and calendar information). Even today, half of sales reps cannot get the access to data they need, and only a third are using analytics to prioritize and qualify leads.[19] Sales-enablement platforms like Revenue.io have begun using advanced analytics and AI to analyze all this content consumption, buyer engagement, and seller activity data from many sources. They use those analytics to recommend content, visualize engagement with stakeholders in key accounts, and build customer engagement metrics that quantify account health. Corey Torrence of Blue Ridge Partners reiterates the importance of providing frontline customer-facing employees real-time coaching and guidance at scale. "To make the greatest use of scarce time we must equip sellers with better information about where the buyer is positioned in the buying cycle and meet them there with the information, content, and plays the buyer needs much faster."

Augmenting Your Selling Channels with Real-Time Data-Driven Selling Guidance and Coaching

Advanced sales operations teams like HPE and Cvent are connecting selling technology portfolios to create data-driven algorithmic selling ecosystems that dramatically improve the ability of sellers to deliver value during client interactions. Here are four emerging data sources.

The first is what is called email, calendar, or "exchange" data. Sales solutions providers have become adept at capturing and analyzing the email and calendar data of sales and service agents from exchange servers, Microsoft Teams, and collaboration systems like Slack. This data augments CRM account and opportunity data to create a much richer picture of buyer engagement, seller activity, and pipeline health.

The second is what we call "content data." Most organizations are now systematically tracking content distribution, engagement, and consumption with buyers and prospects from digital asset management, sales enablement, or marketing automation systems. The data this content distribution creates is like tracer bullets that map buyer engagement, flesh out buyer teams, and signal buyer intent.

A third primary data group is first-party data. Most organizations have robust owned digital sales infrastructure to engage customers online. These include websites, blogs, mobile apps, marketing automation, ecommerce, social media, and email platforms. These platforms have now incorporated automated data entry, data capture AI, lead scoring, Natural Language Processing (NLP), and revenue acceleration technologies that allow them to capture a much higher percentage of this data in CRM systems or Customer Data Platforms.

And the fourth and emerging data set is recorded conversations. Perhaps the most valuable customer data set to emerge in the last 10 years is the ability to record, transcribe, and analyze customer conversations in phone calls and videoconferences at scale. This type of data is commonly called conversational intelligence. The percentage of inbound and outbound sales and service calls that are being captured and digitally recorded has grown a hundredfold in the past several years with the scale adoption of collaboration platforms like Zoom, AI-guided agents, contactless selling, and conversational intelligence tools. As an illustration, over 200 million participants interact using the Microsoft Teams collaboration tool in a single day.[10]

This customer engagement and seller activity data are quickly becoming like oxygen in sales. This data is available to any organization that wants to use it. And it can breathe life into the revenue engine. "It does not take an army of PHd data-scientists to capture, organize and monetize this data," according to Howard Brown, CEO of Revenue.io and a pioneer in conversational intelligence. "Yet only a surprisingly small fraction (under 5%) of organizations actually do. This is gold right at the surface."

Unfortunately, much of this data exists in many different systems because each solution generally has its own data set. This creates data silos. For example, many popular sales engagement and conversational intelligence tools use single streams of digital engagement and conversation data to help sales reps with sequences, priorities, and outreach. But they don't natively integrate with CRM so that data can be combined and used to support other use cases like coaching, guidance, and performance measurement. This is a problem that needs to be solved, according to Jeff McKittrick. "There is more data around the revenue stream available than ever, but without the right analytics and ability to get the selling insights quickly to front line sellers at the pace of business, it's all just noise," says McKittrick. "Operations teams need to mine that stream of customer engagement data to uncover the right signals of buyer sentiment, intent, and objections to help expensive sales, customer success, and sales engineering resources perform at their best in live selling conversations."

Customer data that exists in a silo has limited value. If you are trying to augment and align your marketing, sales, support, and success teams to deliver the best possible experience for your buyer, as well as your seller – then you will benefit from a full picture of the information that led to that phone call. Sellers need to know things like how many support tickets and issues the customer has, and whether the way they answer questions indicates fear, interest, or ambivalence. Managers need to know what reps are really great at, what value they can create in their conversations, and where they need training. Those are the keys to deliver more revenue, more sustainable growth, and a happier customer base.

Growth innovators are using AI to "connect the dots" between these massive new sales engagement data sets to the five ways they create immediate value: delivering better channel performance, resource allocation, people management, measurements, and product channel readiness.

"What's critically important that people don't understand, is sales reps need insights that are actionable in real time—That is the big difference maker," reports Howard Brown. "As the 'clock speed' of modern selling increases to keep pace with customers' expectations, the triggers, prompts, and alerts that inform frontline sellers need to happen faster and faster. In many cases in real time."

While that seems complicated, it is very doable. Figure 7.4 provides a blueprint for using advanced analytics to connect and transform your engagement data into insights that guide, augment, and enable frontline sellers. The engagement data outlined in this blueprint already exists – or is right below the surface – inside most organizations. The beauty of today's tools and the democratization of technology is that you can quickly mine the gold beneath the surface in your organization by making it feasible to pilot real-time seller guidance and one-to-one coaching at scale. It also makes the change management involved fairly minimal. And measurement is quantifiable because the system generates some robust metrics from these data sets that prove what works and what doesn't. This makes it easy to look at the performance of that pilot group against other performers across your organization.

Using advanced analytics to create and capture value in these four ways can dramatically improve the historically low returns on sales assets – including people, data, technology, and content.

(continued)

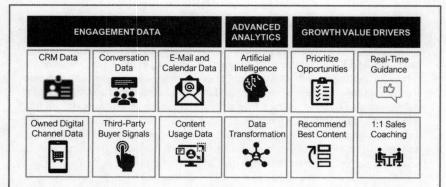

FIGURE 7.4 Connecting the Dots Between Sales Engagement Data and Business Value

For example, HPE, which sells software and services to large enterprises across 150 geographies, found better ways to combine sales force automation, analytics, and AI-enabled coaching from Revenue.io with a legacy Salesforce. com and call center technology to dramatically improve seller engagement, productivity, speed, and visibility. This combination of capabilities removed many of the obstacles facing the inside sales reps tasked with local presence selling in critical geographies. As an outcome, these inside reps were able to generate 400% more sales opportunities in their calls. "Revenue.io helps our Inside Sales teams make more deals and increase our connection rates," said Dana Clark, director of WW Inside Sales Processes at HPE, "while providing a market-leading platform to drive greater sales."[42]

Cvent was able to increase the productivity of their Sales Development Reps (SDRs) by over 20%, without sacrificing call quality, by enabling a collaborative coaching culture using conversational intelligence to help manage, monitor, and coach reps in real time. "The ability to listen to reps' conversations in real time allowed Cvent sales managers to spend more time coaching and less time waiting for a rep to identify a meaningful call and listen in," according to Jen Schlueter, Senior Manager of Strategic Projects and PMO at Cvent.[44]

Senior growth leaders must force themselves to look past this background noise. CXOs must provide their sales operations and enablement teams with clear strategic and financial criteria to help them evaluate, consolidate, and evolve their growth technology portfolios. This requires a top-down road map for building a Revenue Operating System that generates more growth and profits from their capital investments in data, technology, content, and digital selling channel infrastructure.

To put your operations team on a path to enabling real-time selling guidance and one-to-one coaching at scale, you need to show this blueprint to any current or prospective sales enablement or engagement solutions providers as a test. If they are the right partner for the long term, they should be able to answer these questions about their ability to enable real-time data-driven selling guidance and coaching:

1. **Can you help us get control of the four core sources of customer engagement and seller activity data that already exist in our business – CRM, conversational commerce systems, marketing, and sales enablement?** Right now, most organizations are not fully leveraging the first-party data they have resident within CRM, marketing automation, and digital marketing platforms to support business decision making or drive measurable growth.

2. **Can you provide real-time guidance at the "moments that matter" in the sales process?** Giving reps access to the right guidance via prompts, alerts, and active guidance based on what is actually happening "during the game" has a much bigger impact than the "post-game replays, evaluations, and reviews" typically provided by conversational intelligence solutions.

3. **Can you help our managers coach reps during sales calls?** Properly integrated, your intelligence, engagement, and enablement platforms give managers the ability to coach sales reps during sales calls instead of before or after. This is a better way to deliver coaching than offline sessions simulating sales conversations or traditional ride-alongs where much of the time is spent between calls and meetings. It also lets you apply your management and expert resources in situations where they can do the most good – helping to close a sale, create differentiation, or save a customer.

4. **Can you give us a complete picture of what works and what does not?** Combining data from sales readiness, enablement, engagement, and conversational intelligence solutions provides a "multithreaded" picture of how well your training, reps, and playbooks perform. Measuring the performance of sellers, coaching them, and providing their training and playbooks in one closed-loop system gives managers the ability to identify and reinforce what is working, and to focus on fixing what isn't.

5. **Can you deliver signals of buyer intent or churn from marketing to our reps?** Every organization spends a high percentage of their budgets on websites, blogs, mobile apps, earned media, contactless selling, and email marketing platforms and programs. These platforms generate the lion's share of customer engagement in your company. AI solutions can get these valuable signals of opportunity, intent to buy, or churn to your sellers so they can act on it.

6. **Will your solution enable our CRM system as a practical and forward-looking system of record for revenue intelligence?** From the perspective of sales enablement professionals and the sales reps they support, if the customer data doesn't exist in CRM, it doesn't exist for all practical purposes. Keeping the data in CRM as the system of record is important because sellers need to have a simple and consistent selling

(continued)

motion – and CRM is always at the center of their day-to-day workflow. They cannot be going to different systems or "panes of glass" to find out things about their customers. And they cannot find out too late about critical signals and insights about the customers they are speaking to. Any conversational intelligence or "revenue intelligence" solution you buy must improve your overall data integrity by enhancing profiles in CRM to create a single source of real-time customer intelligence. Advanced AI solutions should be able to update Salesforce.com CRM completely, automatically, and in real time – making sure conversations are recorded and formatted to conform to the data structures used in CRM.

7. **Can you help us improve data integrity and save sellers time by automatically recording and updating customer data records?** Selling has become more data-driven as almost every customer interaction, selling campaign, and marketing program in your business is informed by customer insights. This has placed such a premium on clean, complete, and up-to-date customer data that many sales executives tell us they are compensating their sellers for their data hygiene. One of the best ways to improve the integrity of your customer data is by automating in a meaningful way the call logging, data entry, and data compliance that reps used to do manually. In particular, the platform ensures that all of the interaction data goes into CRM completely and immediately. This is important because more and more of the programs, coaching, and alerts that run your selling operations are happening in real time to keep up with the pace of buyers.

A good example of a solution provider that is doing all four of these things is Revenue.io. Over the last eight years, they have built an end-to-end RevOps platform that uses AI to connect the dots across the entire sales and marketing technology ecosystem to help frontline revenue teams to prioritize, prepare, and execute effective customer experiences. The platform combines buyer and customer engagement data from conversations with CRM data and third-party buying signals to create a complete picture of seller activities, behaviors, and conversations. They also integrate with other key assets in the growth technology ecosystem – CRM, sales enablement, videoconferencing – to share information and take advantage of insights generated in those systems.

Unlike many promising applications of analytics to grow revenues, this one is not a "bridge too far." Every organization has the fundamental data to get started – recorded conversations, content consumption by clients, CRM, and exchange data from email and calendars. And any organization should be able to leverage the customer engagement and seller activity data they already have to pilot real-time guidance and coaching at scale in 60 days if their CXOs demanded it.

Building Block #3: Customer-Facing Technology – The Owned Digital Selling Infrastructure That Manages Customer Touchpoints

CUSTOMER-FACING TECHNOLOGY	
OWNED CHANNEL INFRASTRUCTURE	MARKETING AUTOMATION
MOBILE INFRASTRUCTURE	E-COMMERCE

As discussed, most organizations have built a large array of company-controlled and company-owned digital channels to address the rising desire of buyers to learn, shop, and buy online. This combination of customer-facing technologies collects enormous amounts of first-party customer engagement data, including customer buying signals and behavior that communicate unmet needs. It's also an environment where the company controls 100% of the message.

This digital selling infrastructure requires a large capital and operating investment that commands most of your growth resources, yet rarely shows up as a discrete budget item. Marketing organizations micromanage media spending with marketing mix models that improve targeting, yet often ignore the wealth of tangible, attributable data in their digital selling infrastructure. This and the people who staff and provision them represent perhaps their largest growth asset—and that asset is underutilized and underperforming relative to its potential.

What Is Digital Selling Infrastructure?

The digital selling infrastructure includes all digital channels that the company uses to engage customers and where it controls 100% of the message. Such channels include e-commerce, websites, mobile applications, and blogs. They can be used to explain products, deliver information, stream services, and assist

(continued)

in purchasing. Our definition extends to any digital marketing, sales, or service touchpoint that engages customers, collects first-party data about them, and is owned by your organization. This definition applies to expensive marketing automation platforms like HubSpot, Adobe (Marketo), or Pardot. It also includes platforms that monitor and communicate using social media like Sprinklr. AI-enabled service chatbots and contactless selling software like Podium that communicate automatically with customers via text are also key components of this infrastructure.

The digital selling infrastructure needs to be fed with content to answer questions, generate earned traffic, and provide reasons to contact clients and prospects. To generate earned media traffic via these channels, organizations will have staffs of people and agencies focused on generating content that manipulates search rankings and drives people to visit and engage. This portfolio of customer-facing technologies collects enormous amounts of customer engagement data that communicates interest, unmet needs, purchase intent, or pending attrition. This portfolio of technology is also very expensive. When you add up all of the spending associated with these assets, they represent a significant capital investment. Likewise, when you add up the costs of all the programs and people associated with running and feeding this infrastructure, it can be a quarter or more of your operating budget for growth. A big issue facing managers is that the digital selling infrastructure is a large capital and operating investment that rarely shows up as a discrete budget item. It has many owners, and lives in many functional silos.

The size, breadth, and mix of capital investments and operating expenses needed to build, support, and run the digital selling infrastructure are enormous when you count all the digital, technology, content, and owned marketing channels that have emerged. Companies now spend more of their marketing dollars on owned marketing and media than on paid media programs from places like Google, Facebook, and digital media. Programs like account-based selling and propensity to buy modeling are replacing the traditional marketing campaign program.

These far more targeted activities draw upon a significant amount of data captured within the owned digital infrastructure. It's disappointing that "owned media" is rarely a budget consolidation category, because not utilizing it this way prevents these programs from fully reporting results as part of marketing spend, or forces their exclusion from most fully loaded ROI models.

Much of the owned digital infrastructure is bought and managed by the marketing function. Consequently, this infrastructure frequently falls into the silo trap. It often becomes disconnected from the technical, process, and data perspective from the sales and service teams to which it is supposed to feed leads and intelligence. That is a big reason why most (62%) marketing organizations are not leveraging the first-party customer data from their digital marketing technology systems in marketing planning and measurement.[15]

Neither are their peers in sales. Only 32% of sales reps report they use information from marketing automation systems in their day-to-day selling.[17]

To monetize the data that is generated by this owned digital infrastructure, managers have to find ways to connect digital interactions to customer profiles, get that information to sales and service teams, and suggest smart ways they can act on it. This requires a blend of advanced analytics, sales enablement, and high degrees of sales and marketing integration.

Account-Based Marketing is a great example of a program that connects dots from marketing data to sales and service actions.

Economics is another hurdle. Any program that tries to monetize these valuable first-party data assets should have an extremely high return on investment. Unfortunately, the economics of monetizing customer-facing technologies are compelling in theory but not yet well understood. The value chain spans too many functional business units and budgets to allow any single manager to make the business case. This ambiguity exacerbates the perception that marketing cannot link its results to tangible sales results. Conventional waterfall and siloed marketing funnels of MQL and SQL metrics are archaic and generally gone, so we need a new dashboard approach to make the economics of owned infrastructure clear.

"Data is the new oil, and we are big believers in that because our tech captures a lot of data," says David Rabin, VP Global Commercial Marketing at Lenovo, in a recent interview with Wharton Business School as part of the "Markets in Motion" research initiative on evolution of the commercial model.[38] "I believe we should be able to measure 70% of what we do. I can measure the basics – registrations, engagement, activity, attendance – in media and events. But there is a 'moat' around marketing – there is still a human factor between marketing engagement and the sales outcome – because a sales rep has to receive that lead, and code it into CRM, and give credit to a marketing action and verify it converts. The problem we as marketers face is the same as our clients. There are thousands of solutions out there who can help us with that problem – 47 new vendors – but we have no capacity to deal with tools that can help us, we simply can't get to them."

This is the real reason marketers like to hide behind front-of-the-funnel "vanity metrics" like clicks, website visits, downloads, and sales qualified leads (SQLs) to justify their investments in digital marketing, media, and technology. The vast majority of inbound digital marketing interactions (95%) are anonymous – which means you cannot tell whether a visitor is a prospect, customer, Russian spy, or even a robot.

The real value of customer-facing technology is realized when an organization has a system for (a) identifying more of the leads coming in digitally, and (b) getting that information to a human who can convert it into value. Sales and service reps are in the best position to use this information to create value either by winning a deal, improving the customer experience, or keeping an angry customer from leaving. "The Revenue Operating System paints a clear picture of the state of your selling system," says Viral Bajaria, the Chief Technology Officer and Co-founder of 6sense.[70] "There are the places where the data exists, and the places where the data needs to be used. First-party data has a lot of richness. The problem is it's disconnected from the CRM. So the CRM data becomes stale. Often it is the least up-to-date system, because nobody goes in to update historical information, and there is a lot of incomplete data in it. Some people try to bypass the system – but ultimately if you want to have salespeople use marketing signals from your websites and third-party signals of intent – you need that data in your CRM – that's why we put so much emphasis on cleaning data, eliminating bad data, filling missing data gaps in data. That's where the ROI is."

Mike Diorio, a Sales Systems Analyst at Datadog, reinforces the simple fact that sales reps need a single system of record to simplify their selling motion and execute more advanced programs like Account-Based Marketing. "I constantly tell our sales team, if it's not in CRM, it does not exist," says Diorio. "Sales forces need a single system of record and workflow to be successful. For us, Salesforce.com is our all-encompassing truth, and everything a rep does needs to be captured there in order to have proper visibility and reporting."

A range of solutions have emerged that offer sales leaders practical ways their organizations can start to connect these stranded customer-facing technology assets to the four sources of value creation outlined here:

1. **Incorporating digital marketing data in customer profiles and frontline selling systems.** A growing number of Customer Data Platforms like Snowflake. Blueshift, and Openprise are automating the process of pulling data in from digital channels and touchpoints – including e-commerce, marketing automation website, mobile, blog, social, and text interactions – so it can be used to help sales and service teams in client conversations, decision making, and offers. Revenue Operations platforms like Revenue.io automatically augment CRM profiles with data from marketing.

2. **Leveraging data from contactless selling technologies with sales, marketing, and service teams.** Several solutions are leveraging the customer engagement data created in contactless selling platforms, including chatbots and AI-guided digital assistants, social media, text, and messaging platforms. Sales Engagement Platforms like Xant.ai and HubSpot Sales Hub are using data from chatbots to append customer profiles and provide guidance to sellers. Customer experience platforms like Sprinklr and Interaction Management Platforms like Podium are extracting insights from social, text, and messaging interactions that make up a growing portion of customer contact so they can be used to inform sales and service actions.

3. **Sharing digital marketing data with sales and service teams.** Marketing Automation Platforms like Adobe Marketo, Oracle Eloqua, SAP eMarketing Cloud, Saleforce.com, and Pardot have the potential to unify and integrate their suites to share data across sales, marketing, and service functions. For example, SAP offers its customers a Customer Data Platform, Emarsys, that makes it fast and easy to unify customer interaction from all three of its functional solutions – SAP Sales Cloud, eMarketing Cloud, and Service Cloud platforms.

4. **Enabling ABM programs to optimize account coverage.** Many B2B organizations are adopting a variety of sophisticated ABM or account engagement platforms from 6sense, Demandbase, and Terminus that apply digital, targeting, and personalized marketing practices to improve sales productivity and key account development. These platforms help them blend advanced analytics, with marketing content, and high degrees of sales and marketing integration to accelerate enterprise selling and redefine the customer journey. ABM is a great example of a program that is much better described and managed as a system that connects dots across the sales, marketing, and service ecosystem rather than a narrow technology category. For example, 6sense uses AI and analytics to analyze buyer engagement data from many different sources to support day-to-day selling by revenue teams. They orchestrate prospect and customer data across many systems. They map that data around account structures to make it much easier to develop, cross-sell, upsell, and penetrate their best customers. They integrate that data with profiles in CRM. They augment that data with third-party data that holds buying signals and identifies anonymous visitors. This is helping growth leaders to leverage their huge investments in sales, technology, CRM, and content management and enablement systems.

Monetizing the Digital Marketing Infrastructure with Selling Teams Using ABM

Most business-to-business organizations are adopting sophisticated ABM programs that apply digital, targeting, and personalized marketing practices to improve sales productivity and key account development. These strategies blend advanced profile and account matching analytics and third-party account information and signals with marketing content, and high degrees of sales and marketing integration to accelerate enterprise selling and redefine the customer journey.

Marketers are investing a lot of money in ABM systems and programs. Research from ITSMA generously suggests B2B CMOs are spending over a quarter (28%) of their marketing budgets on ABM programs.[14] The Duke CMO Survey reports marketers are now investing more money in Customer

(continued)

Relationship Management than they are in Branding.[4] Those numbers may be exaggerated but it's safe to say businesses are spending a lot of money on ABM programs.

Investing in ABM makes sense. Enabled by advanced analytics, these strategies promise to more fully leverage technology and data, better connect marketing efforts to key account sales, and more seamlessly integrate marketing and sales processes. "I define ABM as the new name for the age-old practice of intensely studying the customer and applying that meaningful insight to the development of masterfully choreographed sales and marketing plans," reports Melinda McLaughlin, the CMO of Extreme Reach who took ownership of her company's ABM strategy.[73] "What is entirely new and exciting, however, is that our toolkit for activation of those plans is exponentially more diverse. Then, because many of these new tactics are digital, our actions return data that help the team better understand what is working and what isn't so we can adapt, swerve, and/or pivot in near real time."

Even though ABM focuses on key account selling, it's a truly cross-functional program. More often than not the data and resources are owned by marketing operations. This is because marketing controls most of the growth assets that make these programs run – notably the martech stack, demand generation programs, the customer interaction data they both produce, and the marketing content that fuels them. But these assets alone won't ensure success. CMOs need to be very smart about how they execute because ABM programs have many moving parts and face the same headwinds as every other sales and marketing collaboration in history.

"The end state vision where data and technology enable one sales and marketing motion looks really good on paper" reports Jaime Punishill, the CMO of Lionbridge who just assumed command of his company's ABM program.[73] "But when you get into the details of enabling ABM, most CMOs are in need of a GPS to help guide them through some pretty significant points of failure, scale and leverage. For example, if sales and marketing want to work together on a common customer journey they will need to define and agree on common objectives, processes, incentives and shared accountability. The way B2B firms have historically measured marketing funnel vs. sales pipeline and leads will have to evolve dramatically to support a seamless customer journey and the complexities of engaging many stakeholders using many touchpoints across a large number of accounts."

Managers executing ABM programs too often fall into the trap of defining them as a "technology." Analysts reinforce this belief that the technology does all the work, and solution providers do little to dispel this notion. The reality is a successful ABM program takes a high degree of coordination between sales and marketing and service. "Most industry analysts have historically put us in the Account Based Marketing (ABM) category," says Viral Bajaria of 6sense.[70] "But that doesn't tell the full story – there's so much more. The category is Account-Based Marketing, but in reality we help marketers and sellers and customer success teams. Our mission is to provide 100% visibility into accounts, activity, and opportunities across the entire revenue cycle. So any person in marketing, sales, or customer success can use this information to develop customers – whether that's winning new revenue, retaining existing revenue or upselling the current customer base."

An ABM program will take anonymous digital marketing signals from the website or mobile apps, identify them with clients and accounts based on the master account structure, and ideally communicate those signals to human sales and service reps using CRM as the system of record. On an outbound basis, sales reps need to be comfortable that marketers are communicating the right things to their clients. There is plenty of room for crossed wires and confusion. One sales enablement executive complained that marketing operations brought in an ABM solution without working with sales. The vendor trained sales reps to use the triggers from their platform, instead of the approved process of managing all customer engagement data within Salesforce.com. Reps were confused. Money was wasted. Adoption was poor.

Another problem is that the economics of ABM, while compelling, are not well understood. Over 95% of inbound digital marketing interactions are anonymous to the degree an account rep does not know their customers are engaging with the business. That means if a company spent $10 in fully loaded, owned, and paid marketing expense to get an anonymous inquiry, they really spent $200 for that inquiry. Add in the capital expense of maintaining the digital marketing infrastructure that supports that lead flow and it's even more expensive. The real value of ABM is it makes all of that investment pay off by identifying more of the leads coming in digitally and getting that information to a human rep who can convert it into value. Winning a deal or save an account from leaving. Conventional waterfall and siloed marketing metrics fail to make this economic formula clear.

Growth leaders should focus on four keys to success to ensure their ABM strategies generate results in terms of firm value and financial performance:

1. **Make scalability the core strategic objective of ABM technology investment;**
2. **Evolve performance measurement from marketing-sourced pipeline to customer engagement metrics;**
3. **Improve how fast and efficiently your organization shares customer data and insights; and**
4. **Establish a common economic purpose for long-term investment in ABM assets with sales and finance.**

Focus on Scalability. Scalability is a critical goal of ABM because high-quality account relationship management is very resource intensive. ITSMA Benchmarks suggest that it costs $36,000 per account to deliver highly personalized one-to-one service to an account because it involves high-value human interaction. Those unit economics won't scale across hundreds or thousands of accounts unless technology dramatically changes the cost structure of targeting, servicing, and developing accounts. "For ABM investment to really pay off it needs to scale. We've won awards from ITSMA for the 'white glove ABM' we

(continued)

were able to provide our clients when we concentrated our human sales efforts on a few of our largest customers," reports Mike Marcellin, CMO of Juniper Networks.[73] "The challenge is to use technology, process and personalization to deliver that level of personalized service to thousands of stakeholders in thousands of accounts. To become more scalable, we have done many things: building a data science team to increase our focus on advanced analytics needed to build a customer data repository to support ABM at scale, ensuring we have a state-of-the-art martech stack, and massively ramping up our demand generation efforts."

Make customer engagement the measure of success. Many B2B CMOs believe that the traditional measures of sales and marketing effectiveness based on the demand unit waterfall model – Marketing sourced pipeline, Marketing Qualified leads, Sales Qualified Leads – are flawed. These metrics lead to constant challenges from sales and finance. They waste precious energy on documenting who gets credit instead of improving account profitability. They also make it difficult to reconcile interactions with many individual stakeholders into a coherent picture of account potential, profitability, penetration, and customer lifetime value. Robin Matlock, CMO of VMware, suggests the unit of measurement for ABM needs to evolve from traditional marketing-sourced pipeline and MQLs to customer engagement and account health.

Accelerate the sharing of data and customer insights. Modern marketing produces customer data that allows marketers to identify trigger events that signal buying intent, flag inquiries from important influencers within accounts, and make decisions about next best actions based on past customer behavior. The window of time your organization has to act on that data is small, however – gated by customer time, attention, and expectations for response. This makes speeding data and decisions about an opportunity from the source (e.g. a website, an algorithm in marketing) to a customer-facing employee who can act on it (e.g. a relationship manager or customer service rep) a critical value driver. Academic research by the Marketing Science Institute (MSI) has proven that the ability of an organization to generate, disseminate, and respond to market intelligence – called Organizational Knowledge Sharing – has a quantifiable positive effect on firm value and financial performance in terms of profits, sales, and market share.[6]

Establish a common economic purpose for investing in ABM assets. According to Jaime Punishill, "Sales and Marketing have historically been separate functions with separate goals and KPIs. But seen through the eyes of the customer there is only one customer journey and one aggregated setoff interactions they have with a firm. For ABM to work, marketing and sales will need a common economic purpose and financial incentive if they are going to collaborate around a common customer journey." Agreeing on a common financial goal to support the execution of ABM strategies is critical but can be tricky. ABM programs require more capital investment than conventional marketing campaigns. So CMOs must build a multiyear investment road map to support building out the analytics infrastructure, technology, content, and owned marketing channels required to support ABM, while at the same time balancing short-term demand generation tactics to drive sales. The most financially valid business cases will treat ABM as a force multiplier that dramatically improves the utilization of these growth assets by taking significant human labor sales preparation, content personalization, and marketing program execution.

CHAPTER 8

Blend Data into Insights That Inform Selling Actions, Conversations, and Decisions in Real Time

Unlocking the Potential of Analytics to Ignite Growth

The emergence of advanced analytics, AI, and Machine Learning (ML) – and the massive new sales engagement data sets to support them – represents the most significant opportunity to accelerate sales growth since the scale adoption of call centers (40 years ago), CRM (30 years ago), and digital channels (20 years ago). This revolution in advanced sales analytics offers growth leaders unprecedented potential to improve the productivity of revenue teams, multiply the return on selling assets, and create firm value. This makes the ability to capture and unify customer data and convert it into customer and seller insights that optimize and automate cross-functional sales, marketing, and service workflows a big priority.

Businesses and investors agree that better insights can fuel new revenue and profit growth. Growth leaders are investing heavily to realize this potential. On average, investment in advanced analytics will exceed 11% of overall marketing budgets by 2022.[4] Spending on AI software will top $125 billion by 2025 as organizations weave AI and ML tools into their business processes.[3] Ninety percent of organizations are using AI to improve their customer journeys, revolutionize how they interact with customers, and deliver them more compelling experiences.[36]

The leaders we spoke with were turning these investments into value by using advanced analytics to reinvent customer journeys, automate sales activities, and extract better prices. Others were leveraging insights to optimally allocating sales resources, better managing sales teams, and improving the performance of sales channels.

In parallel, investors have poured more than $5 billion into over 1,400 AI-fueled sales and technology companies to meet this demand.[66] So it's no surprise that over 90% of the top 100 solutions we identified in our analysis of the 100 technologies transforming the commercial model are using advanced analytics, AI, and machine learning to better enable sales, marketing, and service teams.[26]

Individually these innovators are connecting the dots across the sales and marketing technology portfolio to optimize resource allocation, direct revenue teams, enable individual sellers, and measure and motivate performance, while also working to personalize communications, pricing, and offerings. Collectively, this group of platforms are fast becoming the linchpin of the Revenue Operating System. They turn legacy investments in sales and marketing technology, selling channel infrastructure and customer data into selling outcomes that grow revenues, enterprise value, and profits.

At its core, this new Revenue Operating System creates value by unifying and monetizing customer data and insights at the center, while enabling and automating cross-functional sales, marketing, and service workflows at the periphery.

In effect, it's forcing executives to reimagine their technology stacks and go-to-market models around platforms that aggregate and orchestrate customer engagement data rather than CRM. This has led to a Copernican Revolution in how companies generate revenue by harnessing the full potential technology to accelerate profit growth. This revolution is blurring the lines between traditional software categories and making the ability to turn customer data into insights the primary driver of value creation in sales, and the key to increasing the return on selling assets.

The combination of these forces compels growth leaders to change in several ways:

- **Curating platforms that orchestrate commercial insights will create more value.** This places a premium on platforms that can coordinate and deploy customer engagement and seller activity data faster and better than CRM. Businesses are creating value by finding ways to convert big data into insights that prescriptively inform seller decisions, actions, and conversations in real time at the "moments that matter" in the human selling process. "Growth leaders need core central system of decision-making," says Viral Bajaria, the Founder of 6sense.[70] "Every company now has 20, 30, or even 50 plus tools to help them grow. And even more media and marketing partners to reach customers. They need to start to bring the engagement data from all those tools together in one place. To create the center decision-making system. And then once the decision is made, push those insights to the system where you can use that information to create value. There is a place for best-of-breed solutions and a place for platforms in this ecosystem. But at the end of the day you need a system to pull it all together."

- **Relying more on algorithms to define territories, account priorities, and the allocation of selling effort.** The megatrends toward remote selling and the alignment of sales, success, and marketing into one revenue team are releasing the legacy constraints of geography, function, and role on the allocation of selling resources. This is allowing B2B sellers more freedom to leverage AI to define data-optimized territory boundaries, seller assignments, account priorities and the allocation of resources and effort. "In the short term, sales organizations are deploying algorithms that help with the basics of account prioritization, lead qualification, recommending the content or sales action that will lead to success, and reallocating sales resources to the places they can have the most impact," reports Leonard Lodish, Professor of Marketing at the Wharton School of Business.[32] "More sophisticated organizations using AI tools can also create algorithmically derived customer response models to help take the guesswork and gut feel out of aligning sales resources across geographies, accounts, and business lines."

- **Connecting sales and marketing solutions into closed-loop systems that better support planning, measurement, and execution of the day-to-day selling motion.** AI is rapidly converging the traditional sales and marketing software categories in ways that will make frontline selling faster, simpler, and more consistent. This confluence of capabilities represents an immediate and significant opportunity for B2B organizations to generate the next level of growth from their revenue teams. Growth leaders that configure these platforms in ways that make them simpler to use by sales, marketing, and customer success reps will realize the immense promise of this latest generation of selling technology. The most advanced organizations are demanding that their enablement teams connect their sales enablement, sales engagement, sales readiness, and conversational intelligence capabilities into closed-loop processes that deliver real-time guidance and coaching at scale to every member of the frontline revenue team.

- **Providing managers greater visibility into seller activity, customer engagement, forecast commitments, and pipeline health and enabling more data-driven decision making.** Greater visibility is now essential in a post-pandemic economy where work at home, hybrid work, and work from anywhere practices have become the norm. It gives sales managers the information they need to better manage, measure, coach, and empower remote revenue teams at the edge of the organizations to make the right decisions faster. Sales leaders are building KPIs based on seller activity and customer engagement that provide more transparency of seller performance, customer engagement, and forecast commitments that pipeline health and enable more data-driven decision-making. Building KPIs based on activity and engagement makes practical sense in the face of remote selling and the fact that linear waterfall metrics don't accurately reflect the ways customers buy or revenue teams sell. Analytics and AI also allow them to create better incentives for all customer-facing resources based on account profitability and contribution to firm financial performance.

This means getting better control over the customer engagement and buyer activity data that they already have.

Like the heads of sports teams, marketing, sales, and service leaders need to orient their teams toward a common goal. In other words, they need to use advanced analytics and AI to turn sales engagement data into a common set of measurements and financial incentives that get sales, marketing, and services working toward the wins of firm value, customer lifetime value, and profits.

Professor Adi Wyner, who leads the Sports Analytics and Business Initiative at Wharton Business School, sees close parallels between the cultural and business transformation that sports teams have experienced in the past few decades and the challenges sales and marketing leaders face today. He often points to the challenges faced by Billy Bean, General Manager of the Oakland A's, in the book *Moneyball* as a lesson about leading transformation from the top. Bean was forced by competitive circumstances to challenge baseball orthodoxy by using analytics-based approaches in order to find better ways to build and run his team. His efforts to transform his organization ran into the same cultural, organizational, and capability obstacles as sales and marketing transformation programs do. To ultimately succeed, he had to push hard to invest big resources on building analytics capabilities, acquire the right talent at the right price, and give general managers more power and control over coaching tactics, game strategies, and play calling. "Billy Bean was remarkable not because he discovered the value of walks as a predictor for player performance – but because he was a leader who allowed himself to listen to what the analysis was telling him when it contradicted conventional wisdom and entrenched beliefs of his organization to find ways to transform his business" according to Professor Wyner.[105]

To make this a reality, sales leaders are increasingly looking to a new set of analytic tools – including customer data platforms, sales engagement platforms, and sales analytics and automation solutions – that can convert data into information, and information into value. These tools are taking on the hard work of coordinating data across channels and making it available to sales, marketing, and service reps in real time. In practice, businesses are putting these solutions in place in ways that integrate with, augment, and in some cases, bypass legacy CRM systems to combine and monetize customer engagement and seller activity data.

This represents a material shift in the center of gravity of the systems that support growth to platforms that are able to aggregate, transform, orchestrate, and disseminate customer insights in ways that are faster, more proscriptive, predictive, and actionable. This trend is evidenced by the rapid growth of what are commonly called Customer Data Platform, Sales Engagement, or Revenue Acceleration Platforms. The names may vary, but these types of platforms and solutions are among the fastest-growing companies in our analysis. For purposes of this book, we call that "center of gravity" of the Revenue Operating System the Engagement Data Hub. This chapter will detail how the best organizations are aggregating data from marketing and sales systems and turning it into insights that inform selling actions and resource allocation decisions.

Building Block #4: Revenue Intelligence – Manage and Measure Financial Value

REVENUE INTELLIGENCE	
FORECAST ACCURACY	ACCOUNT HEALTH & LIFETIME VALUE
OPPORTUNITY POTENTIAL METRICS	SELLER PERFORMANCE METRICS

Visibility into opportunity potential, account health, seller performance, and pipeline activity are regarded as the four most important insights managers need to better manage their selling system.[9] Companies that make progress creating more accurate metrics, dashboards, and incentives have a significant advantage over the competition, reports Brent Adamson, distinguished Vice President in Gartner's Sales practice.[129] "Companies that align their metrics and incentives with customer buying behavior will give them a much more accurate picture of the cost of sales, the opportunity cost of selling time, and how different resources contribute to their commercial organizations in terms of commercial outcomes," advises Adamson. "This will allow them to make much better decisions about how to allocate people, technology, data and content resources based on what they are contributing to the top-line, bottom-line and value of the company." (See Figure 8.1.)

Advanced analytics can give you much better visibility into account health, pipeline accuracy, opportunity potential, and the like. These insights can be derived from the data your organization currently collects from customer engagement, product usage, financial transactions, and seller activities.

Building KPIs based on pipeline activity and seller engagement makes practical sense in the face of remote selling and the fact that traditional marketing funnels and linear waterfall metrics don't accurately reflect the ways customers buy or revenue teams sell anymore. Analytics and AI also allow you to create better incentives for customer-facing resources based on account profitability and contribution to firm financial performance.

There are several practical ways that sales leaders take advantage of advanced sales analytics, engagement, and performance management platforms to get greater visibility into seller activity, customer engagement,

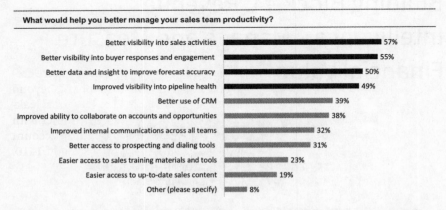

FIGURE 8.1   The Top Opportunities to Better Manage Sales Teams. *Source: Revenue Enablement Institute Survey of 150 sales leaders, May 2020*

forecast commitments, and pipeline health and enable more data-driven decision making. Specifically, they include:

1. **Creating more precise measures of account health and lifetime value.** Sales and marketing leaders like AT&T, Ciena Networks, Marketo (Adobe), and DHL are taking steps to align their metrics and incentives with the activities and behaviors that lead to better selling outcomes, greater customer lifetime value, and improved account health. They are using advanced customer engagement analytics and sales AI to create customer engagement metrics to serve as the foundation for performance measurements based on real-time information about sales engagement, deal attractiveness, content usage, and personal-level interactions to provide management a more accurate proxy of the current buying reality.

2. **Automating and improving sales forecast accuracy.** Sales analytics leaders, such as Aviso and Clari, are leveraging data from across enterprise systems to create more accurate revenue forecasts. Currently only about a third (34%) of sales leaders have intelligent forecasting. Ninety percent of those that use this capability say it helps them do their job more effectively.[17]

3. **Quantifying seller performance, capacity, and consistency.** Frontline sales managers can use AI to significantly measure the performance of the "B and C players" on their revenue teams. They can now use advanced analytics to automate the evaluation and coaching of sales talent, create measures of seller performance based on activity and behavior, and improve the coverage and penetration of key accounts using ABM data and insights.

   The best way to get sales, marketing, product, and service reps working together to improve account health and penetration is to create data-driven incentives and KPIs to foster a common purpose in working as a team to grow customer lifetime value. Sales leaders are starting to use advanced analytics to derive new measures that more accurately quantify the collective engagement and customer experience our teams are creating within accounts. Teamwork-oriented leaders are evolving beyond outdated and dysfunctional waterfall metrics that lead to handoffs, leakage, and waste by putting sales, marketing, and service in conflict with each other. They are creating data-driven metrics that quantify account profitability, pipeline health, and seller performance on a scale of 1–10. They are also drawing on sales analytics solutions like Xactly and Captive IQ to track the behaviors and activities that define team success while laddering up to innovative data-driven customer engagement measures and incentives tied to account health and value creation.

4. **Using simulations to test and evaluate growth strategy scenarios.** Best-in-class companies are using simulation tools to compress time, evaluate multiple scenarios, navigate trade-offs, and accelerate consensus

building. AI-driven simulation-based tools offer faster and more collaborative approaches to generating territory, product launch, account-based marketing, and business unit growth plans.

Using simulation tools to have your leadership team "war game" more scenarios has a variety of benefits when compared to the traditional top-down strategy development approach used by most companies. First, it compresses time to test go-to-market strategies and scenarios seven years into the future. Given that most strategies will not bear fruit or fail until several sales periods after inception, this can be a huge advantage.

Second, AI-driven simulations can manage millions of scenarios and possible resource allocations to find the best combinations to maximize growth. They allow managers to test and balance different combinations of sales force emphasis, calling priorities, customer targets, and treatment types to generate the greatest profit and growth contribution, ROI, and quota attainability. Because they can incorporate dozens and even hundreds of field leaders into the process, simulations allow you to combine bottom-up local market knowledge and performance insights with top-down focus on realizing the greatest profit, revenue, and opportunity share. They also let planners "pressure test" and adapt plans to deal with rapidly changing and different customer and market scenarios. Finally, they accelerate the time between strategy development, tactical planning, buy-in, communication, and implementation by revenue teams.

5. **Using advanced analytics to improve the accuracy, predictability, and quality of growth plans, forecasts, and predictions.** Due to rapidly changing customer behavior, shorter product life cycles, the complexity of omnichannel and virtual selling systems, sales modeling is increasingly critical to sales resource allocation, forecasting, and strategy developments. Advanced modeling technologies have been made practically and financially viable thanks to the broader availability of better data to inform growth strategies and the democratization of analytics.

Modeling allows managers to balance and tune six interrelated inputs – the size, segmentation, and emphasis of the sales force, the design of territories, the segmentation of markets, and the treatment of customers – against corporate growth goals and resource constraints. Modeling also forces management to blend quantitative data inputs and objective empirical analysis with estimates based on management judgment and local market knowledge in ways that must achieve growth priorities, targets, and strategies defined by firm leaderships. "It's important to understand what Machine Learning and AI tools are good for, and what they are not" reports Ron Cline, Head of US Marketing Data and Analytics at the TD Group.[31] "These tool and modeling techniques allow us to analyze more data sources, faster, with more statistically valid results, and less work."

Advanced modeling and analytics techniques can significantly improve the process and the outcomes they achieve in five specific ways. Improving critical assumptions about the sales response function predicts the incremental revenue associated with an incremental increase in selling effort. Better understanding of this relationship is critical because it underlies all sales resources, budgets, quotas, and territory definitions. Modeling also leads to making better assumptions, allowing organizations to evolve beyond simple heuristics or rules of thumb that assume linear sales responses or equal allocation of efforts against all customers and territories, and to more nuanced and accurate assumptions that reflect the true nature of demand and sales response based on decision science.

6. **Creating measures of the financial contribution of long-term growth investment.** Accountability is fundamental to scalable growth, according to Tony Pace, CEO of the Marketing Accountability Standards Board (MASB). "Greater financial scrutiny and improved marketing accountability for the financial return on all marketing investments is fundamental to protecting, unlocking and growing the financial value they create," says Pace, who is also the former CMO of Subway. "Unfortunately, with current budget setting processes, financial reporting standards, and measurement practices – over two-thirds of companies cannot effectively measure their financial return on investments that create value through improving brand preference, the customer experience, sales activation, customer loyalty and cultural relevancy according to the MASB research."

"The central problem is marketing lacks the kind of accountability and metrics that are common along the value chain of the rest of the corporation," according to David Stewart, the editor of the book *Accountable Marketing*.[134] "Marketing remains a 'dark science' where its practitioners can generate desirable results but cannot tell you how they achieved them."

Executives leading Fortive and Lionbridge agree with this reality. "Holding marketing assets, investments, and front-of-the-funnel marketing activity accountable for financial returns is fundamental to profitable growth," according to Jaime Punishill, CMO of Lionbridge.[113] "Financial returns are the only vocabulary you can use to communicate the return on critical growth investments like digital selling infrastructure, selling content, brand building and the customer experience to the CEO, CFO and the Chief Revenue Officer. So we shifted our focus to understanding, measuring, and improving the contribution of the commercial assets we manage – digital technology, data, content, leads, and brainpower – to growth, profits, and firm financial performance."

Fortive Business Systems, an industrial conglomerate, is using analytics to create feedback loops to evaluate outcomes, attribution, and performance across sales, marketing, and customer success. Kirsten Paust, VP of Fortive Business Systems has worked hard to help business units put in place analytics that create feedback loops that measure the sales impact of actions and investments. "The whole idea of accountability for growth outcomes and attribution of revenue is really important in our culture," shares Paust.[130] "That's a critical role for analytics because if we want to excel at sales and marketing as a company then we have to measure it. Our leaders work to really understand the connection between investment in sales and marketing and growth outcomes. This understanding is so critical because it turns sales and marketing into an enabler of growth, not a discretionary expense."

Using Advanced Analytics to Create Better Measures of Seller Performance, Account Health, and Opportunity Potential

Expanding revenue is a team sport. Selling to a digitally empowered customer across many channels requires a wider variety of functional roles, a bigger arsenal of tools and tactics, and much more communication and coordination. As organizations struggle to keep up with an ever-changing customer journey, the role of the marketing and sales executive has evolved into an orchestrator of an increasingly complex marketing and technology ecosystem.

Teamwork-oriented executives like Denise Karkos, Jason Phipps of Ciena, and Robin Matlock, formerly from VMware, are pushing past twentieth-century demand unit waterfall metrics that support linear sales process, handoffs, leakage, and waste by putting sales, marketing, and service in conflict with each other.

Their hard-learned experience has taught them that the traditional measures of sales and marketing effectiveness based on the demand unit waterfall model – Marketing-sourced pipeline, Marketing Qualified leads, Sales Qualified Leads – are flawed on many dimensions. These metrics do not foster teamwork. Nor do they address current customer behavior. Demand unit waterfall metrics lead to constant challenges from sales and finance. And the list goes on. They waste precious energy on documenting who gets credit instead of improving account profitability. They also make it difficult to reconcile interactions with many individual stakeholders into a coherent picture of account potential, profitability, penetration, and customer lifetime value.

To get their revenue teams working together to create customer lifetime value, they advocate putting in place metrics that quantify customer engagement, energy created within accounts, team success, and customer lifetime value. For example, Robin Matlock changed the unit of measurement for the performance of sales and marketing resources, teams, and investments from traditional marketing-sourced pipeline and MQLs to customer engagement and account health. "Getting insights on an account level vs. an individual level was a huge paradigm shift for us," according to Matlock in a speech at the Forbes

CMO Summit.[73] "It means thinking about Coca-Cola as a holistic account as opposed to a lead or tracking this one individual through a buying journey. The buying journey is made up of tens of individuals and an account is made up of many leads. I want to look at the health of an account. The pulse of what is going on in the account and how they are engaging with our marketing activity. The solution is quality of the engagement of the customer. Measuring this at scale is the tricky part. With many stakeholders in the account, tracking interactions across marketing and sales systems is the golden thread."

Denise Karkos, CMO of Sirius XM & Pandora, believes that to successfully align sales, marketing, and customer experience teams around a common set of customer goals and increase control over the entire customer lifecycle, leaders will need a better set of performance measurements and financial incentives for these disparate groups to work together. A key success factor in this new growth equation is to create a common scorecard for customer success based on unified customer engagement metrics that provide go-to-market teams more incentives to work together. The holy grail is to create a common set of financially valid and data-driven incentives where the ultimate scorecard for marketing and sales is firm value, future profits, and revenue growth.

"In order to create a common purpose for your growth team, smart leaders must do two things," says Karkos.[105] "First, he or she must define what a win is. And it starts with defining a common purpose for all the leaders in the organization. For example, at TD Ameritrade our CEO redefined a win as a high Net Promoter Score. This completely changed the organization's focus to customer success. The second job is to create a set of shared operational goals that ladder up to the winning score. To do this right, you need to break it down into functional components that map to day-to-day transactional activities – like engagement quality, levels of service, time to resolution, and customer advocacy. From there you need to derive common incentives – or shared KPIs – for the entire team. Having shared incentives is a powerful way to operate because if forces teamwork and is scalable."

Putting this scorecard for success into operation involves deriving customer engagement quality metrics from the customer data that exists in CRM, exchange servers, marketing automation, and content management systems. The secret is to develop a set of KPIs using advanced analytics that track the behaviors and activities that define team success but ladder up to a common scorecard and set of financial incentives for winning. This creates one common and agreed-on scorecard for success – tied to firm value and financial performance – if all these disparate functions and armies of customer-facing employees are going to work together in any meaningful way. Hierarchical, functional, funnel, and waterfall metrics based on linear sales funnels and independent functional roles will fail to either foster teamwork or address current customer behavior.

Steve Lucas, CEO of iCIMS, believes creating a common measurement system and model for orchestrating the engagement of sales, marketing, and services with all the key customer stakeholders in ways that deliver a superior customer experience is critical to achieving hyper growth in today's marketplace.

(continued)

"One key to winning in the engagement economy is to develop a universal customer engagement quality score that defines engagement excellence to all the stakeholders in your organization," according to Lucas, who famously doubled revenue and tripled the value of the firm to $4.75 billion in 24 months.[133] "That means defining as an organization what a 10 out of 10 looks like in terms of customer advocacy, quality of interaction, content sharing, and other relationship health metrics." Lucas pushed his team at Marketo to clearly define and quantify what a good client relationship looks like empirically on a scale of 1–10. And then used advanced analytics to build composite metrics that quantify and track customer engagement quality on a customer and account level. He kept the bar high on engagement quality. Any account team with a customer engagement score of less than 9 had to take a series of actions to improve customer health. In parallel, he created a vocabulary, criteria, reporting, and most importantly, financial incentives for his go-to-market teams to develop relationships with these "ideal customers." To enforce this discipline of delivering high-quality customer engagement to the highest potential customers, his teams were paid 20% higher commissions when they engaged and developed "ideal" customers. They were paid 20% lower commissions when they spent their energies on less than ideal prospects.

Lucas is not alone. Sales and marketing executives at AT&T, Ciena Networks, Sirius XM, and DHL are taking steps to align their metrics and incentives with the activities and behaviors that lead to increases in customer lifetime value, profit margins, and total contract value. They are using advanced customer engagement analytics and sales AI to create customer engagement metrics to serve as the foundation for performance measurements. These metrics are based on real-time information about sales engagement, deal attractiveness, content usage, and individualized customer interactions to provide management a more accurate proxy of the current buying reality.

For example, DHL used advanced customer engagement analytics and sales AI to create measures of customer engagement quality to give them visibility into opportunities and inform actions to help customers become more successful. AT&T business developed measures and incentives based on customer growth, profitability, and satisfaction (Net Promoter Scores) to help their revenue teams balance the interrelated issues of profitability, value creation, and customer success. Ciena Networks were able to integrate data from sales enablement and operations, marketing, and sales to create a dashboard and Quality of Engagement (QOE) measurements that give their leadership a more complete and real-time picture of the breadth, depth, and frequency and impact they are having on their customers and the level of customer engagement that was happening with key stakeholders in their key accounts. "Our dashboard is like an 'EKG for selling' that gives us a dynamic and digital picture of what is going on in the account," says Joe Cumello, CMO of Ciena.[126] "It lets us answer questions like are we engaging the right levels in the organization? And are those stakeholders attending webinars, participating in 'Demo days,' or downloading materials?"

Building Block #5: Engagement Data Hub – Leverage Advanced Analytics to Connect Growth Assets to Value

ENGAGEMENT DATA HUB	
SELLER ACTIVITY DATA	CUSTOMER ENGAGEMENT DATA
PRODUCT USAGE DATA	FINANCIAL TRANSACTION DATA

Customer data is one of the most valuable assets a company has. For example, creditors valued the customer data assets of United Airlines at higher than firm value, according to Doug Laney, author of the book *Infonomics*.[131] Finding ways to harvest the first-party customer engagement data your company already owns is an obvious way to grow sales with no incremental investment. Unfortunately, only 38% of CMOs believe their investments in analysts, data, and analysis fully support their decision-making process.[15]

Digital marketing programs, digital selling platforms, and third-party data providers generate information that can signal buying intent, propensity to buy, or the risk of attrition. Frontline sellers can use this information to make decisions about next best actions and prioritize urgent opportunities and leads and identify new buyers within target accounts. But they need that information in time to act on it. This makes the ability to speed that information from the source (e.g. a website, chatbot, or mobile app), to a relationship manager or customer service rep who can act on it, a priority. Often in real time. This makes improving the speed of information flow a management priority.

Finding ways to use advanced analytics to collect and monetize the data generated by legacy investments in CRM, sales enablement, and digital selling systems is at the heart of modern selling. On a fundamental level this places a premium on solutions that unify, deploy, and monetize customer data and insights to create value. As we mentioned earlier, businesses and investors universally believe AI and ML can fuel new revenue and profit growth by reinventing customer journeys, transforming the customer experience, and optimizing investments in marketing channels.

Sales systems are transforming into Customer Data Platforms that are faster, more proscriptive, predictive, and actionable. This trend is evidenced by the rapid growth of customer data platforms (like Snowflake, Lytics, Blueshift, and Tealium) and sales engagement platforms (like Outreach.io, Salesloft, and Xant.ai). These solutions are among the fastest growing companies in our analysis of the 100 technologies that are defining and enabling the twenty-first century commercial model.[25]

There are a range of ways to aggregate, consolidate, analyze, and deploy customer engagement data to augment and enhance this foundation of known customer data that help revenue teams save time, make better decisions, allocate resources more effectively, and deliver better customer experiences. Specifically:

1. **Aggregating third-party data from many sources to uncover selling triggers and insights.** Sales analytics solutions like Oracle Sales CX, Insight Squared, Cognism, XiQ, and People.ai are aggregating data from many external sources to uncover event triggers, buying signals, and churn risks in the client and prospect base. Customer data platforms like Hull, Blueshift, Zylotech, and Tealium make this happen by automating the integration and delivery of behavioral and trigger data from digital marketing platforms with sales and marketing teams. The best blend it with first-party account and prospect data from CRM to develop and deliver actionable insights to frontline sales, marketing, and service reps in real time. These solutions automatically log data into CRM systems and append data records to improve data quality and gain a 360-degree view of the customer. Third-party data solutions like Bombora, Discover.org, and Everstring are appending and enriching internal customer and prospect data sets in real time with buyer intent, prospect, and event triggers so sales reps can prioritize opportunities and act quickly while the prospect is still "in market."

2. **Managing and organizing data around account structures.** Account data management and orchestration solutions like Lattice, LeanData, Jabmo, and 6sense are helping account teams to manage and orchestrate prospect and customer engagement data from inside and outside the company around accounts to make it easier for account teams to develop, cross-sell, upsell, and penetrate key accounts.

3. **Automating the consolidation, harmonization, and cleaning of data from customer-facing systems.** A primary use case of customer data platforms is to automate the process of onboarding, orchestrating, and synchronizing data from first, second, and third-party data sources your organization already has in real time. Automating this process helps ensure that customer profiles relay the most up-to-the-minute data. Sales analytics solutions like Insight Squared aggregate

data from email, calendar, content, and call recordings and integrate it with records in CRM. Sales engagement platforms like Salesloft, Out-reach.io, and Xant.ai automate the process of aggregating buyer data, targeting anonymous interactions, and cleaning records. Sales automation solutions like Seamless.ai and Node clean customer data and enrich customer profiles to make them more predictive and usable by frontline revenue teams and the specific applications they use to engage customers.

4. **Aggregating customer activity, seller activity, product usage, and financial transaction data around a common customer profile.** Most high-performing marketers have developed a single view of the customer to direct targeting.[15] They do so by unifying data from many touch points, channels, and media interactions into a common customer profile. Customer data platforms like Treasure Data, Snowflake, and Openprise have automated the orchestration and management of this data across individual customer profiles as well as key accounts. Sales automation solutions like People.ai and Collective[i] automatically log customer interaction data to enrich CRM files and get a 360-degree view of the customer. Other solutions can help enrich customer profiles with third-party prospect, trigger, and behavioral data. For example, sales automation solutions like Seamless.ai and Node clean customer data and enrich customer profiles to make them more predictive and usable by frontline revenue teams and the applications they use to engage customers.

5. **Integrating data from many customer engagement systems.** The modern selling engine relies on data sourced from many channels, systems, and touchpoints to support selling decisions, priorities, and presentations. Most organizations are sitting on large amounts of customer engagement data in a variety of revenue enablement systems – including CRM, exchange (email and calendar), content management, marketing automation, websites, social media, and customer engagement management systems. And that's not counting one of the biggest sources of customer intelligence – data from recorded phone calls and Zoom meetings. Organizations that are able to capture and unify customer data and convert it into insights that enable, optimize, and automate cross-functional sales, marketing, and service workflows will have a competitive advantage over those that don't. Conversational AI solutions like Revenue.io capture, transcribe, and integrate engagement data from live sales calls and AI assisted service agents so it can be used to inform sales coaching, prioritization, and action recommendations. Customer data platforms like Blueshift and Zylotech help to streamline the onboarding and integration of first-party data from across in-house digital marketing, website, and e-commerce platforms.

Combining Data from Many Sources to Create Revenue and Customer Intelligence

Executives at Fortive Business Systems, Pitney Bowes, and Ryder were using customer engagement, product usage, and seller activity data turning to create insights that help them manage customer journeys, better allocating sales resources, better managing sales teams, and improving the performance of sales channels.

For example, Kirsten Paust believes every organization has the opportunity to leverage the customer engagement data that already exists within their organizations to make an impact if they don't let perfection stand in the way of progress. "When it comes to analytics," she notes, "our philosophy is making progress over perfection."[130] "One of our fundamental beliefs on this is to start with the data that you already have," Paust continues. "And over time you can decide to enrich those data sources based on your need to get better visibility into things that will make you more effective. Most of our companies have readily accessible data they can use to help them grow sales. For example, everyone has revenue or sales data they can use to better understand what customers are buying as well as renewal and churn rates. Most also have service records which help them understand who is asking for service and how that service can be improved. Many of our businesses have what we call product telemetry data, which is product usage data that provides invaluable insight into what customers are using, where they are getting value, and where we can help them realize value they aren't getting today," says Paust. For example, Fortive, a conglomerate of industrial businesses, is integrating customer engagement, sales activity, product usage, and telemetry data to support coaching and guidance of revenue teams. "Advanced analytics is a force multiplier that we are putting to work," Paust claims. "More and more of our core commercialization processes are being supported by AI, insights and technology that enables our teams to get to insight and action faster."

Likewise, Ryder Systems is using product telemetry data from the vehicles they rent to inform programs that help sellers sell value and at higher prices. Ryder hired data scientists to aggregate first-party product telemetry and third-party data that can help improve sales performance. The team applied advanced analytics to calculate propensity to buy, Total Cost of Ownership (TCO), and price elasticity to prioritize the highest potential customers for sales to focus on. For example, Ryder uses safety and maintenance data to proactively call on clients to recommend ways they can reduce their TCO by lowering insurance premiums and avoiding expensive downtime. "On the maintenance side, the trucks we maintain have fault codes and all of a sudden the red light goes on because a problem happens," says John Gleason, former Chief Growth Officer at Ryder.[119] "We can get that information from a sensor by working with the OEM and we will call the client and say hey, I know you're on a route from here to there but bring your vehicle in because you're going to have a problem that you're not even aware of. We can schedule that appointment for you online." Gleason continues, "A good example of how we have used third-party data is the Compliance Safety Accountability Score (CSA score) collected and disclosed by the federal government to measure the safety of trucks on the highway, or, if you ever see a truck pulled over by a state trooper because the truck's brake light was out, the trooper will probably notice there were three or four other problems and report it. Armed with this information, we will call on prospects and say your CSA score is amongst the worst in the industry and it's probably impacting your business. I didn't have to wonder if a client had a problem. I called them because they had a problem. From a performance standpoint, if that data allowed us to put sales reps on customers with bad CSA scores and we could demonstrate ways we could fix it and reduce the TCO, it would improve the likelihood to buy."

Bill Borrelle, CMO of Pitney Bowes, views data and insights as the next frontier for unlocking more growth and value for their customers. They have used customer data platforms to develop an engagement data hub that aggregates and leverages customer engagement data from a variety of digital touch points. "Our digital channels, devices, and marketing and sales technologies are generating new IoT of data we can leverage to sell better and improve the customer experience," Borrelle reflects.[121] "We've got an assortment of initiatives under way to leverage new sources of data. We've recently partnered with a customer data platform, Snowflake, to organize all that information about customers to inform better campaigns and customer actions. We're starting to use conversational intelligence and NLP to mine our customer conversations for feedback to help customers onboard, solve their problems, and deliver better service. And we're continuing to find ways to use technology to combine first-party customer data from our digital channels with third-party customer insights to develop richer signals of buying intent, churn, competitive activity and upsell opportunities for our sales teams."

Building Block #6: Customer Intelligence – Use Customer Data to Inform Decisions, Actions, and Conversations

CUSTOMER INTELLIGENCE	
RECOMMENDER ENGINES	ACCOUNT MANAGEMENT
CAMPAIGN OPTIMIZATION	RESPONSE MANAGEMENT

Digitally enabled customers want answers that are faster, better, and relevant. That puts more pressure on sellers to deliver a superior customer experience in the shrinking window of time they are directly engaged with customers. This has accelerated the pace at which customer information must be commercialized and shared across the organization. The speed of selling has gotten so fast that revenue teams often need selling insights in real time to compete.

These pressures have growth leaders looking for better ways to use advanced analytics to turn the customer data in their CRM, sales enablement, and digital marketing systems into actionable insights. The executives we spoke with defined actionable insights as intelligence that can directly inform the decisions, actions, and conversations that frontline sellers must make every day at the moments that matter in the human selling process.

"The revenue team doesn't want big data – they want guidance, recommendations and prioritization on what to do next," explains Howard Brown, CEO of Revenue.io, a business that has helped hundreds of organizations leverage insights to grow. "Sellers need to know what actions will drive value and generate the highest return on their time and attention. We need to use data to focus revenue teams, not overwhelm them. To transform noise into sales guidance."

The need for actionable insights places a premium on systems, processes, and operations that unify, transform, and interpret data from many customer engagement systems to answer critical day-to-day selling questions like:

- What content or offers to present?
- Which stakeholders and decision makers to engage in accounts?
- How to respond to customer questions, RFPs, and RFIs quickly and compliantly?

The pressure to turn big customer data into actionable insights is also a big reason why over 90% of the executives we spoke to are consolidating the operations that support sales, marketing, and success. They've realized they must take a more coordinated approach to managing the data from their sales conversations, marketing systems, and customer service interactions and make it available to their revenue teams faster. No longer can they afford to manage customer data in six or more operational and technology silos.

Solving this problem is one of the most impactful ways data-driven algorithms can create value. AI and advanced analytics are very good at prioritizing and qualifying leads and recommending the next best sales action. These tasks are easier for organizations to execute with limited analytics acumen and data scientists in short supply, according to Professor Leonard Lodish. "There's a broad continuum of applications of AI in the selling model ranging from relatively simple to very complex," reports Lodish.[32] "There are many high-impact and simple to implement sales AI applications most organizations can be taking advantage of today. Organizations are dramatically improving sales performance by using algorithms to help with the basics of account and lead prioritization and qualification, recommending the content or sales action that will lead to success, and reallocating sales resources to the places they can have the most impact. In customer service, AI is opening entire new frontiers in customer experience and success by applying NLP, sentiment analysis, automation, and personalization to customer relationship management."

A wide range of AI tools are now available to help sales teams prioritize opportunities based on buyer intent, recommend next best sales actions, and automate or augment the day-to-day planning, content gathering, and data entry that eats up two-thirds of selling time. While fewer than half (46%) of sales reps currently have data insights on customers' propensity to buy, the majority (62%) of high-performing salespeople see a big role for guided selling that ranks potential opportunity value and suggests next steps.[14]

There are several practical ways leading organizations are converting the customer data they already have into customer intelligence that can inform decisions, actions, and conversations. They include:

1. **Enriching customer profiles with third-party prospect, trigger, and behavioral data.** Sales analytics (Revenue Intelligence) solutions like 6sense, Oracle Sales CX, Insight Squared, Cognism, XiQ, and People. ai are aggregating data from many external sources to uncover event triggers, buying signals, and churn risks in the client and prospect base. Then they blend it with first-party account and prospect data from CRM to develop and deliver actionable insights to frontline sales, marketing, and service reps in real time. These solutions automatically log data into CRM systems and append data records to improve data quality and gain a 360-degree view of the customer. Sales automation solutions like Seamless.ai and Node clean customer data and enrich customer profiles to make them more predictive and usable by frontline revenue teams and the applications they use to engage customers.

2. **Opportunity prioritization based on propensity to buy, intent, and opportunity potential.** Sales reps spend 7% of their time prioritizing leads and opportunities.[20] But a range of solution providers have emerged that support predictive lead scoring and lead prioritization models based on customer engagement data from inside and outside the organization. For example, sales engagement platforms like Xant.ai prioritize daily tasks and plays for sales teams using real-time buyer intelligence from billions of sales interactions. Third-party data providers like Bombora

and TechTarget make those models even better by enriching them with customer intent data that lets them know a prospect is in the market for a solution.

3. **Analytic engines that recommend contextual content and next best-selling action.** Sellers are using AI-enabled recommender engines to make intelligent suggestions about the content, conversations, and actions that will advance the sale in a given situation. At the basic level, they help sales reps find the right content for a particular selling situation. This is useful because sales reps spend almost 10% of their time on call planning and content preparation.[18] Sales enablement solutions like Highspot are now using AI to push specific content based on customer preferences, past success, and client need.

   Platforms like RFPIO use AI and machine learning to analyze question-and-answer interactions from across the organization to provide highly personalized and contextual responses to complex inquiries like RFPs, RFI, and specific questions. This is a discipline called Intelligent Response Management, an advanced concept that uses AI and machine learning to create a knowledge base of content based on actual question-and-answer exchanges between customers and sales reps. The software makes this aggregate knowledge available to entire revenue teams, on demand, with no wait times. A simple query provides the answer your salesperson needs to deliver their best answer, with immediate results whether a rep is writing a text, email, proposal, presentation, or an RFP. They leverage question-and-answer interactions from across the organization to deliver answers fast, in the context and format of the inquiry, and in compliance with regulations and internal standards. Sales engagement platforms like Salesloft and Outreach.io create next-best offer algorithms to recommend content, playbooks, and even in-call guidance with real-time flash cards. This is a big opportunity to improve because only 37% of sales reps report they get algorithmic suggested next steps on an opportunity.[20]

Using AI and Machine Learning to Streamline and Personalize the Selling Content Supply Chain

If data is the oxygen in a modern growth engine, then selling content is the gasoline that provides the fuel.

This is because modern selling is increasingly centered around owned digital selling channels that rely heavily on timely, targetable, personalized, and compliant content. "New school buyers" are demanding faster, more complete and relevant content as they engage with frontline sales, marketing, and service employees across direct, virtual, and digital touchpoints. In response, CMOs are increasing their investment in content and the systems that support its delivery in context, like sales enablement and Configure, Price, and Quotation solutions.

Given this modern selling reality, customer data and sales, marketing, and product content need to be treated as strategic assets. In many cases they are not. This is particularly true for sales and marketing content.

After two decades of dramatic growth in selling content budgets, these assets are generally managed like perishable inventory, stockpiles, or transitory marketing fodder. Many CMOs still focus most of their energy on optimizing the performance of paid media spend. Meanwhile, behind the scenes, the budgets for sales and marketing content – and the people and machines that create and deliver it – have grown to become the bigger part of the growth investment mix at most B2B sales organizations.

This needs to change. Particularly if you expect to generate any reasonable return on your investment in sales and marketing content assets – and, to that end, the digital selling channels they support. Today, these represent the lion's share of B2B growth assets when you add up investments in sales enablement, engagement, and readiness systems, as well as search, social media, and contactless selling channels that are the mainstay of digital marketing today.

Change means tackling the real problems that have hamstrung content management and digital asset management programs for over a decade. One problem is structural – no manager has a span of control broad enough to control the entire content supply chain – which is an enterprise process spanning many stakeholders, silos, and systems.

Another problem is measurement and accountability. When it comes to content, nobody is really counting. An entire industry has evolved to target, measure, and certify media performance, yet few organizations even add up how much money they spend on content. Even fewer have financial models that link the performance of expensive digital channel infrastructure and data-driven selling tools to the content that fuels them.

But the list of challenges is even longer. Current models of content management remain largely manual, slow, expensive – which makes them inherently unscalable. This is largely due to a growing set of operational challenges associated with the enterprise process for planning, creating, organizing, assembling, and distributing content. These include:

1. The increase in the overall volume of content needed to sell.
2. The growing cost and complexity of creating new content.
3. The speed with which that content must be delivered to clients.
4. The growing number of channels through which content must be delivered.
5. The need to scale and personalize content globally, across segments, markets, industries, and geographies.
6. And the need to manage content quality, context, and compliance.

From a financial perspective, traditional content operations simply do not scale in a modern selling model. For example, the cost of localizing, targeting,

(continued)

and personalizing a branded content asset in five market segments is more than 20 times the cost of the original content asset according to the Forbes "Publish or Perish" study. Add new digital channels and one-to-one segmentation at scale, and the cost curve goes to the moon.

The combination of these issues has forced growth leaders to rethink their approaches to managing sales and marketing content across the enterprise. "Creating personalized content at scale with digital speed and control is essential but expensive and complicated unless you transform your processes," according to Jaime Punishill, in a recent executive forum on response management.[34] "You can't write your way around it, you can't anticipate your way around it, and you can't police your way around it. But at the same time, you don't want to pave cow paths by automating stupidity at speed and scale. So how can business leaders navigate the two?"

Progressive executives challenge traditional notions of digital asset management and sales enablement to answer that question. They are looking beyond traditional information hierarchies, writing content to spec, and establishing a "single source of truth" as the citadel and control point of all content. The most successful of them are rethinking the focus of their content efforts in the context of arming their revenue teams to answer customer questions, regardless of person, system, delivery channel, or format. This is the notion of Intelligent Response Management, which looks to leverage AI and machine learning to find scalable, intelligent, and cost-effective ways to manage the quality, speed, and context of the answers across every customer-facing employee, every channel, every stage of the customer journey, and every customer segment.

Intelligent Response Management is becoming a core component of a Revenue Operating System that turns expensive selling assets – selling content, customer data, and engagement technologies – into customer conversations and selling outcomes that grow revenues, profits, and enterprise value.

This notion goes beyond the prevailing content management practices of writing content to spec, creating top-down information hierarchies to organize it. "Older CMOs, like me, grew up with the Dewey Decimal System, which is really about the library sciences," shares Punishill. "That's all about ontologies, taxonomies and tagging content one way or another. It's comfortable, but it's a very old, manual way of organizing the content universe. And if you think about it, most of the information architecture underlying our web sites adopts this library sciences mentality. So, we're all trying to guess how people categorize themselves, the doorway they'll come through, the questions they'll ask, and the buying path they will go down, " relates Punishill. "But most millennials simply want to ask the question they ask Google, or increasingly now voice search, driven by voice activated devices like Siri, Bixby, Cortana or Alexa, or a human on the other end of the phone. Shifting to a response management paradigm is critical because today we have to think about how the buyer will now ask the question – and how quickly and completely you respond. That matters whether it's answered by a sales rep, service rep, or a chatbot, or a voice activated device."

Using response management as the foundation of content recommendation is much faster and simpler than having sales reps using many different digital asset management, content management, CPQ (Configure, Price, Quote), and sales enablement's systems to find, tailor, and deliver the content they need in live selling situations. This is blurring the lines between a wide variety of traditional software categories such as digital asset management, content management, configure, CPQ, and training and development.

Patrice Trichon, the CMO of 1919 Investment Counsel, has decades of experience wrestling with these problems. She emphasizes the importance of using client questions and intelligence to inform the organization, governance, tagging, targeting, and compliance of content as the key point of leverage and scale in content operations. "Managing complex, granular and real-time content is first and foremost about clients," says Trichon.[34] "It really begins with how much information can we get about the client so that we can actually systematize our ongoing interaction with them. That information is essential to defining what type of content we want to deliver to those clients."

Patrice also emphasizes the importance of creating a robust content architecture to define, segment, organize, and manage and distribute selling content from across the enterprise. "We build our content architecture from the bottom up foundationally, by asking what are the critical things we need to communicate in all of our materials? What are the common items that exist in all of our client and selling content – whether it's an Investment Review & Outlook, an RFP, or a fact sheet? That allows us to personalize our content at the highest level," she continues. "Creating this foundational content architecture makes that content development much easier, faster, more scalable, and most importantly more relevant to customers."

The real value of moving from a content management to a Response Management model is that it's inherently more scalable because it uses AI to fuel a virtual cycle, according to Ganesh Shankar, the CEO of RFPIO, and a leading mind in the evolution to Response Management. "Our clients respond to day-to-day questions," says Shankar.[136] "Questions from RFPs, RFQs, and RFIs. But also, service questions, product questions, regulatory and compliance questions. What we've figured out as we add more AI to our systems, is that this can be converted into an intelligence asset. The more questions you respond to, the more you learn, the more intelligence you create to fuel customer engagement. It's a virtuous cycle if you do it right." Shankar points out that the distinction between content management and Response Management is important because it unlocks the potential of your entire revenue team. "This starts with the people in bid response or proposal management, but naturally extends to every customer-facing employee in the business – from sales, to service, to technical support. That also applies to the contactless selling, sales engagement, and chatbot tools that use AI to answer customer questions directly or indirectly. Ultimately, Response Management scales to the degree that you can control, govern, speed up and enhance the way your organization responds to every customer question – again, not just RFPs or RFQs, but proactive proposals, presentations, security and compliance questions, product questions, or service questions."

CHAPTER 9

Extract More Revenue and Margins from Your Teams and Resources

The third element of a Revenue Operating System is to leverage digital technology and advanced analytics to create value by improving the performance and financial contribution of revenue teams. These technologies can accelerate sales growth and extract more revenue, margin, and value from your revenue teams by:

- Optimizing the allocation of revenue team resources to realize a greater share of your target markets
- Developing and retaining high-performing selling talent
- Focusing your selling teams on the best account opportunities
- Ensuring more sales reps achieve quota targets
- Generating more value in terms of price realization, share of wallet, and margin in sales transaction
- Expanding customer contract value, lifetime value, and annualized recurring revenues

One major opportunity, when it comes to getting more revenue from your teams, is to focus on a better system for recruiting, ramping, and retaining top sales talent—to make sure, in short, that you're building a strong, capable team. Doing so will improve revenue growth and sales quota attainment while reducing cost to sell. Ninety percent of the executives we spoke with agree that their sales reps are their biggest growth asset. Yet, in our experience, few manage their sales reps as valuable assets. Most don't realize how poorly those assets are performing on a financial basis or the true cost of attrition on sales, margins, and costs. If the average CFO evaluated their salespeople as financial assets, they would conclude that sales reps are expensive (between 10–40% of firm spending), that they require significant maintenance and upkeep (training and management), yet underperform (most fail to achieve quotas) – and have a useful life of less than two years. Why? Because of the fragmented way most organizations recruit, develop, measure, manage, and motivate their reps. In most cases, no single person is responsible for measuring, managing, or improving the performance of the talent pipeline. The financial consequences of these disconnects on your revenue goals, selling costs, and margins can be severe. A 5% increase in sales rep attrition across your sales team can increase selling costs 4–6% and reduce total revenue attainment by 2–3% overall, according to research by Blue Ridge Partners.[137] In addition to the negative impact on selling costs, lost opportunity, and revenue goal attainment – the revolving door of salespeople can damage customer relationships.

"If you don't invest in training and enabling your people, you wind up spending a significant chunk of resources dealing with rep churn, finding new reps, and ramping them," according to Frank Jules, President of AT&T Business.[120] "In the end, very few of them will develop into the top talent you need to outperform the competition."

Another way to create value is to use analytics to "shrink the bullseye" and "cut the long tail" of customers. Doing so can multiply the impact of every selling interaction and individual in your business. The reason for this is, while every business leader understands the 80/20 rule when it comes to targeting customers, most don't actually apply it. In our experience, most organizations tend to target too many customers and develop too few of them. For many businesses the "customer curve" remains too long and sellers continue to chase "tail accounts" that are unprofitable to pursue. There are good reasons for these tendencies – the optimism of sellers, the desire to realize more market potential, and the pressure to generate the most revenue growth from scarce selling resources. But they are also rooted in bad habits like not challenging entrenched belief systems. Another bad habit is using "gut feeling" assumptions to size and rank opportunities instead of data. A third is relying too much on historical sales data instead of predictive insights about the future when planning.

A system based on facts can change this. The secret is to convert the customer engagement data you already have into insights. Sellers don't need more data. They need actionable insights that inform account priorities, resource allocation decisions, and the level of effort to apply to specific target customers. For example, it is possible to develop highly accurate targeting models that more skillfully predict which customers are going to buy from you soonest, at the highest price, and with the least selling effort using your existing CRM and transaction data. "When we compare customer assignments based on data-derived propensity to buy models with those based on the estimates of sales teams and local market leaders, we typically see improvement of 20% or more in conversion, sales quota attainment, and account development," reports Jim Quallen, a Managing Director of Blue Ridge Partners who has helped dozens of B2B sales organizations deploy such models.

Using your data assets to better align and allocate your selling resources with market opportunity is another way you can create more revenues and value.

Recent advances in sales performance management software, analytics, and modeling approaches can dramatically simplify complex territory defini-tion and quota design problems. They can also make the process of planning, managing, and updating territories and seller quotas faster, less labor intensive, and more accurate.

Not only that, but recent advances in analytics, modeling, and sales performance management tools provide the opportunity to dramatically improve the territory and quota planning process, the quality and impact of its outputs, and the resources, labor, time, and effort involved in managing it. These advanced modeling techniques offer the potential to improve the accuracy, effectiveness, and predictability of territory and quota plans. For example, businesses that digitize their territory alignment process increase revenue up to 15% through better resource allocation, tight alignment bet-ween sales territories and the go-to-market strategy, improved sales produc-tivity, and goal attainment, according to research by the SMA.[138]

Building Block #7: Talent Development - Attract, Develop, and Retain Commercial Talent

TALENT DEVELOPMENT	
FIND NEW TALENT	RAMP NEW SELLERS
DEVELOP SKILLS AND CAPABILITIES	RETAIN TOP TALENT

Frontline sales managers can use sales enablement and readiness technologies and AI to significantly improve cross-selling, account penetration, and the performance of the "B and C players" on their revenue teams. They can now use these tools to better evaluate, educate, and focus sellers. Sales enablement and readiness tools can automate the evaluation and development of sales talent. Analytics can create measures of seller performance based on activity and behavior. They can also improve the coverage and penetration of key accounts using customer engagement and seller activity data. This can create significant value for a variety of reasons:

- Most (57%) sales leaders regard visibility into seller activity and performance as their top sales productivity challenge.[9]
- Even more (62%) lack confidence in their organization's ability to cross-sell, upsell, or expand key account relationships, according to Miller Heiman.[37]
- Sales teams are not very effective at coaching and guidance, according to a survey of sales managers and performance professionals.[9]
- Managers have largely failed to leverage the potential of advanced analytics to improve accountability and reinforcement. The survey identified visibility into adoption, behavior change, and use of sales skills and tools in selling situations as the biggest opportunity to improve sales performance.

This doesn't have to be the case. There are a dozen commonsense ways that organizations can improve the process of attracting, recruiting, developing, and retaining top sales talent. These include connecting training and development systems into a closed-loop process and using AI to better support training, establish better measures of seller performance, and simplify the seller experience. What's key is managing this effort as one enterprise process and one closed-loop system. An effective first step is to assign an executive to manage and measure the performance of the process of recruiting, ramping, and retaining sales talent across the company. Improving seller attribution, seller satisfaction, and the cycle time to ramp new sales reps even a few percentage points can lead to large improvements in margins, costs, and revenue attainment.

Sales managers and performance leaders (from sales operations, sales enablement, and learning and development teams) at growth-oriented businesses are developing new management capabilities and skills as they struggle to manage, enable, and motivate remote selling teams. In response, sales managers are increasing their adoption of sales enablement technologies and sales analytics to generate the engagement, speed, and productivity essential to being productive in a virtual setting and adapting to the new buying reality.

In particular, they are putting in place systems and programs that lever- age data to create value. These include:

1. **Establishing integrated coaching, skill development, and rein- forcement processes.** Remote learning is now a fact of life because face- to-face training delivery is not a practical option as most organizations have cut travel (84%) while encouraging employees to work at home. In response, frontline sales managers are looking at integrated learning and development solutions like MindTickle, Allego, and Ambition to enable an integrated sales development approach that is both highly efficient and a "closed-loop" in that it connects training to behavior to performance. These solutions blend video role plays with AI evaluation and guided selling to connect development and reinforcement to in-the-moment selling activities. These solutions incorporate conversational intelligence and activity tracking to measure how training translates into actual cus- tomer engagement and account success.

2. **Improving your visibility into revenue team performance.** The lack of visibility into pipeline activity, seller actions, buyer engagement, and account health are setbacks to remote selling productivity. Sales engagement platforms like Outreach.io give frontline sales managers management tools and dashboards built on individual client and account engagement data that allow them to see pipeline health and activity of any rep, and to drill down as needed to coach, guide, and assist reps in advancing opportunities. Sales automation platforms like Gainsight and Totango give account leads and service managers visibility into account health by aggregating, analyzing, and organizing customer data from many legacy systems to provide real-time signals of churn, service issues, and upselling opportunities.

3. **Creating measures that close the loop between seller performance, training effectiveness, and customer outcomes.** Sales leaders are starting to use advanced analytics to derive new measures that more accurately quantify the collective engagement, energy, and customer experience their teams are creating within accounts. They are drawing upon sales analytics solutions to track the behaviors and activities that define team success. At the same time, they are building toward inno- vative, data-driven customer engagement measures and incentives that are tied to opportunity potential, account health, and seller performance on a scale of 1–10. Integrated learning and development solutions like MindTickle, Allego, and QStream use AI to evaluate selling skills and performance based on activity analysis, conversational intelligence, and performance against standards.

4. **Making one-to-one coaching at scale part of an integrated learning and development process.** Historically, sales managers have been limited by their span of control and free time for sales call monitoring or ride-alongs, so they are only able to monitor sales calls and actively coach a limited number of reps. The ability to record sales conversations and compare them to selling outcomes and best practices by integrating with CRM, training, and enablement systems can create a real-time, closed-loop information flow. This gives a sales manager the ability to actively be there at critical points in the actual sales conversation such as common objections, competitive mentions, or signals of attrition. It also lets them understand what training has been adopted, and whether it is successful at changing customer behavior. Continuous, real-time, and individualized coaching allows sales managers to actively manage and develop many more reps. It also accelerates how quickly new reps ramp to full productivity. For example, ChowNow, a leading online ordering platform for restaurants, was able to knit together the systems that support their Sales Development Reps (SDRs) to eliminate manual work, share best practices, and provide real-time coaching in the moments that matter. ChowNow had to double the number of SDRs to exploit exploding demand in the online ordering system market in the wake of the pandemic. Their Growth Operations team unified and enhanced their sales and marketing technology portfolio to make it faster and easier to ramp and support so many new reps. They used AI-enabled tools from Revenue.io to connect the dots across different systems to automate manual work, create best practices libraries, and enable one-to-one coaching from anywhere, at scale. By aligning tools that support the rep coaching and engagement, ChowNow was able to ramp reps to productivity faster (in 60% less time), promote them sooner, and retain them longer (rep attrition dropped by 75%). "Conversation AI is our lifeline right now," according to Stephanie Sullivan, director of Growth Operations at ChowNow.[42] "Sales managers have to listen to calls as part of the job – it's nonnegotiable, because it's by far the best way to train. And we have seen dramatically faster rep ramp time for our SDRs as a result."

Creating a Closed-Loop System for Sales Rep Education, Readiness, Reinforcement, and Measurement

Most organizations have deployed sales training, learning, and development systems and methods. Many organizations have had unsatisfactory outcomes. The sales managers and performance professionals we surveyed rated sales coaching and guidance as one of the most difficult things to do. And managers have largely failed to leverage the potential of advanced analytics to improve accountability and reinforcement. The same survey identified visibility into adoption, behavior change, and use of sales skills and tools in selling situations as the biggest opportunity to improve sales performance.

These circumstances have many sales operations and training leaders re-evaluating their sales learning and development investments, resources, and strategies in light of the pandemic's persistent impact.

To develop their teams faster and better, sales leaders are looking for ways to dramatically increase the historically low return they are getting on their investments in sales technology, data, and people assets while leveraging limited resources. Unfortunately, most of the survey respondents told us the sales enablement and readiness technologies in which they have invested were not providing them with their hoped-for levels of visibility, engagement, speed, and sales rep.

"In my experience building digital sales platforms at Hitachi and Cisco, sales training effectiveness and reinforcement can be significantly improved by giving sales reps the right tools, knowledge, and reinforcement at the right time in their sales context," shares Jeff McKittrick of WalkMe.

The pressure to quickly reskill sales teams has been amplified by the massive shift to remote selling and a hot job market. Sales leaders are being forced to train dozens, hundreds, or thousands of sales reps in new selling tactics and tools to help them engage more effectively in virtual channels and adapt to the faster operating cadence of digital sales. Because of the rate of change, most are trying to do this training in real time rather than pulling large sales teams out for classroom-based training and role playing as they would have done in the past.

"You can have the best technology, but if you don't have the right people leveraging that technology and you don't have the right people anticipating the future needs of your client base, your growth is not going to be sustainable," says Jennifer Mauldin, Chief Customer Officer of Inmar Intelligence.[125] "What's driven our success from our inception is that we're a learning organization."

There is enormous opportunity to develop your sales organizations faster while enforcing the right behaviors in execution by taking a more integrated and virtual approach to sales development, enablement, and measurement – because there are so many threads to weave together between these functions and systems. The technologies and programs that underlie sales development, management, and measurement are usually highly fragmented and spread across HR, training, sales operations, and sales development because most organizations buy and deploy such systems and assets in a siloed fashion. As a result:

- Learning management systems are disconnected from the sales enablement systems where sales playbooks reside;
- The sales analytics and AI used to measure sales activity, adoption, and behavior are not linked to sales readiness and training; and
- Feedback and reinforcement suffer because very little of this information is available to sales managers to support grading, coaching, reinforcement, and performance measurement.

(continued)

"There's no good business or technical reason that learning management, readiness, enablement and advanced sales analytics need to be separate and disintegrated," according to Jeff McKittrick, VP of Sales Execution at WalkMe. "All are in common use across most sales organizations. But they exist largely in silos because the functional experts that buy, manage, and deploy the systems and assets that underlie sales development have no financial incentive to connect the dots across them."

Sales leaders must make linking sales readiness to sales effectiveness a priority. They can no longer afford to automate only "part" of the learning and development process. The urgency and cost of rapidly reskilling sales forces to prepare them for virtual selling will compel organizations to treat them as one system. This will provide sales leaders, managers, and effectiveness executives an end-to-end approach to building skills that can measurably lead to sales and profit outcomes.

Don't waste the crisis. The pressure it creates is an excellent platform to drive change by insisting these expensive and important growth assets work together and do so effectively.

To move at the speed of the market, learning and development organizations must find ways to combine their systems to make them faster, more virtual, and accountable.

By connecting these dots, you can create an integrated sales development approach that is both highly efficient but also a "closed-loop" in that it connects training to behavior to performance (please see Figure 9.1). For example:

- Training and skill development can be assigned and executed virtually by taking advantage of video role play and pitch management systems. These allow reps to practice and develop role play, product demo, and "situation-specific" presentation skills remotely using video platforms.
- These video role plays can be inspected and graded consistently and at scale using a mix of AI-assisted scoring and human assessment by peers and managers.
- The best of these can be catalogued and connected to a master content library of plays and best practices that can be targeted by process stage, persona, product, industry, or pain point.
- These plays can be tagged for deployment in real time using advanced AI and guided selling tools that recommend the next best sales play or most relevant content, based on buyer engagement, response data, and the context of the selling situation.
- Managers can track and measure how this effort and training translate into actual customer engagement and account success by building data-driven KPI that quantify outcomes based on actual seller activity, customer engagement, and success.
- The entire process should fuel a feedback loop that continually reinforces skills, refines plays, adapts to customer needs, and tightens the connection between training and results.

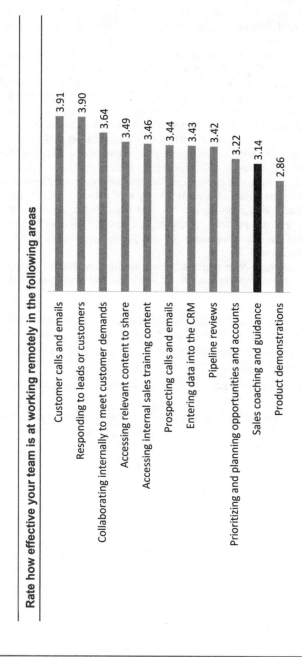

Rate how effective your team is at working remotely in the following areas

- Customer calls and emails — 3.91
- Responding to leads or customers — 3.90
- Collaborating internally to meet customer demands — 3.64
- Accessing relevant content to share — 3.49
- Accessing internal sales training content — 3.46
- Prospecting calls and emails — 3.44
- Entering data into the CRM — 3.43
- Pipeline reviews — 3.42
- Prioritizing and planning opportunities and accounts — 3.22
- Sales coaching and guidance — 3.14
- Product demonstrations — 2.86

Revenue Enablement Institute Remote Selling Report

FIGURE 9.1 The Top Ways Customer Behavior Is Impacting Remote Selling Productivity

(continued)

Not every organization can take all these steps at once. But most of the underlying technologies and assets are in place in most large and complex sales organizations. Connecting any of these building blocks together will represent a significant step forward compared to the status quo or waiting for the next opportunity to conduct traditional classroom training (which could be 12 months away). For example, Scott Kelley, SVP of Sales, Customer Success, and Revenue Operations at GHX, is looking to technology as a way to enable continuous learning at scale. His team is implementing best-in-class revenue enablement strategies to deliver content and training to all teams that interact with customers. "We've used a revenue enablement tool to expand and standardize our training capabilities," says Kelley.[123] "It's allowed us to tap into deep subject matter expertise across the company to create team and function-specific trainings." Kelley has built a system to streamline the targeting and customization of training, an environment for teams to practice, get feedback and improve, a process for knowledge and skill certification, and ultimately a team that serves as trusted advisers to customers. These same pillars of training are applied to onboarding new team members as well as newly acquired companies to ensure a quick ramp up and increased speed to value.

The business objective of taking an integrated learning and development approach should be to improve your sales readiness and performance in four specific ways:

1. **Reinforcement** in the context of day-to-day sales activities with real-time, micro-learning, and easy-to-use training guides;

2. **Accountability** with automated and AI-assisted evaluation, grading, and feedback and behavior-based KPI;

3. **Scalability** by integrating to the existing sales process workflow and sales enablement assets; and

4. **Cost-effective delivery** by using techniques like virtual role playing that allow reps to practice remotely and get feedback and coaching quickly.

Building Block #8: Revenue Optimization – Allocate People, Time, and Effort Against Opportunities

RESOURCE OPTIMIZATION	
SALES RESOURCE ALLOCATION	OPPORTUNITY PRIORITIZATION
SELLING TIME OPTIMIZATION	OPTIMIZE COVERAGE AND TARGETING

Some of the most practical and impactful ways data-driven algorithms can create value is to help managers to better allocate sales resources to the right accounts, territories, and tasks. "Organizations are dramatically improving sales performance by using algorithms to help with the basics of account and lead prioritization and qualification, recommending the content or sales action that will lead to success, and reallocating sales resources to the places they can have the most impact," reports Professor Lodish of Wharton.[32]

What Is Territory Planning and How Does It Unlock and Accelerate Revenue Growth?

Territory planning is the process of creating a workable plan for targeting the right customers, establishing goals for income, and ensuring sales growth over time. It involves making sure your sales team is targeting the right customers. A territory plan documents a structured approach to a defined set of customers, such as named accounts, in a geographic territory, or industry, in vertical or horizontal markets, or in market segments. Territory planning is an ongoing activity that maintains account and territory alignment across functional groups on your revenue team such as sales, sales support, account management teams, and channel partners. An effective sales territory plan can make your team more productive, improve customer coverage, increase overall sales, and reduce costs. On the other hand, unbalanced territory plans and constant changes in territory division can hurt productivity as well as the working relationships between clients and account managers, and those among various sellers.

This is because a wide range of AI tools are now available to create algorithmically derived customer response models to help take the guesswork and gut feeling out of aligning sales resources across geographies, accounts, and business lines.

Sales leaders are taking advantage of advanced analytics to optimize the allocation of sales resources and seller time with data-driven algorithms that increase the return on selling resources in a variety of ways. These include:

1. **Automating the territory design and quota assignment process.** There is a big opportunity to optimize the deployment of sales resources by developing data-driven models that map the response functions by market, territory, and segment. Staffing and allocating sales resources across territories is often done by the seat of the pants or gut feelings at best. Sales performance management solutions like Varicent, Xactly, SAP Sales Cloud, and Optymize digitize and automate the territory and quota planning process of designing territories. For example, optimizing territory design alone can increase sales by 2–7%, without any change in total resources or sales strategy.[140] This is because an optimally designed and well-balanced territory plan can improve seller productivity by 10–20% and save costs according to research by the Alexander Group.[139]

   Organizations are using automated workflow processes to get efficiency gains of two to three times when compared with counterparts using manual or spreadsheet-driven processes.[141] Data-driven automation can help streamline the planning cycle from 60 to 35 days by automating the collection and analysis of many data inputs. It also can improve collaboration across the 6–12 different organizations that need to align territories and quotas with the overall go-to-market, compensation, and corporate growth strategy of the company.[139]

   Solutions like these can also blend CRM data with customer engagement data from other parts of your business to automate and optimize the development of sales incentives and quotas and to improve payment accuracy and resolution.

2. **Algorithmic segmentation, targeting, and coverage modeling.** Sales reps spend 7% of their time prioritizing leads and opportunities.[20] But a range of solution providers have emerged that support predictive lead scoring and lead prioritization models based on customer engagement data from inside and outside the organization. For example, sales engagement platforms like Xant.ai prioritize daily tasks and plays for sales teams using real-time buyer intelligence from billions of sales interactions. Third-party data providers like Bombora and TechTarget make those models even better by enriching them with customer intent data that lets them know when a prospect is in the market for a solution.

3. **Account prioritization and profiling based on propensity to buy, intent, and potential.** Leading organizations are developing highly accurate propensity to buy targeting models from their existing CRM and transaction data and third-party intent data from providers like 6sense. These models can more accurately predict which customers are going to buy from you, with the least selling effort, and which ones are not likely to buy or will require too much work to convert. When compared with the estimates of sales teams and local market leaders, these models are usually more accurate at predicting who will buy, and who will not. When combined with human insights about local markets and customer relationships, they become even more predictive and accurate. Propensity to buy targeting models takes less time than human targeting. The targeting also gets smarter over time, starting a cycle of measurable and continuous improvement. Most organizations see near-term gains of 20% or more in conversion, sales quota attainment, and account development when they use propensity to buy models to focus their resources, according to research by Blue Ridge Partners.[142]

4. **Selling time optimization.** A range of sales automation technologies are now able to automate, assist, or eliminate a range of low value-added tasks that nibble away at sales rep time, productivity, and motivation. Sales automation software, including DialSource, People.ai, and Seamless.ai, effectively automate tasks including CRM data entry, data management, finding information, list building, and repetitive selling tasks like dialing, screening calls, and capturing contact information. Digital adoption software like WalkMe makes it faster and easier to find and use mission critical sales tools that provide competitive intelligence, selling content, automate RFPs, record sales calls, and recommend next best-selling actions.

5. **Using advanced analytics to improve the accuracy, predictability, and quality of plan inputs.** Professors Leonard Lodish and V (Paddy) Padmanabhan have taught "Leading the Effective Sales Force" to a generation of growth leaders over the past decade at Wharton and INSEAD.[143] They believe it is no longer enough to rely on history or rules of thumb in making sales force allocation decisions. The precise historical data available to sales managers is increasingly able to help them to rationally decide on sales force size, territory boundaries, and call frequencies for each account and prospect that maximizes firm profits.

John Gleason, EVP and Chief Sales Officer for Ryder Systems, sees the use of analytics to optimize sales roles, coverage, cooperation, and territories as the next big opportunity to accelerate growth. "I'm a big believer in trying to grow sales without growing the sales organization or cost to sell," says Gleason.[119] "The more I can use analytics to make sure our reps aren't wasting time with prospects they're not likely going to be successful with, the better. We've spent a lot of time in that particular area." Ryder is using advanced analytics to redefine territories and refine the roles and responsibilities within the sales organization to provide better product expertise, cross-selling opportunities, and customer experience.

Another way Gleason has Ryder leveraging analytics is by focusing sales reps on the highest-opportunity accounts. "There's an enormous number of prospects out there—probably 20 million companies that rent trucks, seven million class three through eight leased vehicles, and a hundred thousand or so businesses that need warehousing," he reports. "That's a lot for 50 salespeople to call on. Analytics have become increasingly important, because when you have a smaller sales organization generating around $3 billion, you can't waste a lot of time knocking on doors, so to speak. We became increasingly data driven. We put in much better processes to understand the characteristics of buyers, their current contract status with other providers, who are the decision makers, and when those decision makers change."

Digitizing the Process of Planning, Managing, and Optimizing Sales Territories and Quotas

As businesses grow and evolve their go-to-market approach to better develop the market, they add new selling channels, products, and market segments into their coverage model and selling strategy. These additions lead to more data inputs, seller roles, and functional stakeholders to include in the territory and quota planning process. As a result, there are more variables to analyze, more scenarios to consider, and more trade-offs to balance.

As a rule of thumb, the average B2B organization can take 60–70 days to plan and design territories when dealing with, on average, five different organizations (e.g. marketing, product, finance, human resources, and sales) and a limited number of data inputs to defining territory boundaries (e.g. historical baseline data, corporate growth targets, sales forecasts, and staffing budgets). Adding more stakeholders and data to the process will make your plans better and more aligned with the go-to-market process, which is important. Still, more stakeholders and data inputs can also significantly increase the amount of time it takes to achieve a consensus about territory definitions, particularly if an organization is managing the entire process on a spreadsheet.

For example, increasing the number of organizations involved in the territory and quota planning from three to six or more can double the amount of time it takes to plan, design, and align sales territories with other elements of the go-to-market mix. Adding more data inputs to the process – such as estimates of seller productivity and profitability, customer scoring and ranking data, workload estimates, and customer journey metrics – can dramatically increase the work and time involved in curating data, analyzing different scenarios, and modeling trade-offs between cost, coverage, control, and growth.

"Today, the majority of organizations manage the territory and quota planning process using spreadsheets or home-grown systems to manage these increasingly complex processes," says Michael Smith. "As a consequence, most of these (two-thirds) fail to finish planning before the sales period starts, which means many revenue teams start off the year without a fact-based upon assignments."

Replacing spreadsheet-based planning can have significant benefits. Companies that digitize their territory alignment process increase revenue, shrink the planning cycles, and improve the overall achievement of sellers.

Recent advances in Sales Performance Management (SPM) solutions and tools provide the opportunity to dramatically streamline and improve the territory and quota planning process, the quality and impact of its outputs, and the resources, labor, time, and effort involved in managing it. There are five primary ways new technologies can streamline, automate, and enhance the territory and quota planning process.

1. Digitizing the planning and design of sales territories and sales quota assignments.

2. Helping to visualize, communicate, and align those plans across the enterprise.

3. Helping sales managers, sellers, and incentive professionals to manage sales territories and quotas.

4. Building dashboards for ongoing evaluation, reporting, and stakeholder decision support.

5. Streamlining and speeding up the process of making mid-period adjustments and plan reviews

There are a variety of tools and advanced technologies that can enhance and improve the process for planning, designing, managing, and evaluating territory and quota plans. SPM software is a fast-growing technology that tackles salesperson assignments and territories, quota management, incentive compensation administration, and sales and incentive performance reporting. Current solutions provide sales leaders and their operations teams management greater control, richer insight, and faster decision making. "The highest performing organizations are using advanced analytics and AI to move information across traditional working silos to find ways to generate more revenues, improve operating efficiency and manage risks like sales rep churn," according to Marc Altshuller, CEO of Varicent.[144] "The next generation of sales performance management software allows revenue operations and sales leaders to integrate the plan, operate and pay process to create smarter and more balanced territory plans and quotas that can adapt quickly to shifting market realities."

(continued)

Sales organizations are increasingly using SPM solutions to recalibrate forecasts, recast seller performance expectations, and use analytics to better manage sales territories and quotas in rapidly changing environments. Some of the more impactful ways to digitize territory and quota planning include:

- **Automating the process workflow**, including data entry, analysis, and collaboration with stakeholders. "Organizations that have automated workflow processes are seeing efficiency gains of two to three times when compared to counterparts using manual or spreadsheet-driven processes," according to Michael Smith, who has helped over 300 B2B organizations unlock more growth from existing selling assets in the last decade.
- **Develop scenarios** to test different resource allocations, sales assignments, roles, and territory configurations to find ways of managing more accounts with fewer reps and modeling the financial impact including forecasting costs, outcomes, and commissions based on potential changes. "The number of possible ways you can structure territories and allocate seller time effort and activities is nearly infinite in multi-channel organizations with many selling roles, segments, and products in their portfolio," according to Cam Tipping, whose SABRE simulation tools are being used by business schools and global revenue teams to model and simulate their territory plans using real-world scenarios. "Sales performance management solutions and business simulations make it much easier for operations teams, territory managers and individual sellers to explore the potential of the many different ways they can allocate time, effort, and while fine tuning their day-to-day mix of customer, product, and activity priorities."
- **Seller performance management** offers advanced analytics that provide more accurate and empirical measures of seller productivity, performance, and profitability. These are important design parameters for bottom-up calculations of seller workload, capacity, and sales quota assignments. They also make it easier to track performance of sellers within a selling period. Today, only a fraction of organizations (6%) are able to give their sales teams access to the daily reports of progress and status, or near real-time data, they need for day-to-day sales territory management and decision support.[42]
- **Automating quota management,** including mapping visualizations and dashboards for ongoing evaluation and decision support, helps make quota tracking "active" and provide sales managers the KPIs they need to actively manage performance of their territory teams and individual reps against those goals.
- **Dashboards** that automate the collection and reporting of key metrics required for actively managing quota attainment and providing decision support in real time. For example, 57% of companies use dashboards to monitor territory performance and opportunity metrics to monitor territory performance and health; this was cited as the biggest gap in territory management, alongside a need to move from "gut feeling" and anecdotal management feedback to more data-driven KPIs to guide decisions and adjustments.[141]

Building Block #9: Revenue Enhancement – Increase Revenue Yield with Better Packaging, Pricing, and Personalizing Offers

REVENUE ENHANCEMENT	
PRICING	PERSONALIZATION
VALUE ENGINEERING	DIGITIZATION

Sales teams can use analytics to improve the 4Ps of selling by optimizing pricing dynamically based on willingness to pay, and by personalizing products and proposals to deliver and capture more value from sales transactions. For example, more disciplined and algorithmic pricing offers up to five times the profit potential of cost and growth initiatives because it can expand margins by 3–10% with existing resources and improve earnings multiples with limited investment. Pricing is the most efficient way to improve a firm's profitability, according to Professors John Zhang and Jagmohan Raju of Wharton Business School in their book, *Smart Pricing*.[102] Improving a firm's price by 1% effective price increase without changing anything else normally will increase profitability by over 10%, according to Wharton Research Data Services. Your organization can get two to five times the profit leverage from top-line price optimization than it can from efforts aimed at reducing costs.

Another factor impacting margins and selling effectiveness is rising customer demands for more relevant and personalized content. This dynamic has been exacerbated by the dramatic shift to virtual and digital channels accelerating the use of digital media and the collaborative content, videos, and assets needed to fuel them. Eighty percent of firms are increasing the use of digital media to fuel remote selling and the content creation needed to support owned digital channels.[5]

Advanced analytics can improve all aspects of pricing, proposal development, and solution packaging through personalization, automation, configuration, and optimization. These include:

1. **Pricing optimization and innovation.** Research from Wharton Business School shows that pricing is the most critical profit driver in

business, offering two to five times the profit potential relative to growing sales and reducing fixed and variable costs. A data-driven pricing strategy can yield profit margin expansion of 3–10% with existing resources through pricing optimization and innovation.[102] Analytics leaders like PROS, Vendavo, and Zilliant are helping businesses across industries to use advanced analytics to expand profits and create firm value by evolving their processes, systems, and teams four ways:

a. Governance of pricing policies across the enterprise to stop millions of dollars of margin leakage.

b. Automating, simplifying, and speeding the execution of pricing strategy in terms of price setting, discounting, exceptions, and adjustments due to competitive, exogenous, and market factors.

c. Executing sophisticated dynamic and data-driven pricing strategies that expand demand, capture more value, and maximize customer lifetime value, including dynamic, personalized, and demand-based pricing.

d. Driving innovation through pricing by enabling new business models with advanced pricing models that better package and realize value including SaaS, subscription, premium services, sharing, and fractional ownership models.

2. **Enabling data-driven personalized proposals, presentations, and offerings.** Pricing optimization solutions like PROS, Zilliant, and Vendavo are blending customer engagement data with information from CRM and other legacy systems to create more compliant, optimal, and, in some cases, dynamic pricing. CPQ solutions like Qorus, RFPIO, Apptus, and DealHub are using data from CRM systems to make it fast and easy to assemble, create, and personalize proposals, RFP responses, and client materials.

3. **Proposal and presentation automation and personalization.** Customers want more personalized and relevant content. Sales managers believe meeting this need is the best way they can improve sales productivity and effectiveness. Helping your sellers to deliver more dynamic and personalized presentations, proposals, and microsites is a big opportunity to differentiate and improve performance. Configure, Price, Quote (CPQ) solutions providers like DealHub and Apptus are helping revenue teams to meet this need with dynamic personalized presentations, content, microsites, slide decks, and pricing. Qorus and RFPIO are automating the process of preparing and personalizing RFPs and proposals. This is an opportunity, because only 37% of sales reps use CPQ solutions like these today.[20]

4. **Creating content that is ready for digital and virtual channels.** 4D sales reps will need channel-ready content that meets buyers' high expectations for relevance, personalization, visualization, and collaboration in a

remote setting situation. To meet the needs of modern buyers, virtual sales reps will need to rely more heavily on virtual, video, and collaboration platforms. This means personalized, immersive video and Augmented Reality (AR) and Virtual Reality (VR) content will become more important as online buyers place a premium on the quality and context of content. Organizations that sell tangible or experiential offerings are looking to 3D content creation platforms like Kaon Interactive, Spatial, and Unity to create the channel-ready content that delivers a more immersive experience in digital, mobile, and VR platforms.

Advancing the Science of Personalization: How Pandora Is Using AI and Machine Learning to Enable One-to-One Personalization at Scale

The quest to deliver one-to-one personalization at scale is a huge business need and fast becoming a fundamental component of the go-to-market system. Businesses that are able to exploit the power of AI and ML to better understand customer behavior and personalize their customer experience will outperform their competition.

Advanced personalization and recommendation systems are the brains behind every customer-facing technology in your business – including voice-enabled devices, configurable offerings, sales enablement systems, dynamic pricing, response management systems, and personalized ads.

Ninety percent of organizations are using AI to improve their customer journeys, revolutionize how they interact with customers, and deliver them more compelling experiences.[36] Seventy-five percent of Netflix users select films recommended to them by the company's machine learning algorithms.[145] To realize this potential, businesses in every industry are pouring money into the talent, tools, and data to exploit the potential of AI to grow revenues, profits, and firm value. AI hiring grew 32% in the past year.[144]

Despite all the hype and expectations around the ways AI will transform business, the reality is that mainstream adoption of AI in customer engagement is still in its early days. The runway for innovation is long, and there are myriad ways that AI-enabled personalization can improve margins, conversion rates, and firm value.

One of the biggest obstacles preventing businesses from realizing the full potential of AI in commercial applications is the inability of executives to prioritize, direct, and allocate resources to the most profitable AI applications. "Most of the success and failures to harness the power of AI to transform business lies in management understanding of how to apply, deploy and direct these powerful tools" according to Kartik Hosanagar, Professor of Technology, Digital Business, and Marketing at the Wharton School and author of the influential book *A Human's Guide to Machine Intelligence*.[147] Another factor delaying the

(continued)

business impact of AI is that it takes an enormous amount of learning data to develop robust ML models.

Few businesses have the level of experience, learning data, and technical acumen that Pandora does when it comes to developing AI-driven personalization and recommendation systems. Pandora literally jump-started the development of their recommendation systems with the Music Genome project 20 years ago, and has since had access to one of the largest learning data sets and the best data scientists in the world.

"Pandora was born 20 years ago from what was called the USIC Genome Project which became the first music recommender system for consumers," according to Scott Wong, VP of Machine Learning for Foundation, Search, and Voice Science at SiriusXM and Pandora.[148] His team builds reusable machine learning systems that power recommendations and discovery across Sirius XM, Pandora, and other products. Over the last two years, he worked to integrate the best science data and technology from Pandora, Sirius XM, and a powerful long-term platform. "The initiative started with a team of professional musicologists sitting down and listening to music tracks day in and day out annotating over 450 different attributes about those tracks. They looked at things like the time signature, harmonics, vocals, genre, time periods, instrumentation language, and tons of different dimensions about what is really under the hood in any given song."

That foundation of data gave Pandora what Wong calls a great "cold start" scenario for building a recommendation engine before they even had access to customer interactions and other learning data.

When Pandora did start to access listener data to refine their algorithm, their progress and the quality of their prediction models improved dramatically. "The music genome project really enabled us with the first round of content-based strategies for the recommender system. But after people started using the product and actually listening, it provided us the implicit and explicit feedback that's really the source of digital gold when it comes to machine learning. Listener feedback data really enables the development of advanced and predictive recommender systems," says Wong.

Content-based recommender systems like this are valuable because they are very good at identifying and recommending highly relevant content, songs, or products regardless of preconceived notions, popularity, or other influences, according to Hosanagar's book. That's hugely important in a world where every business is trying to differentiate its products, services, and brands through personalized and highly contextual experiences.

From that foundation, Pandora evolved their approach to combine other data signals and modeling techniques, such as collaborative filtering, which was popularized by Amazon, to take their predictive models to the next level. This lets them take advantage of both explicit signals from their millions of users (such as thumbs-up ratings) and implicit signals (e.g. how long they listen, what actions they take).

"What's happened over time is we started to combine techniques all at the same time," says Wong. "That flywheel, once you get it going, yields extremely powerful models for predicting and recommending. We started to incorporate other categories of strategies into our recommender systems in addition to the content-based strategy we started with. We employed user-based strategies, which look at whether people like you also like this other thing and collaborative filtering strategies that simultaneously look at which listeners are similar, and which content is similar. All of these can help you explain and learn based on what people do and discover the hidden similarities between content and preferences.

"Our access to millions of listeners is helping us build the next generation of recommender strategies. As an example, we've evolved our models to the point where we can take the best of what humans have – the best eye for analyzing the genes underlying music – and scale it up to a much, much larger catalog of songs. We call the combination using humans as quality machines for scale. One way we've been able to accomplish that is to develop a machine listening system where a model listens directly to the audio of untagged songs in our back catalog and new songs when they come in against the label training data we have from the Music Genome Project. Using this approach, we can predict a lot of those attributes about new music that none of the humans internally have ever listened to. And so collectively when you put all these different techniques together we can power algorithmic radio stations that draw from 30 million different sources instead of two million that are human analyzed. In our business, it lets individual people personalize their own stations to their own tastes, and in aggregate it helps us track what is most successful on which stations."

Wong's team builds reusable machine learning systems that power recommendations and discovery across Sirius XM, Pandora, and other products. Over the last two years, he worked to integrate the best science data and technology from Pandora and Sirius XM into a powerful long-term platform. Today Pandora uses these insights in all aspects of their business. Applications include helping individual people personalize their own stations to their own tastes, tracking what is most successful on which stations, and understanding where, when, and how to upsell a customer.

Most of the recommender engine fundamentals that Pandora has developed are universally applicable to the personalization problems every business faces. Hence, the learning is transferable to industries without such a great head start or access to data science.

For example, one of the big applications of AI and ML at Pandora is to figure out how to upsell a customer on a subscription. In this use case, Wong's team is using their advanced models to answer difficult questions that are common to every business – Who should we target? When is the right time to reach them? And in what context? Pandora's models are able to dig into very granular contextual variables from the promotion type, content, product fit, channel of engagement, and presentation of an offer.

"We've built machine learning models to maximize the effectiveness of how we engage with users in the upsell process. We call that smart conversations. Our models look at all aspects of user behavior – what they are doing in the app at any point in time? Who are the right people to target for upsell? When is the right time to engage them? Should we be including any kind of

(continued)

promotions at the same time? Our models maximize the effectiveness of those interventions by determining the right subjects, the right topics, the best artists for that person. We use recommendations inside the content itself."

Pandora's approach is unique and in some ways more personalized than those taken by peers like Spotify, because Pandora's models are built on a strongly contextual user experience with inputs that are very explicit in terms of the specific albums, artists, and content users prefer. Such sensitivity to user input generates really powerful feedback data for developing models.

Wong paints a long runway and wide array of applications for AI-enabled recommender systems going forward. Pandora continues to push the envelope on the next generation of recommender strategies by incorporating search and voice signals. Search provides early signals on trends and event-driven actions that make recommendations richer. Advances in voice science allow Pandora to explore thematic queries for even deeper insights into user preferences, and the combination of Sirius XM's audio and broadcast capabilities and Pandora's digital streaming data sources gives Wong's team a real edge in evolving their models by cross pollinating listener experiences across millions of listeners, stations, and inputs. In its final state, Wong envisions a one-to-one relationship between the user and the algorithm that adapts to exactly who they are and what they like.

"Just like digital technologies have fundamentally transformed business over the past twenty years, AI is set to do the same over the next 20 years," advised Professor Hosanagar. "AI is no longer just for engineers and data scientists. It's for everyone. Professionals can no longer afford to have a poor understanding of something so fundamental to business and society today."

To help managers who don't have Pandora's experience and acumen to catch up and apply AI to enable personalization in selling, Hosanagar and the team at Analytics@Wharton worked with experts like Scott Wong to create an online executive curriculum – *AI For Business Specialization* – to help managers understand how to apply AI and ML to grow their businesses.[149] To build this curriculum, Hosanagar and his team worked with leaders at Pandora and Google to offer executives the benefit of millions of hours of modeling, analysis, and learning, giving them a leg up in the market.

CHAPTER 10

Tune the Revenue Operating System to Get Maximum Performance

As with any machine, digital technology provides us with different mechanisms to control outcomes. Some of these are inherent to the configuration of the machine. Others are levers that create immediate change. In a car, for example, you can now modulate your drive mode and speed to get more fuel economy on long trips. Shift torque ratios and gears to get more horsepower in a race. Stiffen your suspension and center of gravity to get more agility around curves. Achieving these different performance outcomes involves adjusting variables like torque, fuel and oxygen intake, transmission ratios, and suspension stiffness. These actions used to be done with a clutch, gas pedal, and a gear shifter. More and more these are managed by a computer.

For a computer – you might want battery life for long plane flights, processing power for data management, high-pixel screens for gaming and VR experiences. This requires adjusting variables like energy output, memory usage, processing resources, and screen configuration. The dials and sliders that control these variables are easy to find on the control panel on a modern computer.

Your Revenue Operating System is no different. We've already shown you how to build the right configuration. Now we will discuss how you can tune the dials to maximize performance.

Selling systems can generate vastly different outcomes based on how variables like channel mix, customer treatment types, coverage ratios, selling effort, and product emphasis are set up. For example, a pharmaceutical company was able to drive $25 million in marginal sales contribution – an 8% increase – by changing the size, deployment, and product emphasis of their sales force, according to research conducted by Professor Leonard Lodish of Wharton.[49] We've seen other organizations dramatically adjust the sales performance by shifting the key parameters such as calling patterns, customer targeting, and product emphasis. These efforts can result in rapid revenue growth and better profit contributions – without adding resources and costs at the same rate.

There are three ways you can use advanced analytics to create business impact:

1. **Digitize your planning processes to improve agility in deploying your resources.** Digitizing the process of planning, managing, and optimizing territory boundaries, seller targets, and quota assignments will make those processes faster, less expensive, and more data driven. Not only will this streamline key commercial processes, but it will also provide more timely visibility into the performance of people and programs against goals. The ability to make mid-period adjustments and conduct more frequent plan reviews will drive greater accountability.

2. **Use analytics to make better predictions, forecasts, and investment decisions.** Taking advantage of advanced analytics and AI capabilities – and the massive new sales data sets available to every business – can help you significantly improve the accuracy, predictability, and quality of your plan inputs. The ability of analytics to consolidate data and cross-pollinating it provides better value-added analysis. This translates into better and more accurate planning inputs. Better estimates of seller capacity and future sales. Better predictions about how customers will respond. More accurate sizing of potential opportunities.

3. **Adopt advanced modeling techniques to evaluate more scenarios and build consensus.** Advanced models and algorithms make it easier to develop, evaluate, and optimize many different scenarios. This is especially important because there are so many variables to consider when managing your growth engine. In a sales context, scenario planning and modeling of the key factors and assumptions that predict sales. These variables include the different ways competitors will respond, the ways in which seasons will change demand, or how well territory "boundaries" will line up with opportunity. Getting these estimates as accurate as possible is important if you want to realize the most growth from your scarce selling resources. Likewise, assumptions about sales rep tenure, how fast revenues will be booked, the channels customers want to use, and the best way to staff those channels have a big impact on your top and bottom line. The ability to simulate quick adjustments to any or all of these variables will help you better prioritize and work through difficult decisions

with trade-offs. It will also allow you to pivot your system to shifting market opportunities. Models can speed up the analysis of planning inputs, such as breaking out historic revenue by-products, channels, industries, and geography. They make it faster to adjust the allocation of effort based on what will deliver sales at the lowest cost, highest profits, and greatest top-line revenue.

Digitize Planning Processes to Improve Agility in Deploying Your Resources

You can improve your return on selling assets by digitizing the sales territory and quota planning processes.

The process of designing, planning, managing, and optimizing sales territory boundaries and seller quota assignments has several dysfunctional elements. First, the process itself is complex, lengthy, and prone to error. It's a labor-intensive undertaking for most sales organizations, even in the best of circumstances. Second, the process is slow and fails to keep up with rapid changes in competition, demand, and innovation. Third, it involves many inputs and a near infinite range of possible scenarios that overwhelm any spreadsheet-based approach. Finally, it requires stakeholders from sales, marketing, product, finance, and operations teams to jointly balance factors against sometimes contradictory and/or competing objectives.

To optimally plan, design, and refine territory boundaries and seller quota assignments, we must ensure that they are precise, accurate, fair, profitable, and attainable. Ensuring all of this involves collecting, analyzing, and modeling up to fifty or more qualitative and quantitative data inputs from inside and outside the company.

Recent changes in the economy, buying behavior, and selling models have amplified the complexity of allocating growth resources to opportunity. Managers have to make more frequent adjustments to sales territories and quota assignments to respond to market conditions, customer preferences, and competitors that are changing faster than ever. The frequency of these changes will only increase as selling teams become more and more digital, data driven, distributed, and diverse.

At the same time, a revolution in AI has introduced new solutions and modeling tools that make it faster and simpler to evaluate the growing set of variables involved in allocating commercial resources and investment. Developments in advanced analytics provide the opportunity to improve the Territory and Quota Planning (TQP) process. These improvements affect the quality and impact of the outputs of the TQP process and the resources, labor, time, and effort involved in managing it. Advanced modeling techniques offer the potential to improve the effectiveness and predictability of territory and quota plans. Here are some examples of the positive impact that digitizing your core planning processes can have:

Generating more revenue growth from existing sales assets. Companies that digitize their TQP process increase the revenue they can generate with existing resources. The revenue increase comes from four places: better resource allocation; tighter alignment between sales territories and your go-to-market strategy; improved sales productivity; and improved goal attainment.

The agility to reach the market faster. Organizations that use automated workflow processes are many times more efficient than their counterparts who use manual or spreadsheet-driven processes. Data-driven automation can help take weeks out of the TQP cycle. One way to obtain these results is by automating the collection and analysis of many data inputs. Another advantage of automated tools is better collaboration. They make it faster and easier for your sales, operations, marketing, compensation, finance, and strategy teams to work together to align territories and quotas.

Digitizing your processes is a win-win. It can help you improve sales achievement while reducing selling costs. Organizations that use automated technology for territory design have higher sales achievement with lower selling costs. A digitized process makes it faster and easier to match territories with revenue and profit growth opportunities and reduce overall selling channel costs.

Unfortunately, most organizations are not digitizing these processes. Most still cling to outdated approaches to the territory and quota planning process. Fewer than 20% of selling organizations have a data-driven, quantified understanding of the total market opportunity and untapped customer potential, according to a survey of 870 B2B executives worldwide by Bain & Company.[150]

A big reason for this is you can't digitize a process you have not yet systematized. The fact is most managers say they are not very good at territory and quota planning in the first place. Only 36% of sales executives and performance professionals say they are effective at territory design.[138] Most of them (79%) feel they have inadequate off-cycle and midyear territory evaluation practices.[151]

Why is this? One big reason is too many companies still do this process manually. In the digital age, spreadsheets are still the primary tool for most organizations when looking to manage sales quota and territory planning. As a result, as we've already noted, most organizations largely fail to finish planning before an upcoming sales period starts.

Another reason is the sheer complexity of planning. "The number of variables and permutations involved in modern territory and quota planning have increased dramatically," reports Michael Smith of Blue Ridge Partners. "This additional rigor will yield more precision, higher goal attainment and greater opportunity realization. But businesses that still use spreadsheets to manage their sales quotas and territory planning, they fail to get their updates completed and accepted by the field two-thirds of the time."

Use Analytics to Make Better Predictions, Forecasts, and Investment Decisions

Corporate leaders struggle with any long-term growth formula because so many growth plans are based on guesses, forecasts, and hunches on which growth investments will work. Growth plans tend toward these uncertainties because managers rarely agree on these three fundamental things: the most essential questions about their growth strategy, the true economic rationale for evaluating strategic growth investment, and the fundamental "math of growth."

This is an area where advanced analytics can create a lot of value. Analytics give managers the horsepower, processing power, and facts they need to better assess the trade-offs between conflicting corporate agendas and perspectives. They also make it easier to agree on and align all aspects of the go-to-market model – from sales force strategy to market segmentation to product portfolio, go-to-market, and sales incentive strategies.

Growth strategy, at its core, seeks to allocate business resources in the way that realizes the greatest revenues and profits from the market. While there is no one perfect growth plan for everyone, there is a balance that is probably best for your specific company. A common understanding of both the assumptions and expectations of the plan is required on some level, or else execution will suffer.

"It's important to remember that defining, sizing, balancing, and optimization of growth resource allocation depends on a number of interrelated factors," reminds Cam Tipping, whose SABRE strategy simulation is used in 70 top MBA programs to teach growth strategy. "These factors are always in conflict. Cost vs. customer service. Sales capacity vs. coverage. Seller balance and fairness vs. revenue maximization. Seller satisfaction vs. short-term revenue growth. Sales rep location, skill and expertise vs. market need. This leads to trade-off decisions. There is no right answer. Each organization has its own priorities, methods, or 'algorithms' for balancing these trade-offs to arrive at territory definition and quota assignments that create the most value for the enterprise – in terms of short- and long-term growth, profitability, and firm value."

To be more specific, academic research tells us that there are seven inter-related decision factors that inform the development of growth strategies and plans.[106] These factors include the selling channel designs and go-to-market strategies that every selling system runs on. All of these are defined in the glossary. All of these will require a different mix of qualitative inputs (e.g. judgment); quantitative inputs (e.g. historical data); objective inputs (facts); or subjective data inputs (guesses). Selling channel designs and go-to-market strategies also vary based on how they are derived. For example, some organizations use a top-down approach to divide markets into segments and rep assignments that are uniform and rational. Others use a bottom-up approach that factors in more local market input and the unique capabilities and skills of individual sellers. Neither is perfect. So the best management teams try to use both to get the most accurate plans in place. Mixing and matching these approaches is another way that models and automation can really help. (See Figure 10.1.)

Given this interrelationship between go-to-market variables, it's important to align all of the components of the go-to-market strategy. These seven variables must work in concert with the prescribed territory boundaries and

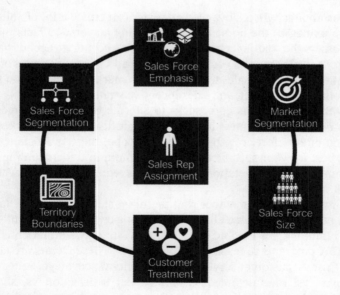

FIGURE 10.1 The Interrelated Decision Factors That Inform Growth System Performance

sales quota assignments that generate revenue and yield from resources. Multiple strategic and tactical objectives are in tension and require active balancing. Coordination among key stakeholders in other functions will ensure that your territory and quota plan aligns with relevant strategies, such as channel strategy, product portfolio strategy, market segmentation, and incentives.

At a high level, you need to balance four fundamental trade-offs when optimizing the growth formula for your company.

- The trade-off between high levels of control over the sales force and market coverage. Too much control may limit sales freedom and miss opportunities. Too little control can result in undisciplined selling, overlaps, and disputes.

- The trade-off between cost and the customer experience. Too much focus on optimizing cost can hurt the lifetime value and quality of important client relationships. Too little focus on costs can waste effort and erode margin.

- The trade-offs between maximizing opportunity and the retention of your sales force. Overly aggressive goals can be unrealistic and increase stress and attrition on the sales team. On the other hand, relaxing growth goals can leave value and revenues on the table and reduce your competitiveness and productivity.

- As organizations move to multichannel, digital, and virtual selling models – they need to rebalance selling team activities, roles, and priorities. For example, engaging customers through direct and digital channels requires a much different type, mix, and sequence of customer engagement and different customer treatment types. The productivity, workload, and capacity of virtual sales reps will be different from traditional field sellers or key account managers. Modern engagement models need to factor in the level of digital engagement, reductions in sales travel due to remote selling. You must also factor in the increased speed and frequency of response that digitally enabled customers have come to expect when you establish activity-based productivity measures.

To fully realize the growth potential of new territory designs, interaction patterns, and customer priorities, it is likely you will need to reengineer their selling architecture. This means adjusting your territories, incentives, engagement models, roles, and customer engagement cadences to generate higher returns from your revenue teams. If you try to manage all these variables using desktop productivity tools like spreadsheets, you will quickly become overwhelmed with the volume of variables and scenarios to consider.

This is an area where advanced analytics, AI algorithms, and models can really help. These tools can help you assess many different scenarios and inform better optimization and resource allocation decisions quickly. For example, these tools will help you evaluate many different scenarios faster, as well as allow you to manage many more variables in reconfiguring selling architecture. They can also support you in optimally matching selling resources with specific market opportunities. In addition, using modeling tools can speed up the development and evaluation of a wide variety of trade-off decisions throughout the planning and optimization process, including but not limited to:

- **Sales resource allocation:** Optimizing the additional revenues and profits associated with increasing staffing in a market. Optimizing in this way involves experimentation with different levels and mixes of staffing based on assumptions about sales response function, rep productivity, the marginal cost of incremental sales, and demand elasticity.

- **Sales force emphasis:** Optimizing the incremental profit and revenue contribution vs. level of effort, mix of calling, and products sold. There are thousands of rep, customer, and personal combinations to consider. Still, selling performance, resource requirements, and margins can change dramatically based on these variables. So, exploring many options makes sense if it can be done quickly and affordably.

- **Optimizing territory assignments:** Optimizing sales potential vs. the mix of customers and accounts in a given territory can have a positive impact on sales productivity, total profits, and revenue growth and risk. You can experiment with a variety of different combinations to achieve the optimal territory definitions and assignments for your organization. Advanced models can process and optimize territories to balance a variety of critical variables. Some of the most important ones to consider are: Making sure quotas are equal vs. equitable. The optimal combination of carrots (incentives and lifts) and sticks (gates and penalties) to motivate sellers. Emphasizing selling new as opposed to existing products to maximize margins and customer lifetime value. The best division of time spent with new and existing clients to optimize top-line growth and cost to sell. The degree you should use measures of activity and behavior as opposed to outcome-based metrics to motivate sellers to make the right decisions where to allocate their efforts.

- **Breaking down baseline revenues and revenue forecasts** by product, channel, industry, and geographic mixes: This involves understanding how changes in market coverage will affect your market share, revenue attainment, and cost to sell.

- **Optimizing top-down opportunity allocation.** Top-down quota planning breaks down the total revenue opportunity of a company into smaller units that can be assigned to individual sales reps or teams. There are a variety of ways a business can break down that opportunity based on cost to sell, sales force size, product emphasis, staffing levels, and sales force focus.

Seven Places Where Analytics Can Help You Make Better Predictions, Forecasts, and Investment Decisions

1. **Sales forecasts:** Developing more accurate predictions of future sales based on a mix of actual pipeline data from CRM, historical transaction data, current levels of customer engagement and seller activity, buying signals from individual buyers, and better models of customer response.

2. **Customer scoring and value models:** Better estimating customer potential based on data about opportunity potential, intent to buy, propensity to buy, historical sales, coverage difficulty, and effort to convert.

3. **Opportunity potential:** Sizing the revenue and profit potential of addressable markets based on go-to-market strategy, sales forecast, historical performance baselines, and corporate growth and profit targets.

4. **Seller capacity:** Calculating sales rep capacity based on sales force roles, field input, judgment, expectations of quota attainment, and individual skills and experience.

5. **Seller productivity and profitability:** Assessing estimates and targets for seller performance based on a combination of historical performance, individual capabilities, the specific customers in their territories, and the products they are selling.

6. **The sales response function:** Estimating the relationship between selling effort and actual sales revenue based on external market inputs, the state of the economy, internal conversion rates, and the historical relationship between actual sales and seller staffing and attention.

7. **Workload estimates:** Developing more accurate estimates of seller effort and workload based on granular inputs, such as transaction economics, the different levels of customer treatment, the number of touches and calls in the engagement model, and the desired level of customer experience.

Adopt Advanced Modeling Techniques to Evaluate More Scenarios and Build Consensus

Advanced analytics and, particularly, the use of advanced modeling techniques can help your team plan, manage, and measure the performance of your growth strategy. They allow you to better and more accurately create, test, and improve plans.

Professors Leonard Lodish and V "Paddy" Padmanabhan have taught the "Leading the Effective Sales Force" curriculum to a generation of growth leaders over the past decade at Wharton and INSEAD.[143] They believe it is no longer enough to rely on history or "rules of thumb" in making sales force allocation decisions. The precise sales performance data available to sales managers is increasingly able to help them rationally decide on sales force size, territory boundaries, and call frequencies for each account and prospect.

"Decision science has evolved beyond simple extrapolations of historic performance or management 'rules of thumb' about key TQP planning parameters, such as seller workload estimates, the sales response function, opportunity potential or seller productivity," relates Cam Tipping. "Advanced models and business simulations are empowering sales managers and key stakeholders in product, marketing, and senior leadership to develop much more accurate and nuanced planning assumptions based on quantitative facts and qualitative management judgements that reflect the true drivers of sales performance and customer response which yield much more effective planning outputs. This includes a better understanding about how sales assignments were derived, and why they are in the collective best interest all parties involved."

Using advanced sales analytics and modeling techniques to derive more accurate and predictive planning parameters is an emerging best practice. Data inputs from many different data sources no longer solely rely on extrapolations of historical baseline data derived from simple assumptions. Some data inputs can be derived by modeling sales response functions, sales profitability, customer value modeling, signals of customer intent and readiness to buy, and "win probability."

A fact-based business case for sales resource allocation is now possible. Investment in markets can be empirically determined by developing a sales response model for the markets you serve. Such a model looks at demand and supply information, competitive spending, and the relationship between sales staffing and revenue performance. Other models can calculate incremental profit and revenue contribution of incremental effort, as well as calling patterns and product emphasis.

The ability of analytics to make planning insights more predictive helps sales organizations unlock the potential in their go-to-market approach, which can drive growth, improve yields, and generate the greatest return on growth investment, according to Marc Altshuller, Founder and CEO of Varicent. "The most advanced organizations are using AI to find the predictive elements in their unique data to identify customer opportunities and seller performance issues," shares Altshuller. "For example, it's possible to identify and predict which sellers have the highest probability of hitting their quotas or churning, including the ability to drill down into the detail on the headwinds, tailwinds, traits, and behaviors that explain why they are at risk and what drives their performance. A leadership team can use this granular and predictive data to decide on the thresholds of revenue and thresholds of churn risk they can tolerate in their plan."[144]

Seventy-nine percent of sales teams currently use or are planning to use sales analytics technology.[14] It is possible to calculate much more accurate inputs for several critical data inputs to the planning, management, and measurement of growth resources. Your growth strategy can be improved significantly with advanced modeling and analytics techniques that use the following inputs:

- **Estimates of market potential and opportunity:** By incorporating internal sales baselines over three years or more with external measures of economic activity, demand, buying behavior, and market trends to more accurately quantify and forecast market opportunity or the total addressable market. Improving your estimates with facts can greatly enhance the TQP process because most sales and marketing executives are not using data to support their growth strategy and resource allocation decisions. For example, two-thirds of CMOs could not demonstrate the contribution of marketing to firm sales and profits with the data they have, according to a survey of 500 Global CMOs in the Forbes Marketing Accountability Report.[15]

- **Seller profitability and performance:** By correlating rep activities and outcomes with profit contribution, sales quota attainment, and productivity metrics such as calling volume and conversion rates.

- **Customer and account priorities:** By calculating account potential by combining internal sales baseline data with external firmographic, technographic, and demographic information as well as usage, adoption, and buying intent to determine customer buying potential, penetration, and lifetime value.

- **Sales workload estimates:** By building rep workload and capacity estimates using a wide range of scenarios based on different customer engagement models – the number, mix, nature, and frequency of customer engagement, different levels of treatment by customer type, and the mix of products presented to those customers.

- **Sales forecasts:** By integrating pipeline health and opportunity metrics from CRM with customer engagement, intelligence, intent, and win-probability data from first-party data drawn from customer-facing systems and third-party data sources.

- **The sales response function:** This is the relationship between sales and marketing investments and actions and the contribution they generate in terms of revenues, profits, and business objectives. This is perhaps the biggest assumption underlying all of your growth plans. According to academic research, the optimization of all aspects of sales operations depends on the behavior of response functions, either explicitly or implicitly.[152]

Management's ability to accurately estimate the effects of sellers' efforts on business outcomes is critical to help them make effective and optimal decisions about how to allocate sales resources.

The science of sales response calibration has evolved from simple estimates of the response function (the relationship between effort and results) to far more sophisticated and accurate approaches based on advanced modeling techniques, according to research by Professor Lodish.[153] Most managers allocate their salespeople to markets based on their judgments or simplistic linear "extrapolations" or "rules of thumb" (e.g. if one rep generates $1 million in new sales in a given market then two reps will generate $2 million). Advanced analytics make it practical to create far more objective and complex data-based econometric techniques. These techniques are based on more sophisticated modeling approaches like regression analysis, maximum simulated likelihood, and hierarchical Bayesian analytics. A good place to learn about these techniques is in the "Customer Analytics for Growth Using Machine Learning, AI, and Big Data" executive education course at Wharton developed by Professor Raghu Iyengar.[154]

Advanced modeling techniques can create much more accurate response functions that represent how sales will vary with selling efforts in different scenarios. For example, a model should be able to tell you how much effort is required to maximize sales on a company, territory, or rep level. It should also allow you to see how those predictions will change based on external factors such as competitive, market, and environmental influences. These models are much more accurate, transparent, and measurable than the simplistic historic extrapolation, linear relationships, or "rules of thumb" that managers have used as the basis of estimating the response function.

An emerging best practice for solving the problem of allocating scarce resources is to conduct an econometrics modeling analysis. Econometrics offers a set of equations describing the behavior of customers and markets. Such models are useful because they better predict how sales will increase as you add resources to a given region or market. This is because customers don't respond in a linear fashion. More complex S-shaped (or convex-concave) response functions better predict customer response because they are most common in nature and factor in the concept of diminishing returns.[152]

Algorithmic models and planning simulations can help managers maximize their return on growth assets a number of ways. They can help you refine these critical assumptions and inputs to your plan. They can set up better tests to see if those assumptions are close to the mark. They can see how those assumptions change many periods into the future. Models also allow you to evaluate hundreds or thousands of different allocation scenarios. This is important because there are literally millions of different ways you can go to market, and small differences in your approach can make a big impact. Finally, models help you incorporate input and perspectives of more people on your team faster and with less labor.

Algorithmic models and simulation tools can be a true force multiplier when it comes to sales strategy. They can help you build resource allocation strategies that increase sales while reducing costs, stress test the allocations and assumptions behind those strategies, and bring those strategies to market faster.

This is an important point because at its core, growth strategy is fundamentally the strategic allocation of growth resources and investment. Those allocation decisions are based on dozens of assumptions and predictions about the future. Most of those assumptions, predictions, and scenarios are based on gut feeling, institutional belief systems, and unchallenged assumptions about the value, responsiveness, and attainability of customers and markets.

Executives continue to struggle when they make the critical growth trade-offs, allocation, and risk investment decisions required to adapt to a dynamic, rapidly changing marketplace. This is because their huge investments in marketing analytics are better at improving marketing tactics than they are at informing strategic growth decisions. The A/B testing that your digital marketing teams routinely use to track performance are great at optimizing marketing tactics, campaigns, and little decisions. The problem is they don't tell you how to run your selling system better. As Elissa Fink, former CMO of Tableau, puts it, "There is no A/B test for the big strategy and trade-off decisions the CMO needs to make, where you are either all-in or out."[155]

The more you use data to inform and test your long-term growth plans – the smarter you become about your business, your market, and your decisions.

The Power of Simulations to "War Game" Scenarios, Pressure Test Plans, and Building a Common Purpose

AI-driven simulation-based tools can provide you with a faster, more collaborative way to generate your territory, product launch, account-based marketing, and business unit growth plans. Using simulation tools lets your leadership team "war game" more scenarios. Almost every profession uses simulations to develop complex plans and strategies and to enhance skills and talent. Lawyers use simulations to game different strategies for mock trials. Doctors in training use simulations to practice surgery without the risk of hurting patients. Pilots train on flight simulators so they don't crash when they make mistakes. Simulations are gaining popularity as a sales strategy and planning tool. There are a variety of big benefits associated with using these simulation-based tools, particularly when compared to the traditional top-down approaches to strategy development that most companies use:

- First, a simulation compresses time in testing go-to-market strategies. Most growth strategies will not bear fruit or fail until several sales periods after they are deployed, which means managers and planners can only guess at what will happen in years two, three, and four. You either guess right, or you guess wrong—and everyone has their own best guess. Simulations let groups of people play out different growth scenarios years out into the future. For example, the SABRE business tool mentioned earlier allows teams to "war game" different resource allocation strategies seven periods into the future. This is a huge advantage. "The SABRE simulation is one of the most highly ranked courses in the Wharton MBA program for a reason," according to Professor Dave Reibstein, who has taught the class for several years. "Simulation tools are extremely effective at teaching, testing, and proving out different growth strategies and management perspectives."

- Second, AI-driven simulations can manage millions of scenarios and possible resource allocations to find the best combination to maximize growth. They allow managers from sales, marketing, service, and product groups to collectively test and balance combinations. From which products the sales force should emphasize to which customers to target and prioritize in calling, to the different ways of treating those customers: all of these factors combine to help you generate the greatest profit and growth contribution and ROI, and quota attainability.

- A third benefit is "crowdsourcing" the market knowledge and experience of your team. Simulation tools can incorporate dozens, even hundreds, of field leaders into the planning process. This means using simulations makes it possible to combine bottom-up, local market knowledge and performance insights with top-down focus on realizing the greatest profit, revenue, and opportunity share. The best of both worlds. "Simulations are one of the fastest ways to build a team consensus," reports Cam Tipping. "A simulation tool brings together different points of view and lets you test different approaches. In the end, you get better consensus understanding of the customer response function, and a better sense of how to manage the product portfolio strategy."

- A fourth benefit of simulations is that they allow planners the opportunity to "pressure test" and adapt plans to deal with rapidly changing and different competitive and market scenarios.

- A fifth advantage is speed. Simulations effectively accelerate the time between strategy development, tactical planning, buy-in, communication, and implementation by revenue teams. This is important because most organizations that use spreadsheets and manual planning approaches cannot get those plans updated and agreed upon by seller before the selling year actually begins. That's effectively starting a journey without a plan.

- A final advantage is risk management. All future plans are risky. And while it's nice to say things "take risk and fail fast," most managers really don't want to take big risks with their careers. "Simulations let you guess and screw up without costing you your career," advised Professor Reibstein. "Few of my students have taken big risks on their jobs. But all of them have crashed a plan in a flight simulator game." Experience is the best teacher. One of the biggest advantages of simulations is they let you try different things without consequences. And they give you years of experience in a week."

The Power of Models to Algorithmically Balance and Tune Your Revenue Engine

Sales modeling is both an art and science. This is true even in the most data-driven organizations.

But the speed and complexity of modern selling has made modeling an essential tool for tuning and running your revenue operation system. For example, modeling is increasingly critical to sales resource allocation due to rapidly changing customer behavior, shorter product life cycles, and the complexity of omnichannel selling.

Eight Places Where Advanced Modeling Techniques Can Be Used to Evaluate More Scenarios and Build Consensus

1. **Selling channel emphasis:** Finding the optimal mix of "products in the bag" based on the ability to cross-sell and upsell products, the effort and skills required to sell them, their margin potential, and the potential to sell many products to target customer personas.

2. **Opportunity allocation:** Finding the best way to allocate market opportunity to all customer-facing channels and to employees who optimally balance the ability to generate revenues, profits, and market share with the skills, capacity, and roles of individual sellers.

(continued)

3. **Territory control boundaries:** Using algorithms to define the optimal territory boundaries based on account potential, customer channel preference, time zone and geographic constraints, and the skills and capacity of sellers.

4. **Quota type and definition:** Defining the best structure for setting quotas that balance risk with income security, the ability to attain quotas, and the desire to create a common focus on the customer and on the right behaviors.

5. **Bottom-up targets:** Establishing bottom-up sales rep targets based on a mix of inputs including seller capacity, local market knowledge, customer priorities, workload estimates, and market demand.

6. **Customer and account priorities:** Establishing fact-based customer scoring based on customer value scoring models; relationship strength; and signals of intent, preference, or propensity to buy based on actual customer engagement and CRM data.

7. **The best engagement model:** Calculating the best mix of calling patterns, calling types, calling frequency, and treatment types to yield the most revenue and profit from seller effort and channel infrastructure.

8. **Historic performance baselines:** Evaluating historical sales data by taking into consideration geographic location, industry, selling channel, and product usage to generate the best predictions for opportunity potential, future sales, and territory boundaries.

Managing a selling system requires constantly monitoring and rebalancing the seven interrelated inputs against corporate growth goals and resource constraints. For example, you will need to change the size, segmentation, and emphasis of your selling channels as buyers move to online channels or require higher levels of support. When demand shifts or new markets emerge, you will need to reset your sales territories and market segments. And adjusting the way you engage and treat customers based on their changing needs and potential is a never-ending exercise.

PART IV

How to Get Started and Drive Impact

CHAPTER 11

Deliver Growth with Six Smart Actions

Revenue Operations presents the best commercial model to achieve sustainable and scalable growth, and organic growth creates the most firm value. Thus, Revenue Operations provides the best approach to create firm value.

In Part I, we learned that Revenue Operations comprises two component systems. The first, the management system, aligns the people in your revenue teams. The second, the operating system, combines technology, processes, and data assets to help your revenue teams generate consistent and scalable growth.

In Part II we walked through the management system for Revenue Operations and its 18 elements designed in detail. Coming out of that section, you should decide what the best leadership model is for your business.

In Part III, we reviewed the operating system and broke it down into nine building blocks that connect your growth assets, commercial insights, and value drivers. After that section, you should be thinking about what your Revenue Operating System looks like and how to improve each building block.

Now it's time to put those all together in your business to create value.

Most important, we want to show you how to take effective action and how to link individual actions together to amplify the overall result. Revenue Operations will work for any business, large or small. It will help every player in your organization understand their role on the revenue team and what is needed from them to create firm value through growth. It will create value by establishing the structure for continuous, radical, and even transformative process improvement in marketing, sales, and service performance.

With an understanding of the management and operating systems in hand, the question you are probably asking yourself now is: "How do I get started?" Welcome to the concept of Smart Actions.

Deliver Growth with Smart Actions

Smart Actions are a set of related activities that meet four criteria: they are practical to execute, interconnect multiple building blocks of your operating system, are accretive financially, and link together with other Smart Actions toward a longer-term objective.

1. **Actionable:** They must be effectively achievable with existing assets, skills, capital budgets, and management bandwidth.
2. **Connected:** They should unite multiple building blocks of the operating system together to create more leverage, simplify the selling process, and eliminate key points of failure in your core selling processes.
3. **Accretive:** They will generate short-term financial gains by reducing leakage, improving sales performance, and eliminating waste. They also stack together to generate higher long-term returns on your technology, data, and selling infrastructure assets.
4. **Scalable:** They create the foundation for consistent nonlinear growth that more predictably creates value and margin at lower cost. Smart Actions link together in chains whose effects stack on top of and amplify one another.

Although Smart Actions must be achievable within the current limits of your organization today, they usually serve as incremental steps toward a larger commercial transformation.

Transformation means change, and many people and organizations don't like change. Fear of change threatens business innovation, including the successful deployment of Revenue Operations. Many transformation initiatives have failed because they were too ambitious and required too many cultural shifts. Long-term investments, even good ones, sometimes distract good, effective short-term management. Micro-disruptions like Smart Actions offer a more reliable path to balanced success.

The CEOs, executives, and operational managers interviewed in our research voiced common concerns about the perceived amount of change involved and the time and commitment it will take to realize benefit from a Revenue Operations model. The leaders who succeeded in transforming their go-to-market models, however, came away with three important learnings:

- **Commercial transformation is a process of continuous incremental improvements.** The comprehensive and integrated nature of Revenue Operations may create the perception that these changes must happen all at once to work. Seasoned executives understand that adoption of the Revenue Operations model in the front office can be executed in stages, similar to applying the principles of Lean Manufacturing, Six Sigma, Kaizen, and Total Quality Management in back-office processes.

- **Transformation starts at the top.** Delegating change management too far down in the organization will inhibit or even stall efforts to align marketing, sales, and service. Organizations that have successfully moved the needle, such as Avaya, Cisco, Honeywell, GHX, Splunk, and Pentair, have CEO support for transformation and have put in place the leadership models outlined in chapter 5 to better manage commercial assets, operations, and infrastructure across the enterprise.

- **The cost of not changing is greater than the pain of change.** Maintaining the status quo will often lead to diminished competitive differentiation, unrealized opportunities in the market, higher selling costs, seller attribution, and account churn.

The executives running GHX, iconectiv, Inmar Intelligence, Fortive, and Honeywell have all used Smart Actions to achieve commercial transformation. They are instilling a culture of continuous learning and improvement and are stair-stepping their way through a series of high-impact changes to their selling models.

For example, Peter Ford, VP of Global Sales at iconectiv, improved the performance of his revenue team by taking inspiration from Dave Brailsford, who led the British cycling team to Olympic gold. When Brailsford took over the team in 2002, Britain had won a single medal in its history of competing. Brailsford transformed that team by breaking down each element of their performance and striving for just a 1% improvement rate for each. He utilized marginal transformation processes and, seven years later, the team took seven of ten gold medals.[156]

Six Proven Smart Actions That Work

To get you started, we provide six examples of Smart Actions successfully used by other leading companies. Use them in your business as-is, or with a little customization. Individually, these bite-sized and financially viable stairsteps can be piloted, sequenced, and measured to transform your organization in ways that are politically, practically, and financially achievable across the organization.

They also can serve as templates for you to author your own Smart Actions (keeping in mind the four criteria). Such a template will help you position tactical initiatives against strategic rationale and to communicate expectations and responsibilities. This provides a way to compare, contrast, and challenge even the activities of your own teams and your partners (consultancies, agencies, integrators, etc.). If those groups come back with recommendations better or more tailored to your business, articulating them as a Smart Action should make them understandable and digestible.

As we discussed in Part III, this approach also sets up a common vocabulary around what your operating system has and how it can best be assembled to deliver growth. Models, systems, building blocks, Smart Actions – we used deliberate language in describing Revenue Operations, and you should, too. Even if you call them something else, a common vocabulary across your teams and your partners will dramatically improve communication, collaboration, and commitment across all corners of your business. In our conversations with hundreds of growth executives, six Smart Actions continually came up. Ideally, you can see how one or more of these could help your business start building a more scalable, sustainable selling system today:

1. **Get better visibility into the revenue cycle**
2. **Simplify the selling workflow**
3. **Share marketing insights with frontline sellers**
4. **Develop and retain high performing selling talent**
5. **Make selling channels more effective**
6. **Streamline and personalize the selling content supply chain**

Get Better Visibility into the Revenue Cycle

Our first Smart Action aggregates, analyzes, and transforms your customer engagement data into commercial insights that give you better visibility into the entire revenue cycle. Such insights include opportunity potential, account health, seller performance, and pipeline activity, regarded as the four most important insights managers need to better manage their selling system.

- Visibility is *actionable* because the seller activity data, customer engagement statistics, product usage data, and financial transaction data required to assemble and create these metrics already exists in your organization. The analytic tools and skills to get better visibility have become democratized and available.
- Better visibility through data is *connected* because it requires you to link four parts of your Revenue Operating System together to create value. It combines customer activity data from your customer-facing technology with seller activity data from your revenue operations stack in an engagement hub to provide revenue intelligence.
- It's *accretive* because it will allow you to better measure and manage seller resources, allocate them to the best opportunities, stop wasting time on

accounts and opportunities that are not worth it, and actively manage customer lifetime value.

- It is *scalable* because the systems in your business will continue to generate more and more customer, product, and seller insights that can provide you facts. Advances in analytics tools and your own acumen allow your team to create ever-increasing improvements in performance by more accurately managing sellers, balancing their quota assignments, penetrating top accounts, and tightening revenue forecasts.

- You can align your metrics and incentives with the activities and behaviors that lead to profitable commercial outcomes – things like selling more to customers, at higher prices, and keeping them around longer. You can use advanced customer engagement analytics and sales AI to create customer engagement metrics. These metrics create performance measurements based on real-time information about sales engagement, deal attractiveness, content usage, and persona-based interactions. This provides you a more accurate proxy of the current buying reality.

Figure 11.1 outlines the requirements to execute revenue lifecycle insights. It is based on the successful experiences of metrics-focused businesses, such as Fortive, Ciena, AT&T, and Pentair, which we profiled in chapter 8. Don't think of these templates as a wiring diagram or instruction manual. Think of them more like a chemistry set. If you combine two elements (hydrogen and oxygen) in the right mixture you create something useful and life sustaining – water. In this case, combine your first-party data generated by your technology to create something valuable and useful: a fact-based dashboard.

The key element here is the first-party data generated by your email, websites, calendars, and recorded conversations when customers engage with you. This data will provide a foundation for customer engagement, and seller activity data and will likely reveal a great deal about how your revenue teams are performing across the entire revenue cycle in essential areas like engagement, transaction, cross-selling, and retention.

FIGURE 11.1 Revenue Cycle Insights

Simplify the Selling Workflow

Our second Smart Action connects the dots across your revenue enablement technology portfolio to create more value to simplify and streamline the selling workflow. How this qualifies as a Smart Action:

- Simplification is *actionable*. Organizations have many key assets and capabilities necessary to support the seller workflow, including CRM, digital asset management, and sales enablement tools. Though desirable, you don't need all these tools to make selling simpler for frontline sellers. Nor do they have to be fully connected. Simplifying auditing and codifying the workflow and enforcing it using digital adoption tools will generate significant improvements and returns.

- It is *connected*. Simplifying selling workflow requires weaving your CRM, sales enablement, sales readiness, and digital asset management solutions to eliminate key points of failure, friction, and manual labor in day-to-day seller workflow. These solutions are largely managed in different functional silos in most B2B organizations.

- It's *accretive*. Simplifying the selling workflow allows you to eliminate waste, redundancy, and underutilized technology assets in your revenue enablement portfolio, yielding immediate cost savings. It will also improve your return on assets because it increases the utilization of those tools. Better adoption of the selling process and tools can dramatically improve the productivity and experience of sales reps, which builds the confidence, performance, and loyalty of sellers. Seller stress is a major contributor to attrition.

- It is *scalable*. The more seamless the seller experience and the more sellers adopt technology, then the more technology will serve as a force multiplier that elevates the performance of your entire revenue team.

Figure 11.2 shows a how simplification can be achieved with the creation of a digital selling platform, based on the successful experiences of Hitachi Vantara we profiled in chapter 7.

The key elements here include your core CRM and sales enablement platforms. It's important to incorporate all systems that support the selling process with content: digital asset management, competitive intelligence, "configure, price, quote" (CQP) tools, and dynamic pricing software solutions. Ideally, you can incorporate learning and development and readiness solutions that give you the capability to deliver training in context during the sales process.

Here are four steps you might take to execute this Smart Action:

- First, establish centralized stewardship and reconfigure your commercial technology portfolio across functions.

- Next, conduct a formal assessment of your technology portfolio architecture and road map to reduce duplication, disconnected apps, and

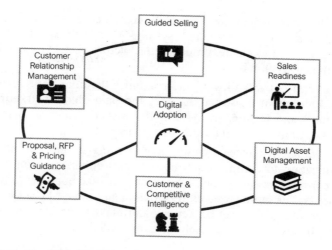

FIGURE 11.2   The Digital Selling Platform

underutilized assets. Also, identify ways to improve value, impact, and the seller experience.

- In parallel, audit the revenue technology portfolio to ID ways to improve utilization, productivity, return on assets, and the seller experience.
- Finally, take advantage of obvious opportunities to improve rep speed, engagement, and time focused on the customer while reconfiguring the commercial technology infrastructure.

Share Marketing Insights with Frontline Sellers

The third Smart Action monetizes the digital selling infrastructure with Account-Based Marketing. Synthesizing the marketing signals from inside and outside your business with your CRM will help execute Account-Based Marketing programs that optimize account coverage and maximize the return on sales and marketing technology

This is smart because:

- This is *actionable.* Every organization spends a big chunk of their marketing budgets on owned, earned, and paid digital marketing and the systems necessary to deliver that information to frontline sales and service teams.

- It is *connected*. It requires you to link customer-facing systems and programs across your technology systems that support customer-facing employees and to create a much better picture of activity and opportunity in key accounts.
- It is *accretive*. It will allow you to maximize the financial return on your large investment in owned, earned, and paid digital marketing media programs and technology systems that support them to help account teams optimize account coverage and penetration.
- It is *scalable*. It creates a closed-loop learning system that allows your organization to continuously improve and enhance account coverage and converge resources faster in order to realize opportunities in those accounts. The more layers of information an account leader has and the more feedback they get on actions and plays to develop accounts, the more effective key account selling teams will be.

Figure 11.3 lays out how to build an ABM program based on the best practices we profiled in chapter 7.

There are three key elements to this Smart Action: your first-party data; specialized software to transform, orchestrate, and map those data streams to existing account structures; and contact profiles that reside in your CRM or other system of record. Once you attach marketing signals to the account profiles, you can use a variety of platforms (CRM, sales enablement, or sales engagement solutions) to share that information to sales reps via alerts, account priorities, recommendations for the best content; and recommended next-best actions to pursue. Such push notifications can also trigger coordinated marketing campaigns that engage stakeholders in the accounts.

The progression of steps to deliver this outcome are:

- Inventory the first- and third-party data streams in your business that might inform a program like this.
- Find gaps in the way your organization aggregates, transforms, orchestrates, and maps anonymous engagement data (people who engage digitally but don't fully identify their affiliation to you) to account profiles and structures in CRM.
- Identify software solutions that can fill those gaps. NOTE: Finding possible solutions here can be confusing because vendors call themselves a variety of names ranging from Account Orchestration, Account Engagement Platforms (like 6sense), and even Revenue Operations platforms.
- Start the process of converting and feeding signals of activity, intent, churn, or propensity to buy to account teams. This does not have to be perfect at first. Any effort to create a closed-loop approach will create real impact and pave the way to future improvements. For example, you can use the data to refine customer targets based on more precise data-driven signals of intent, win probability, fit, and potential. You can also use the

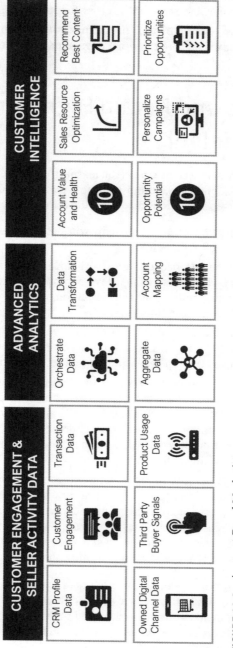

FIGURE 11.3   Account-Based Marketing

data to enable measures that trigger actions to improve the customer experience at every stage of the cross-functional customer journey.

- Continually work toward providing your revenue teams real-time guidance based on core customer engagement and seller activity data sets.

Develop and Retain High-Performing Selling Talent

Our fourth Smart Action integrates the learning and development processes. It unites your sales enablement and readiness platforms to create a closed-loop system for sales rep education, coaching, and reinforcement and measurement.

- This is *smart* because it will help you better develop and retain high-performing selling talent.
- This is *actionable* because most organizations already have the sales training, playbooks, learning, development, enablement, and analytics technology to put this connected solution together. Until now, they have lived in different functional silos.
- It is *connected*. It requires you to link your training and development systems with your sales enablement systems to your analytics teams to better support the rep development and retention process.
- It is *accretive* and will allow you to shrink the time it takes to develop and ramp productive sellers. It will also help you augment selling interactions by improving value selling skills and applying best practices – a major opportunity we reviewed in chapter 9. Most sellers will stay with their current employer if they receive good coaching to help them succeed and develop skills.
- It is *scalable*. A closed-loop system that connects training, behavior, and performance allows you to measure how well sellers absorb and adopt training. It uses actual sales interactions and customer responses to check the real-world impact of training. Managers and sellers become much more precise about which skills a rep needs to work on, and about what gaps exist in their playbooks and value-selling approaches.

Figure 11.4 pulls together an integrated learning and development process based on the best practices we profiled in chapter 9.

The key elements of this Smart Action include many of the solutions and assets in your revenue enablement systems, including sales enablement and learning management systems and the selling content libraries that support them. They also include selling methodologies, selling playbooks, and development program assets that are generally curated by the training and development organization.

FIGURE 11.4   The Integrated Learning and Development Process

To reconfigure your technology infrastructure and better support readiness, training, and development, you can follow this series of steps:

- Audit your learning and development technology portfolio to improve visibility, speed to ramp, skills, coaching and reinforcement, and to identify gaps in the readiness, enablement, and reporting workflow.
- Integrate the learning and development technology portfolio into an integrated and closed-loop process. This process will provide feedback, reinforcement, and visibly into seller activity and compliance. Changes in the vendor landscape should make this easier, as several sales enablement providers are building or buying training capabilities to bolster their solutions.
- Create measures that close the loop between seller performance, training effectiveness, and customer outcomes. These will lay the foundation for AI to evaluate selling skills and performance more precisely and quickly.
- Integrate sales readiness, enablement, and engagement where possible today while creating a consensus road map to direct future investments to improve seller ramp, readiness, skills, and accountability.

Make Selling Channels More Effective

The fifth sample Smart Action automates direct sales and service channels with real-time, data-driven selling. Connecting your sales enablement, CRM, conversational intelligence, and digital marketing systems will make your selling channels more effective.

- This is *smart* because it will allow you to maximize the potential of customer-facing resources during the limited 18% of the customer journeys where buyers actually engage with humans.

- This is *actionable*. Organizations already have the fundamental customer engagement and seller activity data they need – recorded conversations, content consumption by clients, CRM, and exchange data from email and calendars – to pilot real-time guidance and coaching at scale. You just need the executive mandate to access and use it. Using advanced analytics and sales AI tools, you can already get an 80% good-enough picture of buyer engagement and seller activity. Even that can provide real-time guidance to reps about the right response, content, action, or sales play that improves interactions during the moments that matter in the customer journey.

- It is *connected*. It requires you to link recorded conversations from the call center, marketing signals, and insights about customers and ensures that CRM profiles are enriched and up to date with the actual results of calls in real time. This approach connects and aligns CRM, sales enablement, conversational intelligence, and sales engagement systems into one selling motion to create more value.

- It is *accretive*. Better knowledge sharing will improve selling performance, which will show up in conversion rates on sales and service conversations. Sharing information across the company will generate greater returns on your investments in CRM, marketing data, sales enablement, selling content, sales training methodologies, and conversational intelligence. It will also save reps time in planning for calls and inputting call notes into CRM. Importantly, continuous, real-time, one-to-one coaching allows overworked sales managers to actively manage and coach more reps, keeping a tighter connection with the field and accelerating how quickly new reps ramp to full productivity.

- It is *scalable*. It allows sales managers to help more sellers in real time. It enforces the selling motions, playbooks, and methods that document the best practices of your customer-facing employees. To keep up with rapidly changing customer behavior, sales leaders tell us they need to increase the speed at which they deliver selling guidance, coaching, signals of intent, and content recommendations to their frontline sellers.

- The speed of communication internally accelerates to keep pace with the rapidly changing customer behavior. It helps frontline sellers respond immediately and completely to new school buyers while also better reacting to verbal cues in selling interactions.

Figure 11.5 shows what is required to execute real-time, data-driven selling based on the successful experiences of HPE and ChowNow that we profiled in chapter 7.

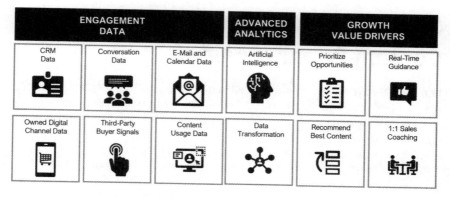

FIGURE 11.5   Real-Time Data-Driven Selling

The key element of this Smart Action includes a sales engagement solution capable of aggregating engagement data from many sources, including recorded conversations, CRM, sales enablement, and marketing signals. That solution must record sales conversations and compare them to selling outcomes and best practices. It does so by integrating with CRM, training, and enablement systems to create a real-time, closed-loop information flow. This eliminates latency throughout the selling process.

The steps you might take to achieve this outcome might follow this progression:

- Find practical ways to get control of the four core sources of customer engagement and seller activity data that already exists: content, email, calendar, and conversational commerce systems. Look to fully leveraging your first-party data that resides within CRM, marketing automation, and digital marketing platforms for business decision making.

- Inventory and map out the different sales enablement, conversational intelligence, and sales readiness solutions and capabilities you already have. Visualize what it will take to support data-driven guided selling and prescriptive insights in real time.

- Pilot real-time seller guidance and coaching where you can. But don't let a quest for perfection get in the way of progress.

- Establish more data-driven measurements, priorities, and pipeline reviews based on actual facts about customer engagement. These will help you to prioritize follow-up on opportunities based on data about probability, potential, engagement, and response.

Streamline and Personalize the Selling Content Supply Chain

Our sixth Smart Action uses advanced analytics and selling solutions to evolve from content management to Intelligent Response Management. This streamlines processes, generating and delivering highly contextual selling content to customers at scale.

Intelligent Response Management is an advanced concept that uses AI and ML to create a knowledge base of content built on actual question-and-answer exchanges between customers and sales reps. The software makes this aggregate knowledge available to entire revenue teams, on demand, with no wait times. A simple query provides the answer your salesperson needs to deliver their best answer, with immediate results – whether a rep is writing a text, email, proposal, presentation, or an RFP.

This notion goes beyond the prevailing content management practices of writing content to spec, creating top-down information hierarchies to organize it, and establishing a single source of truth as the control point of all content. It helps sellers meet buyer expectations for faster, more complete and relevant content as they engage with frontline sales, marketing, and service employees across direct, virtual, and digital touchpoints. Plus it's a lot faster and simpler than having sales reps use many different digital asset management, content management, CPQ (Configure, Price, Quote), and sales enablement systems to find, tailor, and deliver the content they need in live selling situations.

Intelligent Response Management is fundamental to Revenue Operations as it turns expensive selling assets – selling content, customer data, and engagement technologies – into customer conversations and selling outcomes that grow revenues, profits, and enterprise value. This effectively blurs the lines between many traditional software categories such as digital asset management, content management, configure, CPQ, and training and development.

- This is *actionable* because most of the solutions needed to generate selling content already exist—they just need to be connected. The best approach here is to treat the content supply chain like a cross-functional process. That process stems from customer questions and will yield big improvements in performance, throughput, and clarity for future content investments.
- It is *connected* because it makes important selling content available to the sales engagement, enablement, and readiness platform that can deliver to sellers in time to meet buyer expectations for faster, more complete, and relevant material as they engage with frontline sales, marketing, and service employees across direct, virtual, and digital touchpoints.

- It is *accretive* because it dramatically increases utilization of your selling content assets and eliminates waste, redundancy, and underperforming content assets. The dollars add up quickly along this process, such that owned digital selling channels and related content represent a large, growing percentage of your total operating and capital budget. For marketing, 80% of organizations are increasing their investment in content to feed critical selling systems like recommendation engines, sales enablement, and automated chatbots.

- It is *scalable* because it leverages content in more channels and customer interactions and provides an intelligent basis for creating and planning new, more effective content. The more content creation and curation is dictated by direct customer Q&A sequences, the more efficient and effective your content operations will be.

Figure 11.6 represents requirements to keep in mind as you move from content management to intelligent response management using the best practices and client examples we profiled in chapter 8.

There are a wide variety of elements that factor into Intelligent Response Management. They include many of the assets and capabilities that span the cross-functional content supply chain from creation to customer. These include the solutions that generate and store content such as proposal, digital asset management, and competitive intelligence systems, as well as the people (subject matter experts), external agencies, and contractors who create content.

A hub glues this all together and centralizes the management of all content – from organization (taxonomy) to quality control. Central to this hub is having an AI-enabled recommender engine (e.g. RFPIO) to make

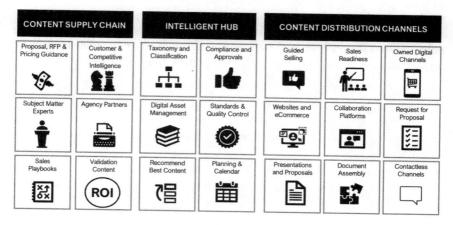

FIGURE 11.6 Intelligent Response Management

intelligent recommendations of the best content, conversation, and actions that will advance the sale in a given situation.

This contextual and compliant content should be available to reps and delivered to the customer through any system that reps use to engage with the customer. Internally this would consist of CPQ systems, sales enablement systems, and sales training and readiness systems – but also email, chat, and direct-to-the-customer channels such as chatbots or ecommerce websites that answer questions and suggest content.

Ultimately, in a mature system, end-to-end response management is enabled across the enterprise, delivering contextually correct and up-to-date content through a mix of touch points and channels.

The steps you would take to achieve this outcome might follow this progression:

- First, establish operational ownership, organization, and deployment of selling content and IP across functions.
- Then, organize all cross-functional readiness, validation, playbook, through-leadership, and product content using a common architecture and taxonomy.
- Create a single source of truth for content based on a common taxonomy and architecture to support enablement, readiness, and response management.
- Make content available to support selling action recommendations and plays through a wider variety of enablement, readiness, and revenue enhancement systems.

There are many other Smart Actions you can take to generate more sustainable and scalable growth with your existing commercial resources. The executives we interviewed were taking a wide variety of steps to build out Revenue Operating Systems. We will make these recipes for success available on the website associated with this book over time.

In the next two chapters we will give you examples and financial tools to help you zero in on which of these Smart Actions are the most relevant to your unique business, based on the biggest challenges your organization faces.

CHAPTER 12

Tailor Revenue Operations to Work for Your Business, Big or Small

How Revenue Operations Can Grow Revenues, Profits, and Value in *Your* Business

Any business can unlock more growth and value from their existing revenue teams and growth assets by building the Revenue Operations commercial model outlined in this book.

That said, every business has a unique history, circumstances, and situation offering opportunities and challenges for growth. Revenue Operations can and has accelerated revenue, profit, and value for businesses of all sizes – highlighting lessons and nuances that you can use in your particular business. For example:

- Executives leading **large, complex enterprises** can become more nimble and agile by breaking down functional silos; leveraging prescriptive insights to improve the speed, engagement, and productivity of their selling teams; and demanding higher returns on their data, technology, and content assets.

- CEOs in **slow-growth industries** can generate higher valuations by focusing their revenue teams around a more precise assessment of high-opportunity clients; by creating a culture of continuous improvement in the commercial process; and by eliminating price, margin, and revenue leakage along their customer journeys.
- Organizations undergoing **business model transformation** can accelerate the shift to a more predictable and profitable recurring revenue model by aligning sales, marketing, and customer teams around a common purpose of generating customer lifetime value and a superior customer experience.
- **Hyper-growth cloud companies** can create exponential growth with high levels of net recurring revenues by unifying their operations, revenue teams, and assets around a single customer journey and enabling ABM, one-to-one personalization, guidance, and coaching at scale in real time.

You need to understand where and how you should be transforming your commercial operations to generate the greatest impact (and buy-in!) with the least amount of time and effort. To help you zero in on the actions most relevant to your business, we developed a few common commercial archetypes – four for large enterprises, four for smaller companies – that describe typical growth challenges facing firms in the current marketplace today.

Transforming the Large Enterprise

Large and complex enterprises face significant challenges as they try to accelerate growth at scale and adapt quickly to changes in market demand, new product innovations, and competitive actions.

Complex enterprises with revenues of $500 million or more struggle to grow and adapt to market demand because they are stifled by functional silos. These silos lead to fragmented management of revenue teams, the cross-functional customer journey, and the operations that support marketing, sales, and service. Fragmentation overly complicates the growth technology portfolio and disconnects customer data sets. Points of failure emerge where revenue and margins are lost along the customer journey.

Slow-growing enterprises with limited ability to sustain growth or capture new markets suffer from lower-than-average growth and valuations relative to their industry peers. The average enterprise listed on the S&P 500 grows at 3.9% and has a value of 18 times earnings before interest, taxes, and depreciation (EBITDA).[53] Even large and slow-growing organizations in mature markets can generate more profitable growth by tightly managing their commercial processes. They can also intelligently allocate their growth resources to the activities, accounts, and opportunities with the greatest potential. "Margin maximizers" generate more profit at lower cost to sell by demanding that every growth asset and resource demonstrate a financially valid return, and by tuning their commercial architectures to generate the most profitable sales from limited resources.

CEOs who seek to grow at scale are increasingly unifying the operations that support sales, marketing, and customer support to generate more scalable growth from their revenue teams. To do this, the CEOs of agile enterprises are putting in place growth leaders with a broad span of control over all revenue teams, a mandate to better leverage technology as a force multiplier, and a mission to make the selling system more data driven, digital, and accountable.

Investors and boards are putting pressure on the CEO to generate more predictable, profitable growth in every business. Often, they are asking them to transition their offerings to a recurring revenue model by introducing cloud solutions, SaaS offerings, or subscription services. Business model transformation programs like this require strong leadership from the top to create incentives and structures that align sales, product, marketing, and service delivery teams. Businesses that successfully transform into cloud businesses or other recurring revenue streams are rewarded with earnings multiples in excess of 45 times EBITDA.[54]

Actions Enterprise Leaders Should Be Prioritizing

Every enterprise has its unique set of challenges. The executives running large, complex enterprises have been prioritizing different aspects of the management systems and operating systems based on their circumstances. Here are some of the actions they have been taking based on four different enterprise archetypes (please see Figure 12.1).

Complex Enterprises

Complex enterprises are large matrixed organizations that can struggle to grow because of their size and structure. Functional silos, fragmented management of selling resources, overly complicated technology portfolios, and disconnected customer data sets can stifle adaptation to changing market realities. Complex enterprises must focus and align their revenue teams and

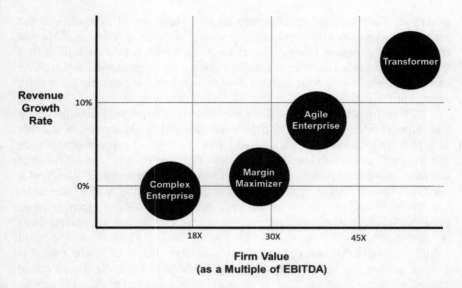

FIGURE 12.1   The Relative Performance and Valuation of Different Commercial Model Archetypes (Enterprises) *Source: Blue Ridge Partners, Pitchbook, Blossom Street Ventures, Dow Jones, Refinitive 2021, Inc 500, NASDAQ*

resources on the highest opportunity accounts and find ways to leverage technology as a force multiplier. The leaders of these businesses prioritize specific aspects of the Revenue Operations model:

- From a commercial architecture perspective, they redesign their market segmentation, account priorities, and coverage model to realize more market opportunity and focus resources on customer value.

- Their analytics teams must make better use of predictive insights to significantly focus account priorities based on potential, propensity to buy, signals of intent, and coverage difficulty.

- Their operations teams evaluate the effectiveness and returns on their technology, data, channel infrastructure assets. To accomplish this, they assess their entire commercial technology portfolio to identify ways to save money by rationalizing the technology and eliminating waste, redundancy, or nonperforming assets. In parallel they ask those teams to better connect the dots across their revenue enablement technology portfolio by simplifying the selling workflow. They also try to streamline the way selling content is created, managed, personalized, and distributed to sellers and customers through all their channels.

Margin Maximizers

Margin maximizers are large but slower-growing enterprises that create value by maximizing margin and price while simultaneously controlling cost to sell. These organizations focus on optimizing the allocation of their growth resources and focusing their sellers on products and activities that generate the most profit contribution. They also invest in revenue enhancement systems that help their revenue teams sell value and migrate selling interactions to digital and virtual channels. These businesses must maximize earnings growth to justify purchase price valuations by PE investors that have grown to exceed 13 times EBITDA. The leaders of margin maximizing businesses are concentrating on these actions and priorities:

- From a leadership perspective, they demand better accountability for financial returns from every commercial investment and asset. To do this, they define financially valid criteria to prioritize, size, allocate, and measure the performance of every team, budget, operation, and enablement asset in the selling system.

- From an operations standpoint, leaders are exerting more control over cross-functional revenue cycle. To do this, they establish a single point of management across the entire revenue cycle from prospect awareness to customer expansion. The goal is to have a single person focused on eliminating the handoffs and "air gaps" in the prospect-to-cash cycle and on stopping revenue and margin leakage.

- Their sales enablement teams invest in revenue enhancement systems that help sellers capture more price and value. To do this, they invest in CQP and fulfillment tools to reduce revenue, price, and margin leakage in the lead-to-cash cycle.

Agile Enterprises

Agile enterprises are large organizations trying to pivot from their core markets to realize market opportunity in new, rapidly growing segments. These organizations invest in product innovations and shift their focus to maximizing the long-term customer relationship. This occurs by cross-selling the full breadth of their expanded product portfolio. Taking this approach places a premium on cross-selling, key account management, and aligning revenue teams on the highest potential accounts. These businesses maximize firm value by using team-based selling approaches to grow total contract value and customer lifetime value. They also pivot their go-to-market strategy to expand addressable markets and drive high levels of growth at scale. Executives leading agile enterprises build out these aspects of their system of growth:

- They adopt real-time data-driven selling. They have tasked their sales enablement and operations team to pilot and enable real-time prescriptive sales guidance and individualized coaching to all customer-facing marketing, sales, and service teams. This helps frontline sellers learn about new products faster and allows managers and specialists to coach them when new cross-sell opportunities emerge in real-time conversations.

- Executives here put in place leadership models that better align revenue teams around the customer with a broad transformation remit and authority. Some organizations like Cisco have adopted the "Tsar" approach by putting a CXO in charge of marketing, sales, and service. Others, like Juniper Networks, have taken a more federated approach to aligning sales and marketing.

- They reengineer the roles on their selling teams to elevate development roles (e.g. Sales Development Reps, Business Development Reps) that better pursue new markets and key account management teams that develop and cross-sell into different buying units in named accounts.

- They link and coordinate their commercial operations to better leverage customer insights and scalable technologies across the enterprise. To do this they create better integration across marketing operations, sales operations, sales enablement, and training and development with the goal of better supporting sellers across the revenue cycle.

- From a technology enablement perspective, they ask their marketing operations and sales enablement teams to collaboratively connect their digital marketing infrastructure with their CRM and sales technology systems in support of Account-Based Marketing. To do this, they connect digital marketing signals, digital marketing programs (e.g. advertising, web assets), and CRM to execute ABM programs. This helps sellers identify key stakeholders to target in accounts, optimize account coverage, and maximize the return on sales and marketing technology.

Transformers

Transformers are businesses transitioning a significant portion of their revenues to a recurring revenue model. Their shift from selling individual hardware, software, and service transactions to recurring revenue streams occurs by repackaging their software or services offerings "as a service" or bundling them into a subscription pricing model. Net recurring revenues, the customer experience, and customer lifetime value become focal points for the revenue team. The average mature SaaS business grows at 19%, which supports double-digit earnings multiples and stable cash flow while covering large, fixed costs.[54] In order to address these unique challenges, the leaders of transformers prioritize these actions:

- From a commercial operations perspective, they are redefining their measurements and incentives. These management systems changes refocus marketing, sales, and service teams on customer lifetime value, retention, and annual recurring revenue as the primary goal.

- From a commercial architecture perspective, they are reengineering selling roles to better focus the revenue team. The goals become customer lifetime value growth, incentives for selling long-term deals, and total contract value growth. As part of this transition, the customer success manager role gets introduced or increases.

- From a commercial insights standpoint, they are developing fact-based measures of opportunity potential, seller performance, and account and pipeline health based on customer engagement and seller activity data.

- Commercial operations teams are also taking steps to shrink the lead-to-cash cycle to improve cash flow. They do this by streamlining the selling workflow and accelerating the sales cycle with enablement, engagement, and readiness solutions. The transition from a transaction to a subscription model delays revenue receipt by spreading it out over time, and this puts serious pressure on cash flow at the inflection point until the annuity streams build up.

- From an insight's perspective, new revenue intelligence dashboards give better visibility into the entire revenue cycle. By aggregating, analyzing, and transforming their customer data into revenue life cycle insights, you can create fact-based measures of account health and customer lifetime value. This helps focus on growing the volume and value of customer accounts.

Achieving Hyper-Growth for Small Companies

Hyper-growth cloud businesses face a different set of challenges as they seek to achieve the growth and recurring revenues required to achieve the valuations their investors expect upon exit. An analysis by Blossom Street Ventures of 49 recent SaaS business IPOs found the businesses were growing at over 50% year-on-year with net recurring revenue ratios over 100%. Investors rewarded these firms' valuations of over 15 times revenue.[53]

Many businesses with SaaS offerings and innovations take on growth capital to fund organic growth but fail to achieve the level of scalable and sustainable growth required to penetrate the large addressable markets they target and to justify the valuation their investors made.

Armed with tremendous investment and growth capital, many organizations pursue a "growth at all costs" strategy. They spend a significant portion of their budget on building revenue teams and go-to-market programs to drive double-digit growth. Without disciplined leadership and a focus on finding ways to create consistent and scalable growth, these businesses can become "gas guzzlers" that fail to generate growth commensurate with the dollars invested or their fair share of the market because they lag the competition.

Other firms achieve high levels of customer acquisition but at the expense of customer experience and user adoption. These organizations risk becoming leaky buckets that lose customers at the back end of the customer journey through churn, lack of user adoption, or low levels of perceived value. These organizations cannot sustain the net recurring revenue ratios required to justify the high valuations their investors and employees are counting on.

The following outlines typical commercial model archetypes for a hypergrowth business, and the key aspects of the Revenue Operations model they need to focus on to take their growth to the next level.

Actions Hyper-Growth Leaders Should Be Prioritizing

Small businesses face their own unique set of growth challenges. Here are some of the actions that leaders of small, hyper-growth businesses are taking to build their system of growth. They are broken into four different fast-growing business archetypes (please see Figure 12.2).

Failure to Launch

Failure at launch describes businesses with high-growth expectations and funding that are unable to generate the high levels of organic growth their investors want to see. These businesses struggle to find the sweet spot in the market, sell their unique value to customers, and win consistently. These organizations are under pressure to achieve greater market share to justify the valuations and growth capital their owners have invested. They try to stem the losses incurred because of inconsistency and failure to leverage scalable

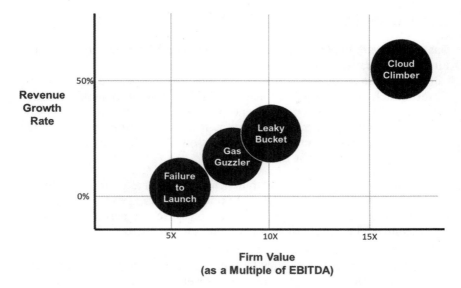

FIGURE 12.2   The Relative Performance and Valuation of Different Commercial Model Archetypes (Hyper-Growth Cloud Businesses) *Source: Blue Ridge Partners, Pitchbook, Blossom Street Ventures, Dow Jones, Refinitive 2021, Inc 500, NASDAQ*

technologies in their commercial models. The leaders of these types of businesses focus on these actions:

- They actively reengineer their commercial architecture to better align selling resources with actionable market opportunity to ignite growth. They do this by refocusing their teams on the territories, accounts, and market segments where they can effectively realize more market opportunity and win more consistently. They also refine the way they cover their target markets, engage with customers, and refocus sellers on the activities that convert business.

- They ask their analytics teams to find ways to "shrink the bullseye" with customer targeting insight by focusing their revenue teams on the highest potential accounts and eliminating "long tail" customers who are not likely to buy. To do this, they are finding ways to use advanced analytics and predictive insights to significantly focus account priorities based on potential, propensity to buy, and coverage difficulty.

- From a commercial support perspective, they ask their operations teams to link together the CRM, sales enablement, sales readiness, and digital asset management solutions in their revenue technology portfolio to eliminate the key points of failure, friction, and manual labor in the day-to-day seller workflow. These systems are largely managed in different functional silos in most business-to-business organizations.

Gas Guzzlers

Gas guzzlers are hyper-growth businesses on a growth trajectory to an IPO. Firms in this category are usually investing a significant percentage of their capital into generating hyper-growth, customer preference, and market share. Unfortunately, they struggle to achieve scalable and sustainable revenues. Gas guzzler revenues do not grow enough to justify rising selling costs, and inconsistent seller performance targets unfocused territories, accounts, and very low returns on commercial selling assets. These businesses focus on connecting the dots in these areas:

- A greater focus on accountability: leaders here ask for much higher degrees of accountability. They do this by defining financially valid criteria to prioritize, size, allocate, and measure the performance of all commercial teams, budgets, operations, and enablement assets.
- Operational ownership of the entire revenue cycle: map the cross-functional customer journey to eliminate the handoffs in the prospect-to-cash cycle and "air gaps" that drive revenue and margin leakage. They seek a single point of management of the customer journey across the enterprise.
- They push their commercial operations to better connect their sales enablement, CRM, conversational intelligence, and digital marketing systems. This makes selling channels more effective. To do this, they use advanced analytics and sales AI tools to help them turn customer engagement and seller activity data into commercial insights. These insights provide guidance and coaching to reps about the right response, content, action, or sales play to use in the "moments that matter" in the customer journey.

Leaky Buckets

Leaky buckets need to look at the combination of annualized recurring revenue plus account expansion revenues, minus revenue lost due to downgrades, cancellations, and churn. SaaS businesses that can acquire new customers at double-digit rates may be unable to sustain net recurring revenue ratios of over 100%. If your net recurring revenues fall below 100%, investors worry that you will lose too many customer relationships without sufficient offset of any revenue gains coming in.

Leakage tends to happen when revenue teams focus too much on acquiring new accounts or lack alignment on the customer experience. When teams lack alignment, significant revenue, opportunity, and margin are lost due to lack of personal accountability. To plug the holes, the executives running leaky bucket businesses emphasize these elements:

- From an operations perspective, they establish a common purpose across their marketing, sales, and service teams to get them working together toward more profitable growth. To do this, they redefine incentives to focus revenue teams on customer lifetime value, retention, and account health.

- They set up a leadership model that better aligns commercial teams around the customer. Due to limited scale and scope these organizations tend to favor a CXO leadership model. The Chief Revenue Officer role is especially popular in hyper-growth businesses.

- From a commercial insights perspective, they ask their analytics teams to give them better visibility into account health and selling activity across the entire revenue cycle. They use this data to measure and manage all the key factors leading to customer churn – satisfaction, loyalty, onboarding, success, and retention. As part of this initiative, they create metrics and fact-based incentives to get frontline sellers working with success teams on longer-term recurring revenues.

Cloud Climbers

"Cloud Climbers" are fast growing cloud-first businesses that see double-digit revenue growth rates by focusing on speed to market, optimizing the customer experience, and scaling selling technologies and channels. The average SaaS business IPO grew at over 50% with net recurring revenue ratios over 100% and firm valuation of over 15 times revenue.[53] To maintain this pace and meet extremely high investor expectations, they add sellers to expand their revenue teams at a rapid clip. Public investors put pressure on Cloud Climbers to provide visibility on future growth, especially annual recurring revenues and total contract value. The leaders of these businesses prioritize specific elements of their growth system.

- They unify their commercial operations to leverage customer insights and scalable technologies across the enterprise. To do this, they take advantage of engagement data from recorded conversations, content consumption by clients, CRM, and exchange data from email and calendars. They also pilot real-time guidance and coaching at scale with their frontline sellers. Using advanced analytics and sales AI tools, most cloud climbers can get an "80% good-enough" picture of buyer engagement and seller activity to provide real-time guidance and coaching to reps about the right response, content, action, or sales play to use in the "moments that matter" in the customer journey.

- From a commercial architecture perspective, they reconfigure roles on the revenue teams and segmentation of their markets. They see this as a way to capture a greater share of their large addressable market and keep their teams focused on sustaining net recurring revenues and growing customer lifetime value.

- From a commercial enablement perspective, they are asking sales enablement, operations, and training and development teams to knit together their sales enablement, training, learning, and development solutions. They aim to shrink the development and ramp-up time for new sellers to add capacity and combat attrition, which is higher in technology sectors. They are creating a closed-loop system for sales rep education, readiness, reinforcement, and measurement.

In the next chapter we will teach you financial tools to help prioritize the most profitable actions your organization can take to generate more sustainable and scalable growth. These tools will help you get the funding, consensus, and leadership support you need to take the required steps to improve.

CHAPTER 13

Make the Business Case for Your Growth System, from Activity to Impact

Prioritize Actions That Will Generate Short- and Long-Term Value

The Smart Actions outlined in chapter 11 create short- and long-term value. They generate short-term financial gains by reducing leakage, improving sales performance, and eliminating waste, while also stacking to generate higher, longer-term returns on your technology, data, and selling infrastructure assets. Smart Actions also create longer-term value by building out an operating system for scalable and sustainable growth at lower cost. These activities are strategic growth investments that change customer behavior in ways that generate future revenues, cash flow, pricing power, and profits.

The challenge comes in proving impact to justify funding and investment. You must overcome a few common obstacles, if you want to build a financial case for taking Smart Actions to connect the dots across your growth technology ecosystem.

First, remember that Smart Actions span functions. Finding a single established budget and owner for cross-functional initiatives is a challenge. Teamwork, sharing, and coordination must exist to gain funding, or the initiative will fall back into organizational, technology, and data silos. Often it's easier to purchase senseless or illogical solutions that fit within an existing budget than to acquire a smart, cost-effective solution that spans many budgets.

Second, conventional measures of sales and marketing effectiveness, such as revenue attribution and sales waterfall metrics, have fundamental flaws and fail to clearly describe how a business grows. They may help optimize media, campaigns, and tactics but do little to justify strategic capital investments. Such measures have reputations as "black boxes" where the connections between activities are poorly understood. Too many gaps still exist along the chain of custody between activity and financial impact.

Take, for example, the classic demand funnel. Sales enablement professionals often rely on linear sales waterfall models with flawed assumptions about how customers buy and how a modern operating system operates. The notion of a lead being generated by marketing and then transferred to a seller contradicts the required alignment of revenue teams around the customer and sabotages a seamless customer experience.

More fundamentally, these measurement models tend to ignore key drivers of value growth in a business. These drivers include things like building customer equity, improving channel effectiveness, and sharing information on financial performance and firm value across the revenue team, according to Professor Dominique Hanssens, Distinguished Research Professor of Marketing at the UCLA Anderson School of Business whose research focuses on short-and long-run impact of marketing on business performance. For example, while building customer equity, improving digital channel effectiveness, and sharing information across revenue teams have all been proven to be causal of firm value, according to academic research, few business leaders really understand how.

Third, Smart Actions involve a mix of operating expenses and capital expenditures. This makes funding difficult because few managers and finance executives have a good understanding of the financial relationship between growth CapEx, firm value, and financial performance. The growing role of data, analytics, CRM, content, sales enablement, and digital marketing channels within the Revenue Operations model puts more pressure on something managers already struggle with: balancing long-term strategic investments with short-term performance tactics. A modern selling system needs funding for a multiyear technology and digital channel road map to support scalable and sustainable growth. Unfortunately, funding review processes favor short-term initiatives and programs that pay off quickly. You will need a very credible financial rationale for the changes you intend to make.

For example, look at the visibility Smart Action outlined in chapter 11. Quantitative analysis of the performance of 300 marketing organizations by Forbes and the Marketing Accountability Standards Board found that organizations investing in data-driven measurement processes, competencies, and systems were achieving significantly higher levels of marketing effectiveness and business outcomes.[15] The research demonstrated that marketers who pursue higher levels of accountability are achieving 5% greater returns on marketing investments and 7.5% better growth outcomes from those investments. The analysis also revealed that these high-performing marketers – who were exceeding growth goals by over 25% – had a significantly more data-driven approach to measuring, optimizing, and reallocating their offline and online marketing investments.

Sharing marketing insights with frontline sellers, another Smart Action we reviewed, creates value by improving organizational competence for sharing data and knowledge. Academic and industry research have made it overwhelmingly clear that growth is a "team sport" and that there is a causal relationship between organizational competence in analytics, marketing, information sharing, agility, and cross-functional collaboration with enterprise value.

Research by Professors Alexander Edeling and Marc Fischer of the University of Cologne shows that a 10% increase in organizational competence will drive on average a 5.5% increase in stock price.[8] A separate analysis of 114 academic research studies by the Marketing Science Institute (MSI) found that the generation of, dissemination of, and responsiveness to marketing intelligence across the company are highly correlated with increases in enterprise value – as measured by profits, sales, and market share.[6] The MSI research also found that the ability of an organization to generate, disseminate, and respond to market intelligence has a positive effect on organizational performance in terms of profits, sales, and market share. The same study found that increased interdepartmental connectedness (defined as the degree of formal and informal contact among employees across departments) enhanced firm performance.

The same economics can be applied to every Smart Action we discuss in this book. Developing and retaining high-performing selling talent creates value by improving employee talent, leadership, and engagement. Ramping employees to full performance faster and keeping them around longer while they're productive has a huge impact on costs, sales, and margins. Making selling channels more effective creates firm value by improving channel reach, share, and performance. It also enhances seller performance, leading to higher prices, better relationship equity, and larger deal sizes. Simplifying the selling workflow creates firm value by improving sales and service effectiveness.

Finally, managers often try to run with overly ambitious and sketchy analysis before they can crawl when it comes to measuring performance. In their zeal to be data driven and fact based, many take on too much. It is too common for analysts to create dashboards full of metrics when most leadership teams cannot even agree on the basic arithmetic of how their business grows. Others will invest in highly sophisticated, proprietary, and laser-focused models of marketing performance when their peers in the C-suite don't understand or even agree on points like how much effort or what level of customer experience will be necessary to acquire new customers.

A Financially Valid Framework for Connecting Smart Actions to Firm Value: The Revenue Value Chain

How can you overcome these obstacles and connect activity and impact? Start with the fundamentals and determine how your business grows. Then build models that can evolve from conceptual frameworks into gradually more sophisticated analyses. Soon you will be predicting and prescribing how to grow faster and more profitably.

The Revenue Value Chain (RVC) is a framework to align leadership around a common view of how your business actually grows (see Figure 13.1). The RVC also helps visualize how a Smart Action can credibly demonstrate its impact on firm value.

The Revenue Value Chain is a simple four-step framework that connects growth activities and investments to firm value and financial performance. It accurately and completely describes the causal chain of actions that must happen for growth investments to generate value.

Most organizations struggle to articulate how programs and activities like Smart Actions lead to financial results. No action, whether it is a campaign or the deployment of a software platform, will create firm value on its own. An action can only create value if it changes behavior. It must make customers respond more, choose more, pay more, refer more, buy faster, or stay longer. Using the Revenue Value Chain, these changes to customer behavior can be mapped to business outcomes – and the business outcomes in turn can be mapped to company financial performance.

The RVC model will help your team better understand the "math of growth." It will support your team in establishing its own common economic purpose for growth investment in your business. This will provide you a financially sound basis for developing business cases, budgets, and fact-based measurements. It also lets you articulate a more scientific formula for growth. By documenting assumptions clearly using this framework, you can conduct tests and ongoing research to continuously improve the financial contribution of your growth investments.

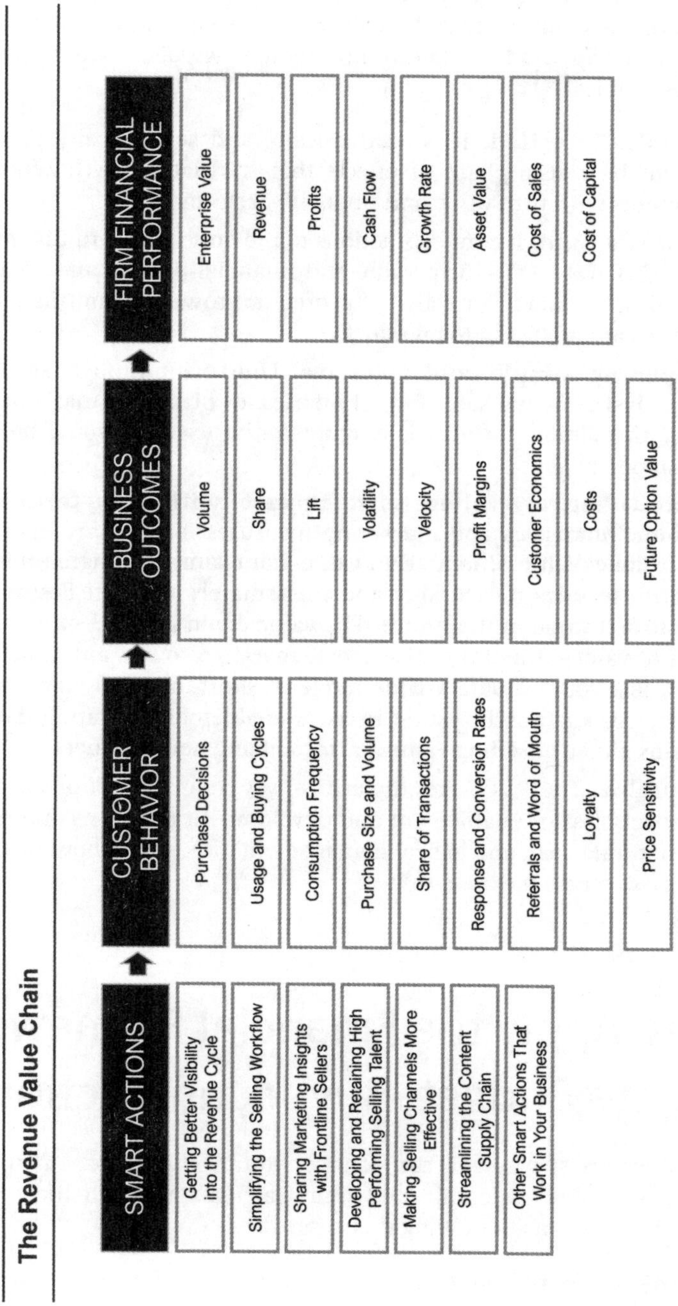

The Revenue Value Chain

SMART ACTIONS	CUSTOMER BEHAVIOR	BUSINESS OUTCOMES	FIRM FINANCIAL PERFORMANCE
Getting Better Visibility into the Revenue Cycle	Purchase Decisions	Volume	Enterprise Value
Simplifying the Selling Workflow	Usage and Buying Cycles	Share	Revenue
Sharing Marketing Insights with Frontline Sellers	Consumption Frequency	Lift	Profits
Developing and Retaining High Performing Selling Talent	Purchase Size and Volume	Volatility	Cash Flow
Making Selling Channels More Effective	Share of Transactions	Velocity	Growth Rate
Streamlining the Content Supply Chain	Response and Conversion Rates	Profit Margins	Asset Value
Other Smart Actions That Work in Your Business	Referrals and Word of Mouth	Customer Economics	Cost of Sales
	Loyalty	Costs	Cost of Capital
	Price Sensitivity	Future Option Value	

FIGURE 13.1 The Revenue Value Chain

This approach has many of the advantages for calculating the return on growth actions and investment. Unlike flawed revenue attribution models, sales funnel metrics, and marketing mix models we discussed earlier, this simple approach is:

1. **Academically vetted.** It is academically and scientifically proven to establish the causal chain of effects that translate growth action and investments with firm value and financial performance.

2. **Financially valid.** It connects actions to the only scorecard that matters to the CEO and CFO – firm value and financial performance. The outputs of this formula tie directly to the organic growth commitments those executives are reporting to investors.

3. **Transparent, simple, and objective.** Unlike multitouch attribution models, dysfunctional sales funnel metrics, or black box marketing mix models, this simple formula is easy for senior executives and boards to understand.

4. **Balanced between short-term impact with long-term value creation.** Most sales and marketing measures bias toward short-term gains at the expense of long-term value. For example, a price promotion will increase sales measurably and immediately but will destroy your ability to sell value in the future. The value chain is based on the causal drivers of value—the things that create margin, growth, and value. Such a chain lets you evaluate a wide range of short- and long-term growth investments, such as investing in sales enablement, curating data and programs aimed at selling value, or introducing new products.

5. **Measurable.** The RVC takes the critical yet complex task of measuring the impact of sales enablement and development programs and turns it into a natural, clear, and logical management discussion about how these actions can create business value.

How to Apply the Financial Framework to Create Budget, Buy-In, and Action

Perhaps the smartest way you can connect your Smart Actions is to walk-crawl-run your sales leadership and financial team through the math of growth. You might consider taking this approach:

1. **Start by agreeing on the basic arithmetic of growth for your business.** Get all the senior stakeholders in a room and use the RVC as

the basis for uncovering and highlighting basic facts, beliefs, and assumptions about how growth actions and investments contribute to revenues, profits, and firm value. The team must agree on the growth equation for your business. By that, we mean the causal chain of effects that explains how a Smart Action creates changes in customer behavior, how customer behaviors create business outcomes, and, finally, how those business outcomes generate improved financial performance.

This will help your leadership to collectively agree on a basic equation that describes how your business grows. It will also help resolve basic disconnects between sales, marketing, and service teams who are doing the selling, and the CEO and CFO who are evaluating growth investments. These disconnects include such questions as: *How is this technology helping us sell better? Is our sales methodology helping us sell value? Will this account-based selling program pay off? Is our training helping us improve margins?* Ultimately, the value chain approach will help you create a common vocabulary for your financial executives and leaders, one that can be used to effectively communicate the value of building your selling system.

2. **Then document the core assumptions behind your proposed action.** Once your team can agree on the basic math of growth for your business, it's important to document collective assumptions about the interactions between marketing activities, customer behavior, and financial outcomes. Documenting and agreeing on the core assumptions about growth (i.e. elasticities, hypothesis, beliefs) makes it much easier to develop financially valid KPIs, credible business cases, and scenario planning tools to direct investments, budgets, and resource allocation.

   Documenting core assumptions fosters better collaboration as the different functions work from a common set of measures and incentives that they trust and accept. On a human level, it is much better to argue about assumptions than about a program idea. People can hate a certain software package, but they cannot argue with demonstrable sales lift, margin growth, price premiums, and transaction volume. Don't worry if you cannot document or prove all your assumptions. Nobody can. Every business investment carries risk. Instead, make sure your assumptions are clear, complete, and transparent and, if you do your homework, it's a safe bet that nobody else will have any better evidence than you do. It is shocking how many budgets and investments are made based on undocumented assumptions, faulty math, or institutional belief systems that go unchallenged. Even if your assumptions are challenged and a better idea is put forth, the business benefits because now you have two profitable actions to pursue, not one.

3. **Use those assumptions to create a business case that connects Smart Actions to firm financial performance.** Once your team can

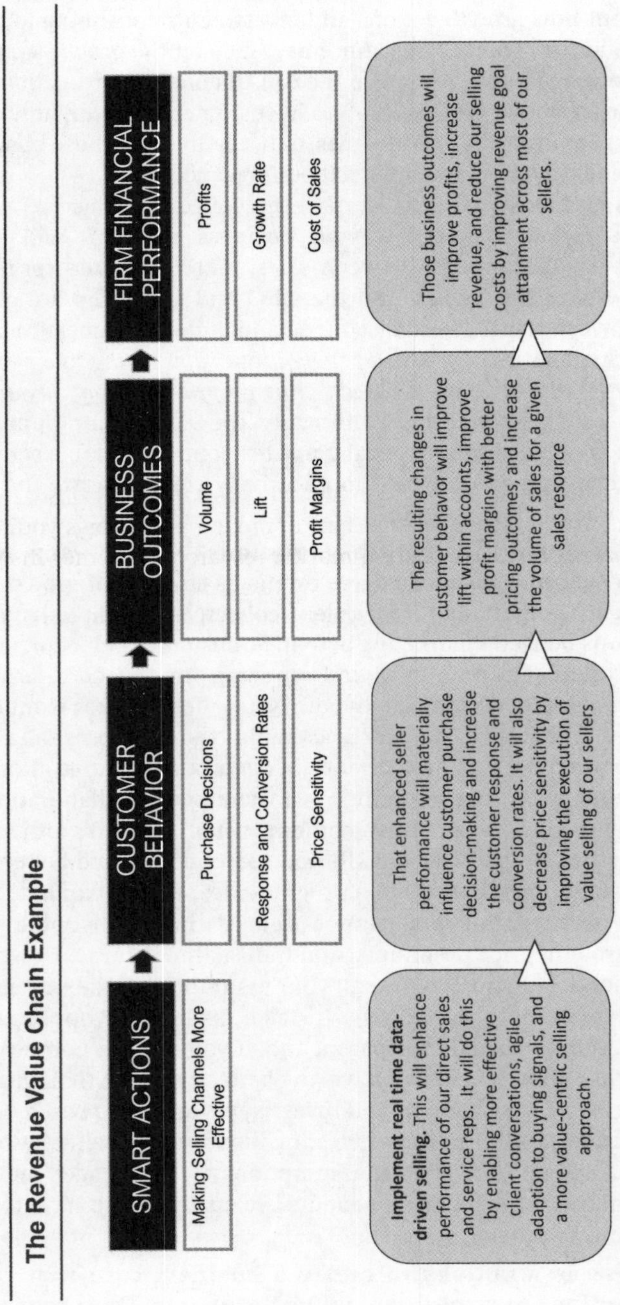

The Revenue Value Chain Example

SMART ACTIONS	CUSTOMER BEHAVIOR	BUSINESS OUTCOMES	FIRM FINANCIAL PERFORMANCE
Making Selling Channels More Effective	Purchase Decisions	Volume	Profits
	Response and Conversion Rates	Lift	Growth Rate
	Price Sensitivity	Profit Margins	Cost of Sales

Implement real time data-driven selling. This will enhance performance of our direct sales and service reps. It will do this by enabling more effective client conversations, agile adaption to buying signals, and a more value-centric selling approach.

That enhanced seller performance will materially influence customer purchase decision-making and increase the customer response and conversion rates. It will also decrease price sensitivity by improving the execution of value selling of our sellers

The resulting changes in customer behavior will improve lift within accounts, improve profit margins with better pricing outcomes, and increase the volume of sales for a given sales resource

Those business outcomes will improve profits, increase revenue, and reduce our selling costs by improving revenue goal attainment across most of our sellers.

FIGURE 13.2 The Revenue Value Chain (Example)

agree on the basic math of growth for your business, it's important to document collective assumptions about the interactions between marketing activities, customer behavior, and financial outcomes. Documenting and agreeing on the core assumptions about growth (elasticities, hypothesis, beliefs) makes it much easier to develop financially valid KPIs, credible business cases, and scenario planning tools to direct investments, budgets, and resource allocation. This also fosters better collaboration as the multifunctional works from a common set of measures and incentives that they trust and accept. Here is an example of how you might create a business case for making your selling channels more effective by implementing the real-time data-driven selling system outlined in chapter 10. (See Figure 13.2.)

4. **Use your research, customer insights, and program tests to validate, refine, and model your growth equation.** Documenting and quantifying growth assumptions provides scientific discipline to help the analytics team to first describe how growth happens, then predict how growth will happen, and ultimately prescribe how growth can happen faster and more profitably. This approach also allows your analytics team to better leverage existing market research, customer insights, and program tests to validate critical growth assumptions to the degree that they can. If more confidence and predictability are required, the analytics team can be much more surgical and precise as they design further research, in-market tests, and models to build marketing performance measurement and models that are increasingly accurate, predictive, and prescriptive.

CHAPTER 14

Practical Tools to Take Control of Your Revenue Cycle

O ur goal in writing this book was ambitious – to teach the next genera-tion of growth leaders a system to steadily drive growth in the twenty-first century.

In the first part of this book we defined Revenue Operations and its impact. In the next, we articulated the six key pillars that make up the management system for growth. Our goal was to help you decide which lead-ership model works best for aligning marketing, sales, and customer success in your business. We then outlined the building blocks of a Revenue Operating System. Here we provided a practical but durable framework to help you con-nect the dots across your technology, data, process, and team investments in ways that can help you grow faster at lower cost. This framework can help you prioritize the capital and operating investments you need to make to acceler-ate growth.

In this final section, we've brought it all together to get you started building your own system of growth. We introduced the concept of Smart Actions and provided you tools and examples to best implement Revenue Operations for your own company.

In chapter 11, we helped you identify a good place to get started on your journey. We outlined six Smart Actions that your organization can take to better align revenue teams, operations, systems, and processes to ignite growth. These represent the most common and financially viable steps the organizations we interviewed were taking. Individually, each action can be piloted, sequenced, and measured to create financially viable and bite-size stairsteps that move your organization through a transformation in ways that are politically, practically, and financially achievable. Collectively, the sum of these steps can yield transformational results. Consider these a place to start. Or use them for inspiration to build Smart Actions of your own.

In chapter 12, we showed you examples of how businesses of all different types are putting these Smart Actions into practice to build systems of growth that address their unique growth challenges.

In chapter 13, we taught you a financial framework that helps you connect these Smart Actions to firm value and financial performance so that you can build the consensus, budgets, and buy-in you need to act and bring your organization with you.

In this final chapter, we provide practical tools to help you and your team to visualize and prioritize the smartest steps you can take in the short, medium, and long term to grow faster and more profitably.

To do this, we have synthesized all of the lessons in this book into a one-page menu of 18 common capabilities that the best organizations are developing to build a system for scalable and consistent growth (see Figure 14.1). This menu is a complete summary of all the best practices and Smart Actions we covered in this book. It may be a good way for you to identify the practices you think will be most useful in your organization. Highlight the ones that make the most sense for your business to explore taking.

The menu expands into a maturity assessment that is structured to help you evaluate how well your current capabilities match up against the best practice in each area. Over the following pages, we have broken down each of the 16 dimensions into four levels of competency. Each level of competency is described in a way that will help you compare it with the current situation at your company. We've numbered them 1–4 to make it easy for you to grade your organization uniformly across these. Try circling the level you think corresponds to your organization.

Once you have graded your organization across the 16 dimensions, think about in which three or four areas you would want to upgrade your capability to the next level. This gives you a rigorous basis for creating a road map for improving your selling approach in ways that lead to more consistent and profitable growth. Each of these incremental steps you prioritize creates the basis for discussing measurable value, what a proof of concept pilot would involve, and whether you can get buy-in and agreement to fund it. Individually, the steps you choose to take should create value or become critical building blocks for more ambitious improvements. Over time they should add up to make a significant impact on growth, profits, and firm value. This road map represents an illustrative and commonsense blueprint for how your organization can sequence and scope the changes involved in commercial transformation.

The assessment gives you a good sense of the most financially attractive places to try to improve. With some additional thought, it is possible to identify the most financially viable ways to "stair-step" your organization toward a more scalable and consistent system of growth. Once you have graded your organization across the 16 dimensions, think about what would be the economic benefits of upgrading your capability to the next level. You can use the list of eight ways Revenue Operations creates financial value from chapter 2 as a guide. For each incremental improvement you consider, ask yourself what is the economic benefit of taking this action? If you answer yes to any of the following eight questions, you are on the right path:

1. Will it help to monetize your customer data, digital technology, and channel infrastructure assets by informing selling decisions, optimizing resource allocation, and supporting higher prices and better conversion rates?

2. Will it make it simpler, faster, or cheaper to complete selling tasks?

3. Will it differentiate the customer experience?

4. Will it enable "scalable" technologies that make it much faster and easier to personalize responses and coach sellers in real time?

5. Will it motivate the revenue team to build customer lifetime value and net recurring revenues?

6. Will it improve visibility into selling performance?

7. Will it motivate team selling?

8. Will it turn your investments in selling technology into force multipliers that help your revenue team "punch above their weight"?

Once you have zeroed in on the actions that make the most sense, you have the foundation for building the business case for taking that action and justifying the investments involved. You can use the Revenue Value Chain outlined in chapter 13 for inspiration, or build Smart Actions of your own.

The goal of Revenue Operations is to transform the commercial model. The path to getting there is a series of individual actions that incrementally improve revenues or costs or the customer experience. "Business transformation and growth do not rely on a single event but rather a series of well-thought-out operational strategies that are adopted and implemented across a company," according to Sam Errigo, the Chief Operating Officer of Konica Minolta, who has transformed the company from a hardware business in a declining market to a growing technology services business. "Revenue Operations addresses this concept by providing a practical formula for CEOs and business leaders to generate more consistent and scalable growth that can be executed one step at a time." We hope this book helps you start the process of pursuing small changes that incrementally improve selling performance today – and that those incremental gains add up to big gains in revenues and profits over time.

The Revenue Operations Maturity Assessment

A CXO Blueprint for Aligning Sales, Marketing, and Customer Success Teams and Optimizing the Performance of Commercial Processes, Operations, and Assets

DIMENSION	DEFINITION	CORE COMPETENCIES
	Top-down leadership to empower and endorse the transformation of the commercial model to unify sales, marketing, and service into one revenue team and become more accountable, data driven, and customer focused.	**1.0 Accountability.** Demand full accountability for return on enterprise selling resources, assets, and investments.
		2.0 Ownership. Establish a single point of decision-making for the enterprise revenue process, assets, investments.
		3.0 Change Management. Provide top-down leadership to empower the organization to transform the commercial model.
	Reconfigure the operations that support growth and enable salespeople to provide coherent, end-to-end management of all customer-facing employees, assets, infrastructure, investments, and the customer journey.	**4.0 Common Purpose.** Establish a common purpose across sales, marketing, and customer success teams.
		5.0 Organization. Establish cross-functional organizational structures to support salespeople across the enterprise.
		6.0 Commercial Process. Establish and manage a cross-functional commercial process across the enterprise
	Redesign the commercial architecture to maximize return on selling assets by improving the speed, visibility, productivity, engagement of frontline selling teams and reducing lower cost to sell.	**7.0 Go-to-Market Strategy.** Redesign the go-to-market architecture to improve performance and engagement.
		8.0 Sales Force Design. Adjust the sales force design to improve performance, engagements, and costs.
		9.0 Sales Performance Management. Modify assignments, territories, and incentives to align resources and opportunity.
	Turning customer engagement and seller activity data into commercial insights that create value and inform decisions, actions, and conversations at the "moments that matter" in the sales process.	**10.0 Data-Driven Selling.** Convert revenue data into prescriptive revenue intelligence that informs day-to-day decisions in real time.
		11.0 Key Performance Indicators. Establish fact-based reporting analytics, KPI, and dashboards of commercial performance.
		12.0 Predictive Selling Insights. Use analytics to create better predictions, parameters, and scenarios to inform investment, allocation, and emphasis.
	Building a common core of commercial capabilities that enable salespeople and maximize the contribution of selling assets and investments to revenue and profit growth outcomes.	**13.0 Enablement and Engagement.** Reconfigure the commercial technology infrastructure to better support revenue team enablement.
		14.0 Readiness and Development. Reconfigure the commercial technology infrastructure to better support readiness, training, and development.
		15.0 Revenue Enhancement. Deploy technologies to enhance the lead-to-cash cycle and capture more revenue, margin, and price realization.
	The strategic management of the commercial data, technology, content, and IP assets to maximize utilization, impact, and return on investment.	**16.0 Content Assets.** Establish operational ownership, organization, and deployment of selling content and IP across functions.
		17.0 Data Assets. Establish a common architecture and owner to monetize customer data assets
		18.0 Technology Assets. Establish centralized stewardship and reconfiguration of the commercial technology portfolio across functions

FIGURE 14.1 The Revenue Operations Maturity Assessment

REVENUE OPERATIONS MATURITY MODEL

COMMERCIAL LEADERSHIP

Provide top-down leadership to unify sales, marketing, and service into one revenue team and empower management to transform the commercial model to become more accountable, data driven, agile, and customer focused.

COMPETENCY	LEVEL 1: BEGIN	LEVEL 2: BASIC	LEVEL 3: ADVANCED	LEVEL 4: BEST-IN-CLASS
1.0 ACCOUNTABILITY. Demand full accountability for return on enterprise selling resources, assets, and investments.	1.1 Decide on corporate performance goals that define success for all GTM functions and cascade down to customer-facing teams.	1.2 Define financially valid criteria to prioritize, size, allocate and measure growth resources and capital investment.	1.3 Create feedback loops to evaluate outcomes, attribution, and performance across sales, marketing, and customer success	1.4 Establish full accountability for financial outcomes for all growth teams, investment, and infrastructure assets.
2.0 OWNERSHIP. Establish a single point of decision making for the enterprise revenue process, assets, and investments.	2.1 Assign an individual to evaluate Revenue Operations to identify points of failure and alignment opportunities.	2.2 Assign an executive to provide cross-functional project management and allocation decisions.	2.3 Establish a CXO executive to lead commercial transformation and coordinate all revenue team functions.	2.4 Centralize all decisions about cross-functional resource allocation, infrastructure investment, and commercial architecture.
3.0 CHANGE MANAGEMENT. Provide top-down leadership to empower the organization to transform the commercial model.	3.1 Create a culture of change by demanding continuous improvement in all commercial processes.	3.2 Establish a change management office empowered to redefine processes, measurements, and systems from the top down.	3.3 Establish common purpose with shared goals and incentives for all customer-facing employees.	3.4 Centralize all operations supporting growth under a CXO with a broad transformation remit and authority.

FIGURE 14.1   *(Continued)*

REVENUE OPERATIONS MATURITY MODEL

COMMERCIAL OPERATIONS

Reconfigure the operations that support growth and enable salespeople to provide coherent, end-to-end management of commercial teams, assets, infrastructure, investments, and processes.

COMPETENCY	LEVEL 1: BEGIN	LEVEL 2: BASIC	LEVEL 3: ADVANCED	LEVEL 4: BEST-IN-CLASS
4.0 COMMON PURPOSE. Establish a common purpose across sales, marketing, and customer success teams.	4.1 Create common definitions of opportunity and performance outcomes for all organizations.	4.2 Clarify opportunity ownership, priorities, and responsibilities at every stage of the customer journey.	4.3 Create common measures based on account and pipeline health for all customer-facing employees.	4.4 Create common incentives based on customer value for all customer-facing employees.
5.0 ORGANIZATION. Establish cross-functional organizational structures to support salespeople across the enterprise.	5.1 Create a RevOps Center of Excellence to coordinate cross-functional team activities and develop core capabilities.	5.2 Integrate sales operations and sales enablement with dotted line reporting to centralized operations function.	5.3 Integrate sales and marketing operations and reporting with dotted line reporting to a central operations function.	5.4 Fully integrate all revenue operations, enablement, and analytics with solid line reporting to a central operations function.
6.0 COMMERCIAL PROCESS. Establish and manage a cross-functional commercial process across the enterprise.	6.1 Map the cross-functional commercial process to clarify roles, handoffs, and key points of leverage, scale, customer abrasion, and revenue leakage.	6.2 Clearly define roles, opportunity definitions and criteria for handoffs and adjudication for all functions.	6.3 Reengineer the cross-functional commercial process to eliminate friction, handoffs, delays, and revenue leakage.	6.4 Integrate the systems and data infrastructure that support the cross-functional commercial process to improve visibility, speed, engagement, and productivity.

FIGURE 14.1 *(Continued)*

REVENUE OPERATIONS MATURITY MODEL

COMMERCIAL ARCHITECTURE

Redesign the commercial architecture to maximize return on selling assets by improving the speed, visibility, productivity, engagement of frontline selling teams, and reduce cost to sell.

COMPETENCY	LEVEL 1: BEGIN	LEVEL 2: BASIC	LEVEL 3: ADVANCED	LEVEL 4: BEST-IN-CLASS
7.0 GO-TO-MARKET STRATEGY. Redesign the go-to-market architecture to improve performance and engagement.	7.1 Assess the go-to-market strategy to quantify opportunities to capture more share and opportunity.	7.2 Refine customer targets based on more precise data-driven signals of intent, win probability, fit, and potential.	7.3 Refine coverage to reflect the impact of new roles, teamwork, and transaction automation and migration.	7.4 Refine and agree upon market segmentation supported by more precise algorithmic models of opportunity.
8.0 SALES FORCE DESIGN. Adjust the sales force design to improve performance, engagements, and costs.	8.1 Assess the sales force design to quantify opportunities to improve performance, margins, and customer lifetime value.	8.2 Redesign the sales force emphasis to rebalance product, engagement, and activity priorities to optimize performance, margins, and customer lifetime value.	8.3 Redesign sales force segmentation to clarify roles of lead generation, specialists, and success to optimize opportunity realization, customer lifetime value, and cost to sell.	8.4 Redesign sales incentive compensation to create common purpose and focus on customer value across functions.
9.0 SALES PERFORMANCE MANAGEMENT. Modify assignments, territories, and incentives to align resources and opportunity.	9.1 Audit the assumptions underlying territory definitions and quota assignments to ID ways to better align resources with opportunity.	9.2 Redefine territory boundaries and quota assignments based on more precise data-driven inputs to reflect changes in business model, automation, selling cadence, engagement mix, and customer behavior.	9.3 Automate the TQP process to improve input parameters, collaboration, scenario development, and update cycles.	9.4 Align incentives across sales, marketing, and customer experience functions to establish common purpose and focus on customer lifetime value.

FIGURE 14.1 (*Continued*)

REVENUE OPERATIONS MATURITY MODEL

COMMERCIAL INSIGHTS

Turning customer engagement and seller activity data into commercial insights that create value and inform decisions, actions, and conversations at the "moments that matter" in the sales process.

COMPETENCY	LEVEL 1: BEGIN	LEVEL 2: BASIC	LEVEL 3: ADVANCED	LEVEL 4: BEST-IN-CLASS
10.0 DATA-DRIVEN SELLING. Convert revenue data into prescriptive revenue intelligence that informs day-to-day decisions in real time.	10.1 Integrate customer engagement and sales activity data to support coaching and guidance of revenue teams.	10.2 Enable real-time guidance across revenue teams based on core customer engagement and seller activity data sets.	10.3 Enable measures that trigger actions to improve the customer experience at every stage of the cross-functional commercial process.	10.4 Enable real-time guidance across revenue teams.
11.0 KEY PERFORMANCE INDICATORS. Establish fact-based reporting analytics, KPIs, and dashboards of commercial performance.	11.1 Establish and agree upon a single KPI dashboard that defines desired outcomes and leading indicators of success with sales, marketing, and customer success leadership.	11.2 Create data-driven measures of customer lifetime value, account health, seller performance, and opportunity potential.	11.3 Develop KPIs to measure the performance of the end-to-end commercial process across functions.	11.4 Create common incentives across functions based on customer lifetime value, cost to sell, and key selling activities.
12.0 PREDICTIVE SELLING INSIGHTS. Use advanced analytics to create better predictions, parameters, and scenarios to inform investment, allocation, and emphasis.	12.1 Establish a center of excellence for developing predictive insights and advanced modeling capabilities.	12.2 Develop analytics capabilities to predict opportunity value, intent, win probability, fit, and coverage difficulty.	12.3 Develop predictive analytics capabilities to create more accurate sales forecasts and pipelines.	12.4 Develop affective analytics capabilities to assess customer sentiment to build empathy and trust in customer conversations.

FIGURE 14.1 (*Continued*)

REVENUE OPERATIONS MATURITY MODEL

COMMERCIAL ENABLEMENT

Building a common core of commercial capabilities that enable salespeople and maximize the contribution of selling assets and investments to revenue and profit growth outcomes.

COMPETENCY	LEVEL 1: BEGIN	LEVEL 2: BASIC	LEVEL 3: ADVANCED	LEVEL 4: BEST-IN-CLASS
13.0 ENABLEMENT AND ENGAGEMENT. Reconfigure the commercial technology infrastructure to better support revenue team enablement.	13.1 Audit the revenue technology portfolio to ID ways to improve utilization, productivity, return on assets, and the seller experience.	13.2 Integrate sales enablement solutions into a digital selling platform to improve speed, engagement, and time focused on the customer.	13.3 Integrate the sales readiness, enablement, and engagement road map to improve speed, engagement, productivity, and accountability.	13.4 Fully integrate sales enablement, readiness, and engagement to support data-driven guided selling and prescriptive insights in real time.
14.0 READINESS AND DEVELOPMENT. Reconfigure the commercial technology infrastructure to better support readiness, training, and development.	14.1 Audit the learning and development technology portfolio to ID ways to improve visibility, speed to ramp, skills, coaching, and reinforcement.	14.2 Integrate the learning and development portfolio into an integrated and closed-loop process that provides feedback, reinforcement, and visibility into seller activity and compliance.	14.3 Integrate the sales readiness, enablement, and engagement road map to improve seller ramp, readiness, skills, and accountability.	14.4 Fully integrate sales enablement, readiness, and engagement to support data-driven coaching at scale in real time.
15.0 REVENUE ENHANCEMENT. Deploy revenue enhancement technologies to enhance the lead-to-cash cycle and capture more revenue, margin, and price realization.	15.1 Audit CPQ and fulfillment tools to save time, enhance the customer experience, and reduce revenue, price, and margin leakage in the lead-to-cash cycle.	15.2 Centralize the management and administration of CPQ and fulfillment tools across functions to maximize adoption and impact.	15.3 Integrate the road map to CPQ and fulfillment tools to accelerate the lead-to-cash cycle, reduce leakage, and optimize price.	15.4 Evolve revenue enhancement capabilities to support one-to-one personalization of pricing, proposals, and onboarding at scale.

FIGURE 14.1   (*Continued*)

REVENUE OPERATIONS MATURITY MODEL

COMMERCIAL ASSET MANAGEMENT

The strategic management of the commercial data, technology, content, and IP assets to maximize utilization, impact, and return on investment.

COMPETENCY	LEVEL 1: BEGIN	LEVEL 2: BASIC	LEVEL 3: ADVANCED	LEVEL 4: BEST-IN-CLASS
16.0 Content Assets. Establish operational ownership, organization, and deployment of selling content and IP across functions.	16.1 Organize all cross-functional readiness, validation, playbook through leadership and product content using a common architecture and taxonomy.	16.2 Establish a single source of truth for content based on a common taxonomy and architecture to support enablement, readiness, and response management.	16.3 Make content available to support selling action recommendations and plays through enablement, readiness, and revenue enhancement systems.	16.4 Enable end-to-end response management across the enterprise, to be up to date, multichannel, and in real time.
17.0 Data Assets. Establish a common architecture and owner to monetize customer data assets.	17.1 Inventory and evaluate customer data sources to establish a common data architecture across first-party and third-party systems.	17.2 Centralize data administration to leverage staff resources and establish common architecture for managing, harmonizing, and leveraging data assets.	17.3 Establish a single source of truth for all customer engagement and conversational intelligence data.	17.4 Integrate customer engagement and revenue intelligence into a Revenue Operating System that aggregates, transforms, and routes data in real time to support all aspects of data-driven selling, coaching, and measurement.
18.0 Technology Assets. Establishment of centralized stewardship and reconfiguration of the commercial technology portfolio across functions.	18.1 Assess the commercial technology portfolio architecture and road map to reduce duplication, disconnected apps, underutilized assets, and ID ways to improve value, impact, and the seller experience.	18.2 Centralize selling tool administration to leverage staff resources and establish common architecture for reconfiguring the commercial technology portfolio across functions.	18.3 Centralize commercial technology investment, prioritization, and implementation across all functions based on value, simplicity, and impact.	18.4 Build a commercial technology road map around core platform partners to facilitate the convergence of enablement, readiness, and engagement solutions and create a highly integrated technology ecosystem.

FIGURE 14.1 *(Continued)*

Glossary

Glossary: A Periodic Table of the Building Blocks of Growth

Building block	Definition
Account-Based Marketing (ABM)	*Account-Based Marketing* is a solution or set of solutions with the capability to identify anonymous website visitors, match them to contact and account profiles, and notify the appropriate person about events and signals that suggest buying intent, risks, or opportunities.
Account Health (and Lifetime Value) Metrics	*Account Health Metrics* are customized measurements of customer satisfaction, loyalty, penetration, and potential that are derived from actual engagement, transactions, usage, and activity levels using advanced analytics.
Account Mapping	*Account mapping* is the process of cataloging, grouping, organizing, and profiling the people that work at a particular target account and matching them with customer engagement data from the different sales and marketing systems they work with from inside and outside your business. Account mapping is central to key account management, cross-sell, and account-based marketing program execution.
Agency Partners	*Agency partners* are business partners who support marketing programs with selling content, program execution, and the deployment of paid, earned, and owned media targeting accounts and prospects.
Artificial Intelligence (AI)	*Artificial intelligence* is the simulation of human intelligence processes by machines, especially computer systems. Specific applications of AI include expert systems, natural language processing, speech recognition, and machine vision.
Campaign Optimization	*Campaign optimization* is the capability to target, test, and refine marketing campaigns and messages based on customer response, engagement, effectiveness, and conversion rates. Campaigns are optimized by refining and adjusting variables such as targeting, messaging, offers, channels, and cadence.

Building block	Definition
Collaboration Platforms	A *collaborative platform* is a virtual workspace asset where resources and tools are centralized with the aim of facilitating communication and personal interaction in corporate project work. Examples of collaboration platforms include Microsoft Teams or Slack.
Compliance and Approvals	*Compliance and approvals* is a capability within content management or workflow solutions that provide governance over the content created, published, and distributed by an organization to ensure it conforms to standards of quality or regulatory and legal requirements.
Contactless Channels	*Contactless channels* are digital channel assets – including chat, voice, digital agents, and automated text – that engage customers without the direct or proactive intervention of human agents. Examples of contactless selling platforms include Podium in automated text and Cognism in chat.
Content Consumption Data (Sales Enablement Data)	*Content consumption data* is a data asset generated by sales enablement platforms that track when selling content – articles, videos, emails, or white papers – are opened, read, otherwise consumed, or passed along by a client or prospect.
Customer and Competitive Intelligence	*Customer and competitive intelligence* is a specialized capability to find and present competitive intelligence such as battle cards, market research, or comparative benefits content to arm sellers with information to address competitive questions, proposals, and offers.
Customer Conversation Data (Conversational Intelligence)	*Customer conversation data* – or conversational intelligence – is data collected from recorded sales and service calls that are converted to data using Natural Language Processing (NLP) and analyzed using advanced analytics for selling signals, triggers, sentiment for compliance, guidance, and training reasons.
Customer Engagement Data	*Customer engagement data* is generated when a customer interacts with a sales and marketing system or representative from within your company as well as in third-party media, websites, and channels. Customer interaction data can be collected in digital ads, websites, mobile applications, chatbots, recorded conversations, and sales transactions captured in marketing and sales systems as well as collaboration platforms.

Building block	Definition
Customer Relationship Management (CRM)	*Customer Relationship Management* is a software asset that serves as the sales system of record for customer information, activity, account structures, and engagement activity. Examples of CRM platforms include Salesforce.com and Microsoft Dynamics.
Customer Relationship Management (CRM) Data	*CRM data* is a data asset that is stored, managed, and updated within the CRM platform including customer information, activity, contact profiles, account structures, transactions, and engagement activity.
Customer Treatment	*Customer treatment* is one of the fundamental interrelated variables that must be balanced in territory and quota planning. A go-to-market strategy should define different ways of treating customers – in terms of time and attention from sales and service reps – but also the nature, mix, and volume of direct engagement, as well as the quality and nature of the customer experience. Different treatment types are used to define a customer engagement model, which is an important input to estimating sales rep workload, cost to sell, and transaction economics of the sales process. Different treatment levels are usually based on customer ranking, potential, or assignment based on customer scoring models (e.g. A/B/C accounts, the 80/20 rule, probability of win algorithms, or customer lifetime value models), account assignments (such as key accounts, named accounts, or accounts targeted for ABM programs by marketing), and also channels (e.g. "inside sales" accounts served through call centers, or "direct accounts" that function primarily through online channels).
Data Assembly	*Data assembly* describes the capability to aggregate customer engagement data from many systems and sources into one operational and usable data set, "data lake," or single source of truth.
Data Orchestration	*Data orchestration* describes the capability that automates the process of combining, cleaning, and organizing data from multiple sources, then distributing it to sales and marketing systems and services where revenue teams can put it to use.
Data Transformation	*Data transformation* is a capability in a variety of software solutions for managing the process of changing the format, structure, or values of customer engagement data to render them usable by selling software systems and individuals. These processes include customer data integration, migration, warehousing, and transformation.

Building block	Definition
Dealer Distributor Channels	*Dealer distributor channels* are third-party partner channels, or middlemen, who support the sale of products by adding unique value – geographic proximity, unique access, industry expertise, as well as client education, service, consulting, systems integration, or assembly and configuration.
Digital Adoption Software	*Digital adoption software* is a software asset that assists and guides users to help them gain the ability to use digital tools as they are intended and to the fullest extent. It is taking a brand-new user and helping them become entirely self-sufficient and competent. Examples of digital adoption software platforms include WalkMe.
Digital Asset Management	*Digital asset management* solutions are software assets that store, index, manage, and distribute selling content in support of sales. Examples of digital asset management solutions include Seismic.
Direct Selling Channels	In *direct selling channels,* sellers engage directly with customers and prospects in a nonretail environment. Direct selling channels include call center and digital channels and are similar to e-commerce and direct-to-customer channels.
Direct-to-Customer (DTC) Channels	*Direct-to-customer (or direct-to-consumer) channels* allow manufacturers and consumer brands to sell, fulfill, service, and support products directly to customers in online channels instead of through traditional distribution channels. It is similar to e-commerce but often involves more complex offerings and product delivery.
Document (Content) Assembly (and Personalization)	*Document and content assembly* solutions are specialized software assets that organize, index, recommend, assemble, and concatenate documents, contracts, proposals, and presentations based on client questions, inputs, or requirements. Examples of document assembly solutions include Contract, Presentation, and Quote (CPQ) solutions.
E-Commerce	An *e-commerce* platform is the software application or platform that allows buyers to discover products, shop, order, pay, and track and return products and services.

Building block	Definition
Email and Calendar (Data) aka Exchange Data	*Email and calendar data – or exchange data –* is a customer engagement and selling activity data asset that is collected from the email and calendar transactions of frontline sellers. Such data can be collected from email servers and calendar applications such as Microsoft Outlook or Google Gmail.
Financial Transaction Data	*Financial transaction data* is generated by sales transactions and is directly tied to revenues, usage, consumption, and product purchases by customers. Financial transaction data provides a basis for calculating sales, sales forecasts, customer lifetime value, the cost of sales, the attribution of sales, and the return on sales investment.
Forecast Accuracy (Metrics)	*Forecast accuracy metrics* are analytical and measurement capabilities that successfully predict sales (in both the long and short term) to support making key decisions about short-term spending and deals for key accounts. Examples of solutions that can improve forecast accuracy are Aviso and Clari.
Guided Selling	*Guided selling* is a capability within sales enablement and engagement platforms that uses advanced analytics to recommend the right content, sales play, or offer to present to a client given their unique needs, questions, or circumstances.
Learning Management System (Training and Development)	A *learning management system* describes a range of software applications that help administer, document, track, deliver, and automate the delivery of educational courses, training programs, or learning and development programs. These solutions support sales rep training and development, coaching, and readiness.
Market Coverage	A *market coverage* model defines how products, solutions, and services are marketed and sold to maximize the addressable market in the most cost-effective way. A coverage model is not equal to territory. The sales coverage model enables companies to set achievable revenue goals, then reach them with thoughtful placement of sales and marketing teams, channels, and individuals in the best territories and highest-value accounts. A coverage model is a cross-functional strategy with inputs from sales, marketing, and finance, factoring in channel strategy.

Building block	Definition
Marketing Automation	*Marketing automation* software automates digital marketing activities such as email marketing, social media posting, and tracking website engagement to provide a more personalized experience for customers
Market Segmentation	*Market segmentation* defines the groups of customers that represent the greatest opportunity and revenue potential to the business overall. Segmentation strategy defines specific groupings of customers to target with resources and marketing programs by geography, markets, industries, customers, or characteristics to design territory boundaries and size market opportunities. Segments are associated with large market opportunities based on homogenous behavior, need, or buying characteristics. Segments are used to target marketing resources on opportunity including demand generation programs, messaging, and products programs. Market segmentation is one of the fundamental interrelated variables that must be balanced in territory and quota planning and one of the six critical external inputs to the process.
Mobile Infrastructure	*Mobile infrastructure* includes mobile applications that support a wide variety of customer engagement objectives including but not limited to marketing, customer service, and support as well as providing the ability to transact, order, and purchase.
Opportunity Potential (Metrics)	*Opportunity potential metrics* are customized measurements of the propensity-to-buy and revenue potential of a lead, prospect, or customer that are derived from actual engagement, transactions, usage, and activity levels using advanced analytics.
Opportunity Prioritization	*Opportunity prioritization* is a capability within sales enablement and engagement software that uses advanced analytics to predict the value and priority of a lead, prospect, or customer based on their propensity to buy, their revenue and profit potential, and the estimated effort to convert that are derived from actual engagement, transactions, usage, and activity levels using advanced analytics.
Owned Digital Channel Data (First-Party Data)	*Owned digital channel* infrastructure data – commonly called first-party data – is a customer engagement data asset that is generated when a prospect or customer engages in owned digital channels including websites, blogs, email, social media, e-commerce, and mobile applications.

Building block	Definition
Owned Digital Channels	*Owned digital channels* are a digital technology asset that helps your organizations engage prospect or customers digitally. These include websites, blogs, email, social media, e-commerce channels, mobile applications, and contactless selling channels like chatbots.
Personalization	*Personalization* is an advanced analytic capability that helps tailor an experience or communication to better suit a customer's personal characteristics, needs, and preferences based on information a company has learned about the individual.
Planning and Calendaring	*Planning and calendaring* is a capability in content management software that helps marketers and publishers plan, schedule, coordinate, manage, measure, and track the creation of selling content from a variety of sources, agencies, subject matter experts, creators, and teams.
Presentations and Proposals	*Presentations and proposals* are selling content assets that support frontline sellers as they engage with customers and prospects.
Product Usage Data	*Product usage data*, or product telemetry data, is data generated and transmitted by a product that provides information about product usage and performance, and tracks what your customers do with your product, when, and for how long.
Proposal, RFP, and Pricing Guidance	*Proposal, RFP, and pricing guidance* is a capability within specialized Configure, Price, Quote (CQP) and dynamic pricing software solutions that uses advanced analytics to guide sellers in writing proposals, making offers, and setting pricing.
Recommend Best Content	*Recommend best content* is a capability from specialized recommender engines and sale enablement software that recommends the next best content to present to a prospect or customer based on transaction history, customer engagement, and third-party data signals.
Recommender Engines	A *recommendation engine* is a type of data filtering tool that uses machine learning algorithms to analyze the characteristics and behaviors that customers and prospects have exhibited in the past to help recommend content, products, and offers to them and to guide them into the best possible customer experience. Recommender systems are used in a variety of applications, ranging from playlist generators for video and music services, product recommenders for online stores, or content recommenders for sales and social media platforms.

Building block	Definition
Request for Proposal (RFP)	*Request for proposals* are documents provided by customers to provide them the information to help them select and buy a complex offering.
Resource Allocation Models (SPM)	*Resource allocation models* are a capability within specialized sales performance management software that helps business leaders and planners to allocate sales teams, resources, budgets, and effort against specific geographic or industry market segments or target accounts and customers.
Response Management	*Response management* is an advanced concept that uses AI and ML to create a knowledge base of content built on actual question-and-answer exchanges between customers and sales reps. The software makes this aggregate knowledge available to entire revenue teams, on demand, with no wait times. A simple query provides the answer your salesperson needs to deliver their best answer, with immediate results, whether a rep is writing a text, email, proposal, presentation, or an RFP.
Sales Automation	*Sales automation* solutions are capabilities within sales automation, enablement, and engagement software solutions that automate non-customer-facing selling tasks including CRM data entry, data management, finding information, list building, and repetitive selling tasks like dialing, screening calls, and capturing contact information.
Sales Coaching	One-to-one *coaching* is a capability within sales engagement solutions that allow sales managers to monitor conversations in real time, easily identify "teachable moments," and interject or coach using prompts to the sales reps.
Sales Force Emphasis	*Sales force focus (or emphasis)* provides top-down direction to sales resource allocation because it dictates where sales resources should be invested and applied. Sales forces can be focused on territories, certain products in the portfolio, or certain types of customers. This determines the focus and structure of sales force by product, geography, market segment, or industry – as defined by the channel strategy, coverage model, and go-to-market approach. Sales force focus is one of the fundamental interrelated variables that must be balanced in territory and quota planning.

Building block	Definition
Sales Force Segmentation	*Sales force segmentation* concerns the different roles of each salesperson in servicing and selling to customers as part of a revenue team or channel strategy as defined by the sales force structures, coverage model, and routes to market. Sales force segmentation is one of the fundamental interrelated variables that must be balanced in territory and quota planning.
Sales Force Size and Structure	*Sales force size* is the number of selling resources – or customer-facing employees – in the field available to engage customers, by role. Sales force size generally considers the major selling roles in the company, which include salespeople (e.g. field sales reps, inside sales reps, account manager, business development reps) and, increasingly, service and support team members (e.g. customer service manager, digital service reps) and specialist reps (e.g. product specialist, industry specialists, sales engineering/ support, or dedicated product overlay rep). To be complete, the sales force size should also factor in marketing support resources that engage customers directly and measurably (e.g. demand generation reps, social listening agents, digital channel support reps) and third-party channel partners such as distributors, resellers, and retailers. Sales force size is one of the fundamental interrelated variables that must be balanced in territory and quota planning.
Sales Playbooks	*Sales playbooks* are selling content assets that are a means of capturing sales best practices and communicating them to salespeople. They concisely describe what a salesperson should do in different situations.
Sales Readiness	*Sales readiness* is a capability in specialized sales training and development software that (1) evaluates how capable a customer-facing employee is at engaging a customer or prospect and driving the conversation toward a specific outcome, and (2) recommends training to fill specific development needs. Examples of sales readiness platforms include MindTickle and Allego.
Sales Rep Assignments	*Sales rep quota assignments* are sales assignments or goals that are to be achieved in a specific period of time. Sales quotas are the total sales of a future period and the duties and activities each salesperson is expected to deliver in a given sales period (quarter or year). Quota assignments are delivered to and agreed on by individual sales representatives and their managers at the beginning of the period.

Building block	Definition
Sales Resource Optimization	*Sales resource* allocation software, often called Sales Performance Management (SPM), describes software, operational, and analytical functions that automate and unify back-office operational sales processes that allocate sales resources, define and administer territories and quotas, set incentives, and measure selling performance.
Sales Response Function	The *sales response function* is the cause-and-effect relationship between sales effort and revenue outcomes, and is the relationship between level of sales effort and sales generated for a given group of customers (or territory). This function is derived from a wide mix of empirical data about rep, pipeline, and customer potential as well as qualitative judgments on customers, markets, and competitive advantage. It generally reflects diminishing returns on sales effort in a finite market – as such it is generally shaped as an "S" and has the potential to provide guidance on the optimal level of sales resource (e.g. calling, staffing, time, and attention) that a company should invest in a given region, segment, or customer grouping. Sales response function is one of the fundamental interrelated variables that must be balanced in territory and quota planning.
Sales Training Methodology	A *sales training methodology* is an intellectual property asset that outlines how your sellers approach each phase of the sales process and, in practice, equips your sales team with a practical, repeatable, scalable framework for sales success.
Seller Activity Data	*Seller activity data* are activity data assets that track seller activity in terms of client calls, communication, emails, and selling actions that are part of the day-to-day selling workflow such as entering data and following up on leads. Seller activity data comes from sales enablement, engagement, email, calendar, and conversational intelligence systems.
Seller Performance (Metrics)	*Seller performance (metrics)* are customized measurements of seller performance, capacity, potential, and compliance that are derived from actual engagement, transactions, usage, and activity levels using advanced analytics.

Building block	Definition
Standards and Quality Control	*Standards and quality control* management is a capability within content management or workflow solutions that provides governance over the content created, published, and distributed by an organization to ensure it conforms to brand and quality standards.
Subject Matter Experts	*Subject matter experts* are people assets who are the experts in your organizations who have specialized product, industry, customer, or set-up knowledge that is useful to customers and prospects making purchase decisions during the customer journey.
Taxonomy and Classification	*Taxonomy and classification* are capabilities in specialized content management, recommender engine, and digital asset management software solutions that help classify, organize, and code information about selling content assets so that they can be targeted, assigned, and distributed to sellers and customers easily.
Territory and Quota Planning (TQP)	*Territory and Quota Planning* are capabilities in specialized sales performance management software assets that digitize, automate, and speed the process of planning designing, managing, and optimizing sales territory boundaries and sales quota assignments.
Territory Boundaries	*Territory boundaries* represent the primary "unit of control" in the territory and quota planning process. Territory boundaries can be defined by a variety of factors – including geography, industry, customer grouping, products, channels, or marketing-defined segmentation – or some combination of these factors in the territory plan. These boundaries ensure that the territory definition aligns with geographic markets, market segmentation, distribution channels, and the target customers served.
Third-Party Buying Signals	*Third-party data* is generated when prospects and customers interact with websites outside of your company. This data is aggregated, identified, and organized by software vendors and sold to marketers to help them append and enhance their internal (first-party) data with information about customers' needs, demographics, firmographics, potential, and signals of customer preference and intent to purchase or churn.

Building block	Definition
Validation Content	*Validation content* is a form of selling content assets that provide validation that your product can do what it is supposed to. These include case studies, client testimonials, ROI models, research reports, analyst reviews, and value selling tools.
Virtual Selling Capabilities	*Virtual selling capabilities* allow sellers to engage customers more effectively remotely. These range from basic connectivity, collaboration, and telephony capabilities but can be as advanced as algorithmic selling, sales enablement, 5G communications, DTC channels, and even augmented reality.
Websites and E-commerce	Website and e-commerce platforms are digital selling infrastructure assets that help engage and sell to customers in digital channels.

References

1 The Modern Marketing Mix, Marketing Accountability Standards Board, Available at: https://www.forbes.com/sites/forbesinsights/2019/04/15/how-transparent-is-your-marketing-spend/#27174a0d3ad1

2 Kelly, Bob, "Unlocking CRMs Value," The Sales Management Association, April 2020, Available at: https://salesmanagement.org/blog/crms-triumph-of-hope-over-experience/

3 AI Summit Industry Insights Report 2020. Forbes survey of 1,093 initial responses. Available at: https://intuitive-design.foleon.com/knect365/ai-summit-insights-report-2020/home/

4 The CMO Survey, Duke Fuqua School of Business, Survey of 2,818 marketers, 2021, available at: https://cmosurvey.org/

5 Reibstein, David, Iyengar, Raghu, and Diorio, Stephen, Markets in Motion, Wharton Business School survey of 352 senior marketing executives, April – June 2020. Available at: https://www.revenueenablement.com/markets-in-motion/

6 Hanssens, Dominique, "Empirical Generalizations About Marketing's Impact," The Marketing Sciences Institute, 2015, Available at: https://www.msi.org/books/empirical-generalizations-about-marketing-impact-2nd-ed/

7 "Real-Time Marketing Accountability: How High-Performing Marketers Are Supporting Strategic Growth Decisions With Real-Time Voice of the Customer Data and Insights," a quantitative research survey of 500 global marketing executives by Forbes, 2018. Available at: http://35.196.99.151/cmo-practice/real-time-marketing-accountability/

8 Edeling, Alexander and Fischer, Mark, "Marketing's Impact on Firm Value: Generalizations from a Meta-Analysis," American Marketing Association, 2016, Available at: https://www.researchgate.net/publication/283827427_Marketing's_Impact_on_Firm_Value_Generalizations_from_a_Meta-Analysis

9 Revenue Enablement Institute, "The Remote Sales Productivity Report," Survey of 150 sales leaders and practitioners, 2020, Available at: https://www.revenueenablement.com/product/the-remote-sales-productivity-report

10 Microsoft usage statistics, 2020. Available at: https://www.microsoft.com/en-us/microsoft-365/blog/2020/04/30/2-years-digital-transformation-2-months/?mod=article_inline

11 Zoom revenue and usage statistics, 2020. Available at: https://blog.zoom.us/90-day-security-plan-progress-report-april-22/

12 Smith, Michael, "The Financial Impact of Adding a Virtual AE Channel to the Commercial Model," 2020. Available at: https://www.revenueenablement.com/the-financial-impact-of-adding-a-virtual-account-executive-to-the-commercial-model/

13 Diorio, Stephen, "Building a High-Performing Virtual Selling Channel," *Forbes*, 2020. Available at: https://www.forbes.com/sites/forbesinsights/2020/04/22/building-a-virtual-selling-channels/#39113173521b

14 Marketing Budget Allocation Trends, ITSMA. 2020 Available at: https://www.itsma.com/research/2020-services-marketing-budget-allocations-trends/

15 Forbes Marketing Accountability Report, A quantitative analysis of the performance of 380 CMOs, Forbes, 2017. Available at: https://blogs.forbes.com/forbesinsights/files/2019/08/Forbes-Marketing-Accountability-Executive-Summary-10.2.17.pdf

16 Gartner Customer Experience Survey, 2018, Available at: https://www.gartner.com/en/marketing/insights/articles/key-findings-from-the-gartner-customer-experience-survey

17 Gartner's 2021 Technology End User Buying Behavior Survey, 2021, survey of 1,500 end users. Available at: https://www.gartner.com/en/newsroom/press-releases/2021-05-17-gartner-cso-sales-leader-conference-americas-day-1-highlights

18 Iyengar, Goorha, "Voice Analytics and Artificial Intelligence: Future Directions for a Post Covid World," Wharton Customer Analytics, 2020. Available at: https://wca.wharton.upenn.edu/white-paper/voice-analytics-and-artificial-intelligence-future-directions-for-a-post-covid-world/

19 Diorio, Stephen, "How Splunk Is Accelerating Growth," *Forbes*, 2021. Available at: https://www.forbes.com/sites/stephendiorio/2022/02/07/leading-business-transformation-at-scale-at-splunk/

20 Salesforce.com State of Sales Report, Survey of 2,900 sales leaders, 2019, Available at: https://c1.sfdcstatic.com/content/dam/web/en_us/www/documents/reports/sales/state-of-sales-3rd-ed.pdf

21 Salesforce.com State of Service Report, Survey of 3,500 Service Leaders and Agents, 2019, Available at:https://c1.sfdcstatic.com/content/dam/web/en_us/www/documents/reports/sales/state-of-sales-3rd-ed.pdf https://c1.sfdcstatic.com/content/dam/web/en_us/www/documents/reports/salesforce-research-third-edition-state-of-service.pdf

22 Research Report: Unlocking CRM's Value, Sales Management Association, 2019, Survey of sales managers and performance professionals. Available at: https://salesmanagement.org/resource/unlocking-crms-value/

23 Revenue.io, 2021 Revenue Operations and Customer Acquisition Benchmark Report, survey of 240 revenue leaders in 2020 by RevOps Squared. Available at: https://www.revenue.io/ebooks/2021-rev-ops-customer-acquisition-benchmark-report

24 Kleber, Sophie, "3 Ways AI Is Getting More Emotional," *Harvard Business Review*, 2018. Available at: https://hbr.org/2018/07/3-ways-ai-is-getting-more-emotional

25 The 21st Century Commercial Model: "A CXO Blueprint for Transforming Sales, Marketing and Services," An analysis of the top 100 technologies that are transforming the commercial model, 2021, The Revenue Enablement Institute. Available at: https://www.revenueenablement.com/the-21st-century-commercial-model-report/

26 The RevOps Framework, Varicent, 2021. Available at: https://www.varicent.com/whitepapers-studies/The-RevOps-Framework

27 "Cisco Announces New Chief Sales and Marketing Officer and New Chief Customer Experience Officer," Cisco, 2018. Available at: https://www.globenewswire.com/news-release/2018/03/28/1454700/0/en/Cisco-Announces-New-Chief-Sales-and-Marketing-Officer-and-New-Chief-Customer-Experience-Officer.html

28 "Cisco's Digital Marketing Transformation," Domo Case Study, 2018. Available at: https://www.domo.com/learn/report/cisco-transformed-their-digital-marketing-with-domo

29 Ives, Nat, "CMO Titles Continue to Wane," *Wall Street Journal*, 2019. Available at: https://www.wsj.com/articles/cmo-titles-will-continue-to-wane-and-thats-a-good-thing-analysts-say-11572258781

30 "The Rise of Revenue Operations, Revenue Operations Performance Benchmarks," Clari, 2021. Available at: https://www.clari.com/blog/the-rise-of-revenue-operations-infographic

31 Diorio, Stephen, "Proving the Financial Contribution of AI to Sales," *Forbes*, 2020, Available at: https://www.forbes.com/sites/forbesinsights/2019/11/20/proving-the-financial-contribution-of-ai-in-marketing-applications/?sh=6178bfa04564

32 Iyengar, Goorha, "Voice Analytics and Artificial Intelligence: Future Directions for a Post Covid World," Wharton Customer Analytics. 2020. Available at: https://wca.wharton.upenn.edu/white-paper/voice-analytics-and-artificial-intelligence-future-directions-for-a-post-covid-world/

33 Diorio, Stephen, "Evolving to Response Management," *Forbes*, 2021. Available at: https://www.forbes.com/sites/stephendiorio/2021/03/25/evolving-from-content-management-to-response-management/?sh=2d94560a65df

34 Diorio, Stephen, "Leading Remote Selling Teams in a Crisis," Revenue Enablement Institute, 2020. Available at: https://www.revenueenablement.com/leading-remote-selling-teams-in-a-crisis-environment/

35 Ransbotham, Khodabandeh, Ronny Fehling, Burt Lafountain, and David Kiron, Sloan MIT Winning with AI Report, 2019, Available at: https://sloanreview.mit.edu/projects/winning-with-ai/

36 Miller Heiman, CSO Insights Sales Performance Report 2019, Available at: https://www.csoinsights.com/wp-content/uploads/sites/5/2018/12/2018-2019-Sales-Performance-Report.pdf

37 Iyengar, Raghu and Reibstein, David, "Markets in Motion Profile: How the Lenovo Is Adapting to the New Market Reality," Wharton Business School, 2021. Available at: https://www.revenueenablement.com/mim-lenovo/

38 Iyengar, Raghu and Reibstein, David, "Markets in Motion Profile: How the Equitable Is Adapting to the New Market Reality," Wharton, 2021. Available at: https://www.revenueenablement.com/mim-equitable/

39 Haas, David, "Baby Boomer Retirement Trends," *Forbes*, 2019. Available at: https://www.forbes.com/sites/forbesfinancecouncil/2019/09/03/retirement-trends-of-baby-boomers/#3be5cca73787

40 Ham, Arno, "Digital Commerce Trends," DigitalCommerce360, 2019. Available at: https://www.digitalcommerce360.com/2019/01/27/2019-b2b-e-commerce-trends-putting-convenience-before-innovation/#:~:text=As%20many%20as%2083%25%20of,product%20choices%20than%20ever%20before.

41 Revenue.io Case Study, ChowNow, 2021. Available at: https://www.Revenue.io.com/case-studies/chownow-case-study

42 Revenue.io Case Study, RE/MAX, 2021. Available at: https://www.Revenue.io.com/case-studies/remax

43 Revenue.io Case Study, HPE, 2021. Available at: https://www.Revenue.io.com/case-studies/hewlett-packard-enterprise

44 Revenue.io Case Study, Cvent, 2021. Available at: https://www.Revenue.io.com/case-studies/cvent

45 Igniting Revenue Operations for 2021 Growth, Alexander Group, 2021. Available at: https://www.alexandergroup.com/insights/revenue-operations-2021-growth/

46 Alexander Group, 2021 Sales Compensation Trends Survey, 2021, Available at: https://www.alexandergroup.com/insights/2021-sales-compensation-trends-survey-executive-summary/

47 Revving up Go-to-Market Operations in B2B, Analysis of 100 high-growth B2B organizations by BCG. Available at: https://www.bcg.com/en-us/publications/2020/revving-up-go-to-market-operations-b2b

48 Lodish, L., "Sales Force Sizing and Deployment Using a Decision Calculus Model at Syntex Laboratories," the Institute of Management Sciences, 1988. Available at: https://operationalincomestatement.com/roi/wp-content/uploads/2015/05/Lodish-1988.pdf

49 Blue Ridge Partners survey of 622 sales professionals and performance professionals December 2020–April 2021. Available at: https://sloanreview.mit.edu/projects/winning-with-ai/

50 Marletta, Gerry, "Recurring Revenues Rising," *CFO Magazine*, 2019. Available at: https://www.cfo.com/cash-flow/2019/02/recurring-revenue-rising/

51 HubSpot State of Content Marketing Report, 2020. Available at: https://blog.hubspot.com/marketing/state-of-content-marketing-infographic

52 S&P 500 historical financial data, Fact Set, 2021. Available at: https://www.factset.com/hubfs/Website/Resources%20Section/Research%20Desk/Earnings%20Insight/EarningsInsight_061721A.pdf

53 Abdulla, Sammy, "SaaS IPOs Take $318mm of Investment," Analysis of 49 SaaS IPOs, Blossom Street Ventures, 2021. Available at: https://www.linkedin.com/pulse/saas-ipos-take-318mm-investment-sammy-abdullah/?trackingId=9Mt1jWPGRIaRJ7xjLEModg%3D%3D

54 Abdulla, Sammy, "SaaS multiples for Q2," a financial analysis of 102 SaaS businesses, Blossom Street Ventures, 2021. Available at: https://www.linkedin.com/pulse/saas-multiples-q2-sammy-abdullah/

55 Knowles, Jonathan, "Intangible Assets Represent 80% of Firm Value," 2019. Available at: https://www.linkedin.com/pulse/intangible-assets-represent-80-value-sp-500-jonathan-knowles/

56 Ocean Tomo, Intangible Asset Market Value Study, 2020. Available at: https://www.oceantomo.com/intangible-asset-market-value-study/

57 Sinclair, Keller, "Brand Value, Accounting Standards, and Mergers and Acquisitions: 'The Moribund Effect,'" *Journal of Brand Management* (2017). Available at: https://themasb.org/wp-content/uploads/2017/04/Sinclair-and-Keller-JBM-2016.pdf

58 Pitchbook, Annual PE Breakdown Report, 2018. Available at: https://files.pitchbook.com/website/files/pdf/2018_Annual_US_PE_Breakdown.pdf

59 Yahoo Finance, 2021 Market Data.

60 US Private Equity Deals Analysis, Reuters, 2021. Available at: https://www.reuters.com/article/us-private-equity-deals-valuations-analy-idUKKBN2B81EA

61 Laney, Doug, "Why Your Company Does Not Measure the Value of Its Data Assets," *Forbes*, 2021. Available at: https://www.forbes.com/sites/douglaslaney/2020/07/22/your-companys-data-may-be-worth-more-than-your-company/?sh=756bff5e634c

62 Laney, Doug, "Your Company's Data May Be Worth More Than Your Company," *Forbes*, 2020. Available at: https://www.forbes.com/sites/douglaslaney/2020/07/22/your-companys-data-may-be-worth-more-than-your-company/?sh=756bff5e634c

63 Diorio, Stephen, "Unlocking the Full Growth Potential of Big Data," *Forbes*, 2020. Available at: https://www.forbes.com/sites/forbesinsights/2018/12/17/unlocking-the-full-growth-potential-of-big-data/#4493598f52e9

64 Spencer, Stuart, "CMO Titles Will Continue to Wane," *Wall Street Journal*, 2019. Available at: https://www.wsj.com/articles/cmo-titles-will-continue-to-wane-and-thats-a-good-thing-analysts-say-11572258781

65 Roetzer, Paul, "Funding for AI Sales and Marketing Companies Exceeds $5.2 Billion," MarketGain Institute, analysis of VC investment in Artificial Intelligence, 2019. Available at: https://www.marketingaiinstitute.com/blog/funding-for-ai-powered-sales-and-marketing-companies-exceeds-5.2-billion

66 ChiefMartech.com, 2020 Martech Landscape, 2020. Available at: https://chiefmartec.com/2020/04/marketing-technology-landscape-2020-martech-5000/

67 Diorio, Stephen and Rogers, Bruce, "Publish or Perish Report," *Forbes*, 2018. Available at: https://www.forbes.com/sites/brucerogers/2015/04/29/publish-or-perish-why-the-cmo-must-become-a-publisher-to-drive-growth/?sh=37acececc310

68 Revenue.io Case Study, Equity Trust, 2021. Available at: https://www.Revenue.io.com/case-studies/equity-trust-reviews-6x-more-calls

69 Sales Operations Program of the Year, Forrester/Sirius Decisions, 2020. https://www.siriusdecisions.com/summit-us/sessions/sos_programs-of-the-year-sales-operations_hitachi-vantara

70 "How 6sense Supports the 21st Century Commercial Model," Interview with Viral Balaji, Founder and CTO of 6sense, The Revenue Enablement Institute, 2021. Available at: https://www.revenueenablement.com/re100/6sense/

71 "How Highspot Supports the 21st Century Commercial Model," Interview with Robert Wahbe, Co-Founder and CEO of Highspot, The Revenue Enablement Institute, 2021. Available at: https://www.revenueenablement.com/re100/highspot/

72 Diorio, Stephen, "Proving the Financial Contribution of Account-Based Marketing to the Business," *Forbes*, 2020. Available at: https://www.forbes.com/sites/forbesinsights/2019/12/10/proving-the-financial-contribution-of-account-based-marketing-to-the-business/#21d069b77df9

73 Matlock, Robin and Haas, Janet, "Marketing Marketing to Management," Forbes CMO Summit, 2018. Available at: https://www.forbes.com/video/5980590891001/marketing-marketing-to-management---cmo-summit-2018/?sh=14f3b6102257

101 Eric Olsen, Frank Plaschke, and Daniel Stelter, "Threading the Needle: Value Creation in a Low-Growth Economy," Infosys, 2010. Available at: https://www.infosys.com/newsroom/features/pdf/file59590.pdf

102 Raju, Jagmohan and John Zhang, Z. *Smart Pricing: How Google, Priceline and Leading Businesses Use Price Innovation for Profitability* (Prentice Hall, 2013). Available at: https://executiveeducation.wharton.upenn.edu/wp-content/uploads/2019/12/Raju-Smart-Pricing.pdfXx

103 Diorio, Stephen, "Private Equity and the New Science of Growth," *Forbes*, 2019. Available at: https://www.forbes.com/sites/forbesinsights/2019/03/01/private-equity-and-the-new-science-of-growth/?sh=5a5b91fa2370

104 Diorio, Stephen, "Creating an Economic Purpose for Long-Term Growth Investment," *Forbes*, 2020. Available at: https://www.forbes.com/sites/forbesinsights/2019/12/04/creating-a-common-economic-purpose-for-long-term-growth-investment/?sh=5b1073594723Xx

105 Diorio, Stephen, "Growth Is the Ultimate Team Sport," *Forbes*, 2020. Available at: https://www.forbes.com/sites/forbesinsights/2020/02/27/growth-is-the-ultimate-team-sport/#28b20be13bcdXx

106 Mantrala, Albers, Caldieraro, Jensen, Joseph, Krafft, Narasimhan, Gopealakrishna, Zoltners, Lal, and Lodish,"Sales Force Modeling: State of the Field and Research Agenda," *Marketing Letters*, September 2010. Available at: https://www.academia.edu/14631455/Sales_force_modeling_State_of_the_field_and_research_agendaXx

107 Ghoshal, Sumantra, Piramal, Gita and Bartlett, Christopher A. *Managing Radical Change* (Viking Press, 2000). Available at: https://www.hbs.edu/faculty/Pages/item.aspx?num=4855

112 LinkedIn, 2020 Emerging Jobs Report, 2020. Available at: https://business.linkedin.com/content/dam/me/business/en-us/talent-solutions/emerging-jobs-report/Emerging_Jobs_Report_U.S._FINAL.pdf

108 Interbrand 2021 Brand Rankings, 2021. Available at: https://interbrand.com/best-global-brands/cisco/

114 Diorio, Stephen, "Driving Non-Linear Revenue and Profit Growth at Rev.com," *Forbes*, 2021. Available at: https://www.forbes.com/sites/stephendiorio/2021/07/07/driving-non-linear-revenue-and-profit-growth-at-revcom/?sh=1906bc1c6bd2

113 Diorio, Stephen," How Jaime Punishill Is Accelerating Growth at Lionbridge," *Forbes*, 2021. Available at: https://www.forbes.com/sites/stephendiorio/2021/01/06/how-jaime-punishill-is-accelerating-growth-at-lionbridge/?sh=6dc63a481f1e

116 Diorio, Stephen, "Turning Juniper Networks into an Agile Growth Business," *Forbes*, 2021. Available at: https://www.forbes.com/sites/stephendiorio/2021/10/20/turning-juniper-networks-into-an-agile-growth-business/?sh=4789db46745c

113 Diorio, Stephen, "Aligning Growth Resources with Market Opportunity at RGP," *Forbes*, 2021. Available at: https://www.forbes.com/sites/stephendiorio/2021/09/27/aligning-growth-resources-with-market-opportunity-at-rgp/?sh=3dfb13012174

118 Diorio, Stephen, "Driving Organic Growth at insightsoftware," *Forbes*, 2021. Available at: https://www.forbes.com/sites/stephendiorio/2021/08/31/driving-organic-growth-at-insightsoftware/?sh=5c8b7f26662a

119 Diorio, Stephen, "Accelerating Intelligent Growth at Ryder," *Forbes*, 2021. Available at: https://www.forbes.com/sites/stephendiorio/2021/08/23/accelerating-intelligent-growth-at-ryder/?sh=462bdffb10bc

120 Diorio, Stephen, "Driving Growth in a Rapidly Changing Market at AT&T," *Forbes*, 2021. Available at: https://www.forbes.com/sites/stephendiorio/2021/04/21/driving-growth-in-a-rapidly-changing-market-at-att/?sh=793ccdd07fe1

117 Diorio, Stephen, "Driving Sales Transformation at iconnectiv," *Forbes*, 2021. Available at: https://www.forbes.com/sites/stephendiorio/2021/05/27/driving-sales-transformation-at-iconectiv/?sh=6b2e17244a8a

122 Diorio, Stephen, "How John Jacko Is Leading Growth at Pentair," *Forbes*, 2021. Available at: https://www.forbes.com/sites/stephendiorio/2021/01/19/how-john-jacko-is-leading-growth-at-pentair/?sh=756e5f772f41

123 Diorio, Stephen, "Transforming the Selling Model from Within at Honeywell," *Forbes*, 2021. Available at: https://www.forbes.com/sites/stephendiorio/2021/03/08/transforming-the-selling-model-from-within-at-honeywell/?sh=4ceeb1d059e9

120 Diorio, Stephen, "Driving Industry Leading Growth and Client Experience at mPhasis," *Forbes*, 2021. Available at: https://www.forbes.com/sites/stephen-diorio/2021/07/01/driving-industry-leading-growth-and-client-experience-at-mphasis/?sh=16c0295d46c1

121 Diorio, Stephen, "Enabling a Digital Transformation at Pitney Bowes," *Forbes*, 2021. Available at: https://www.forbes.com/sites/stephendiorio/2021/04/29/enabling-a-digital-transformation-at-pitney-bowes/?sh=2575a61131cc

126 Diorio, Stephen, "Alignment Between Sales and Marketing Drives Growth at Ciena," *Forbes*, 2021. Available at: https://www.forbes.com/sites/stephen-diorio/2021/02/17/alignment-between-sales-and-marketing-drives-growth-at-ciena/?sh=35f53d105cbf

123 Diorio, Stephen, "Leading Commercial Transformation at GHX," *Forbes*, 2021. Available at: https://www.forbes.com/sites/stephendiorio/2021/07/20/leading-commercial-transformation-at-ghx/?sh=52bfbe957db3

128 Diorio, Stephen, "Leading Sustainable Growth at Flexential," *Forbes*, 2021. Available at: https://www.forbes.com/sites/stephendiorio/2021/06/03/leading-sustainable-growth-at-flexential/?sh=3e60d1416313

125 Diorio, Stephen, "Driving Digital Transformation for Clients at Inmar Intelligence," *Forbes*, 2021. Available at: https://www.forbes.com/sites/stephendiorio/2021/08/02/driving-digital-transformation-for-clients-and-inmar-intelligence/?sh=34e155c55a78

130 Diorio, Stephen, "Enabling Growth Through Continuous Improvement at Fortive," *Forbes*, 2021. Available at: https://www.forbes.com/sites/stephendiorio/2021/06/01/enabling-growth-through-continuous-improvement-at-fortive/?sh=5204cf4d6b41

127 Sirius Decisions 2019 RevOps Research Survey. 2019. Available at: https://go.forrester.com/blogs/revenue-operations-and-cmos/

132 Diorio, Stephen, "Driving Growth and Transformation at Avaya," *Forbes*, 2021. Available at: https://www.forbes.com/sites/stephendiorio/2021/06/16/driving-growth-and-transformation-at-avaya/?sh=2a7c07801b11

124 Diorio, Stephen, "Making Customer Engagement the Common Scorecard for Growth," *Forbes*, 2021. Available at: https://www.forbes.com/sites/forbesinsights/2020/02/26/making-customer-engagement-the-common-scorecard-for-growth/#5fa4f49c2188

130 Diorio, McKittrick, Munster, and Smith, "Tipping, Data-Driven Sales Resource Allocation in a 21st Century Commercial Model," The Revenue Enablement Institute, 2021. Available at: https://www.revenueenablement.com/wp-content/uploads/2021/07/Data-Driven-Sales-Resource-Allocation-Paper-7.14.21-FINAL-V1.2.pdf

131 Laney, Doug. *Infonomics: How to Monetize, Manage, and Measure Information as an Asset for Competitive Advantage* (Bibliomotion Inc, 2018). Available at: https://www.amazon.com/Infonomics-Monetize-Information-Competitive-Advantage/dp/1138090387

132 Diorio, Stephen, *Beyond e: 12 Ways Technology is Transforming Sales and Marketing Strategy* (McGraw Hill, 2001). Available at: https://www.amazon.com/Beyond-Technology-Transforming-Sales-Marketing/dp/B000OFYHVE

133 Smith, Michael, "The Financial Impact of Adding a Virtual Account Executive to the Commercial Model," The Revenue Enablement Institute, 2021. Available at: https://www.revenueenablement.com/the-financial-impact-of-adding-a-virtual-account-executive-to-the-commercial-model/

134 Stewart, David, *Accountable Marketing: Linking Marketing Actions to Financial Performance* (MASB, 2016). Available at: https://www.taylorfrancis.com/books/edit/10.4324/9781315639703/accountable-marketing-david-stewart-craig-gugel

135 Haskel, Jonathan and Westlake, Stian, *Capitalism without Capital: The Rise of the Intangible Economy* (Princeton University Press, 2018). Available at: https://www.amazon.com/gp/product/B071P3VGHQ/ref=dbs_a_def_rwt_hsch_vapi_tkin_p1_i0

136 "How RFPIO Supports the 21st Century Commercial Model," Interview with Ganesh Shankar, the CEO of RFPIO, The Revenue Enablement Institute, 2021. Available at: https://www.revenueenablement.com/re100/rfpio/

137 Smith, Michael, "The Growing Talent Crisis in Sales," The Revenue Enablement Institute, 2021. Available at: https://www.revenueenablement.com/the-growing-talent-crisis-in-sales/

138 "Optimizing Sales Territory Design Report," The Sales Management Association, 2018, Available at: https://salesmanagement.org/resource/optimizing-sales-territory-design/

139 "Accelerate Territory Management and Analysis Processes," Alexander Group. Available at: www.alexandergroup.com/insights/accelerate-territory-management-and-analysis-processes/

140 Zoltners, Sinha, and Lorimer, "Why Sales Teams Should Reexamine Territory Design," *Harvard Business Review*, 2015: Available at: https://hbr.org/2015/08/why-sales-teams-should-reexamine-territory-design

141 Sales Comp Administration Survey, Alexander Group International, 2018. Available at: https://www.alexandergroup.com/insights/2018-sales-compensation-hot-topics-survey-executive-summary/

142 Quallen, Jim, "Using Advanced Customer Analytics to Shrink the Bulls Eye and Expand Revenues," The Revenue Enablement Institute, 2021. Available at: https://www.revenueenablement.com/propensity-to-buy-models/

143 "Leading the Effective Sales Force (LESF) Course," Lodish, L, Padmanabhan, P, INSEAD, 2021. Available at: https://coursalytics.com/courses/leading-the-effective-sales-force-insead-business-school

144 "How Varicent Supports the 21st Century Commercial Model," Interview with Marc Altshuller, the CEO of Varicent, The Revenue Enablement Institute, 2021. Available at: https://www.revenueenablement.com/re100/varicent/

145 Mendoza, NF, "Job Trend Analysis Marks Growth of Data Science, AI Roles," *Tech Republic*, 2021. Available at: https://www.techrepublic.com/article/job-trend-analysis-marks-growth-of-data-science-ai-roles/

146 Columbus, Louis, "Roundup of Machine Learning Forecasts and Market Estimates, 2020," *Forbes*, 2020. Available at: https://www.forbes.com/sites/louis-columbus/2020/01/19/roundup-of-machine-learning-forecasts-and-market-estimates-2020/?sh=19b114925c02

147 Hosanagar, Kartik, *A Humans Guide to Machine Intelligence: How Algorithms Are Shaping Our Lives and How We Can Stay in Control* (Viking Press, 2019). Available at: https://www.amazon.com/gp/product/B07DT1HMT3/ref=dbs_a_def_rwt_bibl_vppi_i0

148 Diorio, Stephen, "Advancing the Science of Personalization," *Forbes*, 2021. Available at: https://www.forbes.com/sites/stephendiorio/2021/10/01/advancing-the-science-of-personalization/?sh=403838af1bb6

149 Wharton School of Business, "AI For Business Specialization," Coursera, 2021. https://www.coursera.org/specializations/ai-for-business-wharton.

150 "Is Your Sales Organization Ready for the Next Recession?" Mark Kovac and Jamie Cleghorn, Bain Survey of 870 B2B Executives, 2020. Available at: https://www.bain.com/contentassets/50ddd4821c8145068c6e179b5da4b592/bain_brief-is_your_sales_organization_ready_for_the_next_recession.pdf

151 "Poised for Growth: Six Trends for Realigning Revenue Management Priorities for 2021," Manufacturing and Distribution industry Trends Report, Alexander Group, interviews with 60 executives. Available at: www.alexandergroup.com/insights/poised-for-growth/

152 Freeland, Winberg C., "S-Shaped Response Functions: Implications for Decision Models," *Journal of Operational Research Society*, 2017. Available at: https://www.tandfonline.com/doi/abs/10.1057/jors.1980.186

153 Lodish, L., "An Interactive Salesman's Call Planning System," *Management Science*, 1971. Available at: https://pubsonline.informs.org/doi/abs/10.1287/mnsc.18.4.P25

154 Wharton Executive Education, "Customer Analytics for Growth Using Machine Learning, AI and Big Data," Wharton School of Business, 2021. Available at: https://executiveeducation.wharton.upenn.edu/for-individuals/all-programs/customer-analytics-for-growth-using-machine-learning-ai-and-big-data/

155 Diorio, Stephen and Fink Elissa, "CMO of Tableau: Helping Marketers Make More Data-Driven Decisions About Growth," *Forbes*, 2019. Available at: https://www.forbes.com/sites/forbesinsights/2017/12/21/elissa-fink-cmo-of-tableau-helping-marketers-make-more-data-driven-decisions-about-growth/?sh=49ec2f575778

156 Clear, James, "Atomic Habits: An Easy & Proven Way to Build Good Habits & Break Bad Ones," Avery, 2018. Available at: https://jamesclear.com/marginal-gains

157 Goorha, Saurabh and Iyengar, Raghu, "Voice Analytics and Artificial Intelligence: Future Directions for a Post-COVID World," Wharton white paper. Available at: https://wca.wharton.upenn.edu/white-paper/voice-analytics-and-artificial-intelligence-future-directions-for-a-post-covid-world/

158 Goorha and Raghu, "Voice Analytics and Artificial Intelligence."

159 Diorio, Stephen, "Simplifying the Science of Selling," *Forbes*, 2021. Available at: https://www.forbes.com/sites/stephendiorio/2021/06/09/simplifying-the-science-of-selling/?sh=65f9ba237924

160 Levine-Weinberg, Adam, "Is American Airlines Loyalty Program Really Worth $31.5 Billion?" Motley Fool, 2020. Available at: https://www.fool.com/investing/2020/06/17/is-american-airlines-loyalty-program-really-worth.aspx

161 Diorio, Stephen, "How Transparent Is Your Marketing Spend," MASB analysis of marketing spend mix, *Forbes*, 2019. Available at: https://www.forbes.com/sites/forbesinsights/2019/04/15/how-transparent-is-your-marketing-spend/#2354be9a3ad1

162 Edelman, David, "You Can't Be Customer Centric If You Can't See the Journey," The Revenue Enablement Institute, 1/12/21. Available at: https://www.revenueenablement.com/you-cant-be-customer-centric-if-you-cant-see-the-journey/

163 Diorio, Stephen, "Leading Business Transformation at Scale at Splunk," The Revenue Enablement Institute, January 2022. Available at: https://www.revenueenablement.com/leading-business-transformation-at-scale-at-splunk/

Index

Note: Page references in *italics* refer to figures and tables.

Accountability:
  Commercial Leadership and, 42–43, *59, 236, 237*
  investment returns and, 225
Account-Based Marketing (ABM), 20, 40, 54, 125, 126
Account coverage, 127
Account health & lifetime value metrics, *98,* 135, 136, 137, 140–142
Account management, *98,* 147, 148, 149, 150, 152
Account mapping, 202
Account priorities, advanced analytics and, 50
Account structures, organizing data around, 144
Adams, Tamara, 49, 65
Adamson, Brent, 21, 24, 136
Adler, Meir, 58
Advanced analytics, 90, 117, 146
  Account-based Marketing program and, *203*
  commercial insights and, 91
  creating better measures with, 140–142
  creating business impact with, 178–179
  personalizing selling content, 208
  pricing, proposal development, solution packaging, and, 171–173
  real-time data-driven selling and, *207*
  revenue cycle insights, 199, *199*
  sales force allocation decisions, 166, 167–168
AI for Business Specialization online executive curriculum, 176
Airbnb, 12
Algorithmic models and planning simulations:
  evaluating more scenarios and consensus building with, 191–**192**
  maximizing return on growth assets and, 188–189
Algorithmic segmentation, targeting, and coverage modeling, 166
Algorithmic selling, 22
Allego, 159
Altshuller, Marc, 169, 186
Amazon, 20, 174
American Airlines, 13
Analytics@Wharton, xviii, 176
Apple, 13
Apptus, 172
Artificial Emotional Intelligence (AEI), advances in, 112
Artificial Intelligence (AI), 90, 97, 104, 146
  acceleration of growth and, 131, 132, 143
  advancing science of personalization at Pandora, 173–176
  customer intelligence and use of, 149–150
  data-driven selling, 18
  Intelligent Response Management and, 150, 152, 208
  simulation tools for evaluating growth strategy scenarios, 137–138
  talent development, 158
Association of National Advertisers (ANA), xviii
AT&T, 42, 45, 137, 142, 156, 199
Attrition, sales reps, 31, 156
Augmented Reality (AR), 22, 97, 112, 173
Automation, enhancement of selling channels and, *114,* 115
Avaya, 33, 43, 52, 63, 83
Aviso, 137

Baby boomers, 16
Bajaria, Viral, 96, 126, 128, 133
Big data, converting into commercial
    insights, 132–133
BigTinCan, 105
Bixby, 152
Blue Ridge Partners, 45, 112, 117, 156,
    157, 167, 181
Blueshift, 126, 144, 145
Blum, Jim, 108
Bombora, 144, 149, 166
Borrelle, Bill, 48, 147
Bottom up targets, advanced modeling
    techniques and, 192
Brailsford, Dave, 197
Brand assets, 13
Brown, Howard, xviii, 107, 118, 119, 148
Burgess, Wade, 46, 52, 57, 69
Business Development Reps (BDRs), 21
Business model transformations, 212
Business-to-business (B2B) growth
    budgets, 10
Business value, revenue growth and, 3.
    See also Firm value

Call centers, adoption of, 131
Campaign optimization, Customer
    Intelligence and, *98*, 147, 150
Canonical, 105, 106
Capitalism Without Capital (Haskel &
    Westlake), 13
Captive IQ, 137
Carlson, Teresa, 63
CEOs, xi, xix, 3, 5, 13, 19, 25, 62
CFOs, 13, 20
Change, fear of, 196
Change management:
    Commercial Leadership and,
        59, 236, 237
    hurdle, overcoming, 32–33
Channel design, Commercial
    Architecture and, *59, 236, 239*
Channel Optimization:
    dealer/distributor channels
        and, *98*, 110

direct-to-customer (DTC) channels
    and, *98,* 110, 116
virtual selling capabilities and, *98,*
    110, 111, 112, 113
Chatbots, 22, 101, 114, 116, 117, 124,
    126, 143, 152, 153
Chief Commercial Officer, 20, 70
Chief Customer Officer, 70
Chief Growth Officer, 70, 71
Chief Marketing Officer (CMO), new
    role for, xii, 24, 69–70
Chief of Staff:
    as Revenue Operations "rock
        star," 83–84
Chief Revenue Officer (CRO),
    43, 70, 75
Chief Transformation Officer, 71
Chirico, Jim, 43, 44, 47, 52, 63, 75
Chorus.io, 116
ChowNow, 49, 55, 160, 206
Ciena Network, 46, 78–81, 137,
    140, 142, 199
CIOs, 13
Cisco, 96, 216
Cisco Webex, 22
Citigroup, xviii
Citrix, 8
Clari, 137
Clark, Dana, 120
Cleaning of customer data,
    144–145, 149
Cline, Ron, 138
Closed-loop system:
    integrated learning and
        development and, 160
    for sales rep education, readiness,
        reinforcement, and
        measurement, 160–162, *163,* 164
CMOs, 20
Coaching. *See* Sales coaching
Cognism, 144, 149
Collaboration platforms, 118
Collaborative filtering, 174, 175
Collective[i], 145
Commercial Architecture:

definition and core competencies
of, *59, 236*
go-to-market strategy and, 48,
59, 236, 239
sales force design and, 47, 48–49,
59, 236, *239*
Commercial Asset Management:
content assets and, 58, *59, 236, 242*
data assets and, 57, *59, 236, 242*
technology assets and, 57–58,
59, 236, 242
Commercial assets:
monetizing, 31
strategically managing return on,
99–101, 103
Commercial Enablement:
definition and core competencies
of, *59, 236*
Commercial Insights:
building blocks of Revenue
Operating System and, 92, *92, 98*
data-driven selling and, *38,* 51–52,
59, 236, 240
key performance indicators and,
52–53, *59, 236,* 240
predictive selling insights and, 53–54,
59, 236, 240
in Revenue Operating System, 91, *91*
Commercial Leadership:
accountability and, 42–43,
59, 236, 237
change management and, 43,
59, 236, 237
definition and core competencies
of, *59, 236*
that unifies marketing, sales, and service, 37, 41–44
Commercial Operations:
definition and core competencies
of, *59, 236*
Commercial process, 46–47, *59, 236, 238*
Commercial transformation, continuous incremental improve-
ments in, 196
Common purpose:

creating across the organization, 68
Configuration, pricing, and quotation
(CPQ) tools, 56, 153, 200
Configure, Price, Quote (CPQ) solution
providers, 172
Consensus building, advanced
modeling techniques and, 178,
185–189, 191–192
Consistency, value creation and,
89–90
Contactless selling:
channels, 114
Content assets, Commercial Asset
Management and, 58,
59, 236, 242
Content data, 118
Content management, 10
Intelligent Response
Management *vs.,* 153
Conversational intelligence, 159
tools, 112, 116
Conversica Drift, 116
Cost reduction, 90
CRM technology, 91–92
CROs, 20
Cross-selling, advanced modeling
techniques and, 191
Cumello, Joe, 70, 78, 79, 80, 142
Customer analytics, 10
Customer and account priorities,
advanced modeling tech-
niques and, 192
Customer behavior:
adapting to, 64
changing, growth formula
and, 15–17, *16*
Customer communications, cadence of,
changed growth formula and, 17
Customer conversation data
(conversational intelligence),
112, 116, 118, 147
Customer data assets:
collateralizing, 13–14
Customer Data Platforms, 126,
135, 144, 145

Customer engagement reporting measurements, 80

Customer engagement & seller activity data:
  Account-based Marketing program and, *203*
  converting into insights, 156–157
  revenue cycle insights and, 199, *199*

Customer equity, share price and, 12

Customer experience (CX), 31–32

Customer-Facing Technology:
  e-commerce and, *98,* 123
  marketing automation and, *98,* 123
  mobile infrastructure and, *98,* 123
  owned channel infrastructure and, *98,* 123, 124

Customer Intelligence:
  account management and, *98,* 147, 148, 149, 150, 152
  campaign optimization and, *98,* 147, 150
  recommender engines and, *98,* 147, 148, 150
  response management and, *98,* 147, 148, 150

Customer lifetime value, 19

Customer loyalty, revenue expansion and, xvi

Customer profiles:
  enriching, 145, 149
  incorporating digital marketing data in, 126

Customer Relationship Management (CRM), 51, 117
  adoption of, 131
  simplifying selling workflow and, 200
  updating with real-time customer engagement and behavior data, 106–107
  worldwide spending on, 18

Customer scoring and value models, advanced analytics and, 185

Customer Success Managers (CSMs), 49

Customer treatment, 30, 165

Cvent, 118, 120

CXOs, xix, 13, 25, 43, 68, 70

Dashboards, monitoring territory performance with, 170

Data assets, Commercial Asset Management and, 58, *59, 236, 242*

Datadog, 126

Data-driven selling, 38, 51–52, *59, 236, 240*

Data orchestration, 144

Dealer/distributor channels, *98,* 110

DealHub, 172

Deciling, 53

Decision science, 186

Dell, 111

Demandbase, 127

Demand unit waterfall metrics, 140, 141

DHL, 137, 142

DialSource, 167

Digital asset management, 107, *98, 103,* 104

Digital channels, adoption of, 131

Digital selling infrastructure, defining, 123–124

Digital Selling Platform, 108–110

Diorio, Mike, 126

Direct selling, *98,* 110, 112

Direct-to-customer (DTC) channels, 22, *98,* 110, 116

Discover.org, 144

Downie, Chris, 49, 100

Duke CMO Survey, 18, 97, 117

Earned media management, 10

EBITDA, 12, 23, 45

e-commerce, *98,* 126

Econometrics modeling analysis, 188

Edeling, Alexander, 225

Edelman, David, xviii, 44, 95

80/20 rule, 156, 108

Elliott, Gerri, 70

Emarsys, 127

Emotion processing tools, 112

Engagement Data Hub, 93, 98, 135
    customer engagement data *98,*
        143, 145, 146
    financial transaction data and,
        98, 143, 145
    product usage data and, *98,*
        143, 145, 146
Equity Trust Company, 55
Errigo, Sam, 235
Everstring, 144
Extreme Reach, 128

Facebook, 124
Field selling economics, 21, 31
Financial accountability, *16,* 20
Financial transaction data, Engagement
    Data Hub and, *98,* 143, 145
Firm value:
    financial link between growth
        and, 7–10, *8*
    tangible *vs.* intangible assets
        and, 14–15
First-party data, 118, 126
Fischer, Marc, 225
5G communications, 22, 97, 112
Flexential, 19, 49, 100
Ford, Peter, 53, 54, 56, 197
Forecast accuracy metrics, *98,*
    135, 137, 138
Fortive Business Systems, 140,
    146, 197, 199
4D revenue teams, 17, 111, 112, 172–173
4Ps of selling, 171

Gainsight, 159
GEICO, 111
General Electric (GE), xviii, 23, 89
General Motors (GM), 23
Genius Bar (Apple), xv
Ghoshal, Sumantra, 90
GHX Global Healthcare Exchange, 12,
    43, 70, 164, 197
Gleason, John, 114, 146, 167, 168
Gong.io, 116
Google, 8, 17, 124, 152, 176

Go-to-market investment mix, 111
Go-to-market strategy, 48, *59, 236, 239*
Growth:
    financial link between firm value
        and, 7–10, *8*
    organic, xi, 10, 43, 83, 84, 89, 215
    scalable, 8, 20, 103, 139, 195, 215, 234
    science of, research on, xviii
    sustainable, 103
    as a team sport, 19–20, 62, 82
Growth assets:
    description of, 90–91
    managing, 12, 13, 30, 99, 100
    modern growth investment mix
        and, 95, *95*
Growth leaders:
    emerging new generation
        of, 41, 67–71
Growth team, creating common
    purpose for, 141
Growth technology portfolio, 68
Guided selling, 101

Hanssens, Dominique, 10, 224
Haptics, 112
Haskel, Jonathan, 13
Healey, Joe, 77, 78
Hierarchical Bayesian analytics, 188
Highspot, 96, 105, 106, 150
Historic performance baselines, 192
Hitachi Vantara, 55, 58, 96,
    108–110, *110,* 161
Honeywell, 19, 43, 49, 65, 70, 74, 197
Hosanagar, Kartik, 173, 176
Howe, Ben, 9
Howland, Jim, 9
HPE, 118, 120, 206
HubSpot, 7, 101, 116, 124, 126
Hull, 144
Hyper-growth businesses, value and
    growth in, 7

IBM.com, 111
iCIMS, 52, 53 141
iconnectiv, 53, 56, 197

Ideal Customer Profile (ICP), 53
Inmar Intelligence, 103, 161, 197
INSEAD, 167, 186
insightsoftware, 33
Insight Squared, 144, 149
Intangible assets, 12–15
Intelligent Response
  Management, 150, 152
Iyengar, Raghu, xviii, 22, 51, 112, 188

Jabmo, 144
Jacko, John, 46, 48, 64
Jewell, Marcus, 82, 97, 115
J&J, 70
Jones, Reginald, 23
Joos, Don, 65, 66, 67
Jules, Frank, 45, 50, 64, 156
Juniper Networks, 33, 82–83, 96, 97,
  115, 130, 216

Kaizen, 89, 196
Kaon Interactive, 173
Karkos, Denise, 41, 140, 141
Kelley, Scott, 70, 84, 85, 86, 164
Kelly, Bob, xviii, 61, 62
Key performance indicators (KPIs), 51
Kimberly-Clark, 70
Konica Minolta, 33, 235

Lamarca, Giovanni, 68
Laney, Doug, xviii, 14, 100, 143
Lattice, 144
Lautenbach, Marc, 76
Leadership models, 73–86
  the Chief of Staff, 73, 83–84
  the Federation, 73, 77–83
  the Tsar, 73, 74–76
Leadership structure, 63–65
Lead prioritization models, 166
LeanData, 144
Lean Manufacturing, 89, 196
Learning management system,
  98, 103, 104
LinkedIn, 43
Lionbridge, 42, 128, 139

Lodish, Leonard, 133, 148, 165, 167,
  178, 185, 188
Long-Term Impact of Marketing
  (Hanssens), 10
Lucas, Steve, 53, 69, 141, 142
Lytics, 144

Machine Learning (ML), 50, 131, 132,
  138, 143, 150–153, 173–176, 208
Management models, evolution of, 23
Marcellin, Mike, 82, 83, 97, 130
Marketing, xi
  accountability, 139–140
  increasing ambiguity and, xii–xiii
  outdated traditional role of
    leaders in, 67
  skill sets, xiii
Marketing Accountability Standards
  Board (MASB), xviii, 12, 19, 95,
  95, 139, 224
Marketing automation, 98, 123, 127
Marketing Automation Platforms, 127
Marketing Sciences Institute (MSI),
  xviii, 11, 130, 225
Marketo (Adobe), 9, 124, 127, 137, 142
Matlock, Robin, 130, 140
Mauldin, Jennifer, 103, 161
McChrystal, General Stanley, 112, 113
McKittrick, Jeff, xviii, 42, 55, 58, 96,
  108, 109, 119, 161, 162
McLaughlin, Melinda, 128
Microsoft Teams, 116, 118
Millennial buyers, 17
Miller Heiman, 158
MindTickle, 159
Mobile infrastructure, 98, 123
Modeling technologies, advanced:
  to define growth strategies
    and, 138–139
  to evaluate scenarios, 178–179,
    185–189, 191–192
  to improve sales productivity, 157
Morgan Stanley Private Equity, 8, 9
Mphasis, 52
Munster, Greg, xviii, 105, 106

Music Genome Project
(Pandora), 174, 175

Natural Language Processing (NLP),
118, 147, 149
Net Annual Recurring Revenues, 7
Netflix, 173
Net Promoter Score (NPS), 45
"New school" digital buying
behavior, 15
Next-best-action guides, 101
1919 Investment Counsel, 153
Node, 145, 149

Openprise, 126, 145
Opportunity allocation, advanced
modeling techniques and, 191
Opportunity potential, *98,* 135, 136, 136,
140–142, 185
Opportunity prioritization, *98,* 165,
166, 167, 168
Optimize coverage and targeting, *98,*
165, 166, 168
Optymize, 166
Oracle, 81–82
Oracle Eloqua, 127
Oracle Sales CX, 144, 149
Order management tools, 56
Organic growth, xi, 10, 43, 83,
84, 98, 215
Organizational Knowledge
Sharing, 11, 130
Outreach.io, 116, 144, 145, 150, 159
Owned digital channel infrastructure:
Customer-Facing Technology
and, *98,* 123
operating budget spending on, 18

Pace, Tony, 139
Padmanabhan, V (Paddy), 167, 185
Pandora, 141, 173–176
Pardot, 124, 127
Paust, Kirsten, 51, 140, 146
Pentair, 43, 47, 48, 64, 70, 199
People.ai, 144, 145, 149, 167

Perception AI, 112
Personalization, 20, 130, 149, 153
Phillips, Charles, 81
Phipps, Jason, 78, 79, 80, 81, 140
Pitney Bowes, 48, 76, 146, 147
Podium, 116, 124, 126
Predictive lead scoring, 166
Predictive selling insights, 53–54,
59, 236, 240
Pricing, *98,* 171–172
Process workflow automation, SPM
solutions and, 170
Product telemetry data, 146
Product usage data, *98,* 143, 145, 146
Propensity to buy targeting models, 167
Proposal, RFP, and pricing
guidance, 172
PROS, 172
Punishill, Jaime, 17, 42, 128,
130, 139, 152

Qorus, 172
QStream, 159
Quality of Engagement (QOE)
measurements, 80
Quallen, Jim, 157
Quicken Loans, 9, 12
Quota assignment, 178, 179
advanced analytics and, 50
automating process of, 166, 170
Quota planning, digitizing process
of, 168–170
Quota type and definition, advanced
modeling techniques and, 192

Rabin, David, 125
Radical business performance
improvement, 90
Radical Change (Ghoshal), 90
Raju, Jagmohan, 30, 171
Ramp new sellers, Talent Development
and, *98,* 157, 158, 160, 161, 164
Readiness and development, 55,
59, 236, 241
Real-time coaching, 20, 160

Real-time data-driven selling,
206, *207,* 216
Real-time scripting, 101
Recommender engines, 101, 114
Recorded conversations, conversational
intelligence, 118
Recurring revenues:
customer lifetime value
management and, 19
supporting, 32
Regression analysis, 188
Reibstein, David, xviii, 10, 190, 191
Remote selling, 21
Request for proposal (RFP), 104, 108,
109, 150, 153, 172, 208
Resource allocation:
econometrics modeling
analysis and, 188
optimizing with data, 30
sales, advanced modeling
tools and, 184
scenario development and, 170
Resource Optimization:
description of, 93
within Revenue Operating System,
92, 93, *98,* 165–170
Response management, *98,*
147, 148, 150
flawed approach to financial accountability and, 20
Retention of top talent:
learning and development process
and, 198, 204–205
Talent Development and, *98,* 157, 158
Return on asset (ROA), 14
Rev.com, 33, 43, 46, 49, 52, 57, 69, 83
Revenue Acceleration
Platforms, 118, 135
Revenue attribution models, 224, 228
Revenue cycle, 5, *6*
eliminating revenue leakage
across, 29
getting better visibility into,
198–199, *199*
lifecycle insights, 199, *199*

tools for taking control of, 233–235
Revenue Enablement, 92, 103–107
Customer Relationship Management
and, *98,* 103, 104,
106–107, 109, 110
Digital Asset Management system
and, 98, 103, 103, 104
Learning Management System and,
98, 103, 104
within Revenue Operating System,
92, *92, 98,* 103–110
Sales Automation and, *98,* 103, 104
Revenue Enablement Institute, 29
Revenue Enhancement, 93
digitization and, *98,* 171, 172–173
personalization and, *98,* 171,
172, 173–176
pricing and, *98,* 171–172
within Revenue Operating System,
92, 93, *98,* 171–176
value engineering and, *98,* 171
Revenue expansion, 90
Revenue forecasts, 184
Revenue growth, 3
relationship to firm value
and, 7–10, 8
Revenue Intelligence, 93
account health & lifetime value
metrics and, 98, 135, 136,
137, 140–142
forecast accuracy metrics and, *98,*
135, 137, 138
opportunity potential metrics and,
98, 135, 136, 140–142
revenue cycle insights and, *199*
within Revenue Operating System,
92, 93, *98,* 135–142
seller performance metrics and, *98,*
135, 136, 137, 140–142
Revenue.io, 96, 106, 107, 116, 117, 118,
120, 122, 145, 148, 160
Revenue Operating System,
description of, 92–94
Revenue Operating System, building
blocks of, 97, *98*

Channel Optimization building block, *92,* 93, *98,* 110–122

Customer-Facing Technology building block, *92,* 93, *98,* 123–130

Customer Intelligence building block, *92,* 93, *98,* 147–153

Engagement Data Hub building block, *92,* 93, *98,* 143–147

Resource Optimization building block, *92,* 93, *98,* 165–170

Revenue Enablement building block, 92, *92, 98,* 103–110

Revenue Enhancement building block, *92,* 93, *98,* 171–176

Revenue Intelligence building block, *92,* 93, *98,* 135–142

Talent Development building block, *92,* 93, *98,* 157–164

Revenue Operations:
goal of, 235
importance of, 8, 25, 27
two component systems of, 4, 37, 195

Revenue Operations Management System, Six Pillars of, 37–60, 89
Commercial Architecture, 38, *38,* 47–50, *59*
Commercial Asset Management, 38, *38,* 56–58, *59*
Commercial Enablement, 38, *38,* 54–56, *59*
Commercial Insights, 38, *38,* 50–54, *59*
Commercial Leadership, 37, *38,* 41–44, *59*
Commercial Operations, 38, *38,* 44–47, *59*

Revenue Operations Maturity Assessment, *236–242*

Revenue Optimization:
opportunity prioritization and, *98,* 165, 166, 167, 168
optimize coverage and targeting and, *98,* 165, 166, 168

sales resource allocation and, *98,* 165, 166
selling time optimization and, *98,* 165, 166, 167

Revenue Value Chain (RVC), 235

RFIs, 150, 153

RFPIO, 96, 150, 153, 172, 209

RFQs, 153

Rockefeller, John D., 23

Rockridge Growth Equity, 8, 9, 12

Rogers, Bruce, xviii, 100

Ryder Systems, 114, 115, 146, 167, 168

SABRE strategy simulation, 170, 181, 190

Sales, xi
outdated traditional role of leaders in, 67
rising complexity in, xiv–xv
silo mentality and, xi
teamwork across executive functions and, 63–64

Sales analytics, 104

Sales automation platforms 159

Sales coaching 122, 159, 160

Sales enablement, 22, 58, 105

Sales Engagement Platforms, 126, 135, 144

Sales force:
economics, 31
design, 47, 48–49, *236, 239*
size and structure, 168–170

Salesforce.com, 91, 120, 122, 126, 129

Sales forecasts, 185, 187

SalesLoft, 116, 144, 145, 150

Sales Management Association (SMA), xviii, 91, 157

Sales Performance Management (SPM) solutions and tools, 169, 170

Sales playbooks, 101, 204

Sales readiness (sales training), 105, 107

Sales resource allocation, *98,* 165, 166

Sales response function, 185, 187

Sales waterfall models, 224

SAP, xviii
  Demand Generation Board at, 81–82
  eMarketing Cloud, 127
  Sales Cloud, 166
Scalable growth, 8, 20, 103, 139,
      195, 215, 234
Scalable technologies, 29–30, 32, 40
Scenario planning, advanced modeling
      techniques, 178, 185–189,
      191–192
Schneider Electric, xviii
Seamless.ai, 145, 149, 167
Seller activity data, *98,* 143,
      144, 145, 146
Seller assignments, 133
Seller capacity, calculating with
      advanced analytics, 185
Seller experience, 31
  Seller performance metrics, 98, 135,
      136, 137, 140–142
Seller productivity and profitability,
      185, 187
Selling channels, 198, 206–207
Selling content, 100
Selling content supply chain,
      198, 208–210
  Intelligent Response Management,
      208, 209, 209
Selling systems:
  optimizing design variables in, 30
Selling time optimization, *98,*
      165, 166, 167
Selling workflow:
  simplifying, 106, 198, 200–201, *201*
  streamlining at Hitachi Vantara,
      108–110, *110*
Sentiment analysis, 149
Service, xi
  outdated traditional role of
      leaders in, 67
  progressive emergence of, xv–xvii
  silo mentality and, xi
  teamwork across executive functions
      and, 63–64
Shankar, Ganesh, 153

Shareholder return, sources of, 7
Showpad, 105
Siemens, xviii
Silos, 67, 95, 148, 204
  breaking down, 61, 62, 96, 113
  in complex enterprises, 213
  data, 118–119
  technology, 96
  territory and quota planning
      process, 169
Simplification of selling workflow, 106,
      198, 200–201
Simulation tools:
  for evaluating growth strategy
      scenarios, 137–138
  used in various professions, 189–190
Siri, 152
Siris Capital, 65
Sirius XM, 83, 141, 142, 174, 175
Situational Awareness Room (SAR), 113
6Sense, 96, 126, 127, 128, 133, 144,
      149, 167, 202
Six Pillars of the Management System.
      See Revenue Operations
Six Sigma, 89, 196
Skill development, Talent Development
      and, *98,* 157, 158, 159, 160,
      161, 162, 164
Slack, 118
Sloan, Alfred, 23
Smart Actions, 195, 233, 234
  definition of and four criteria for, 196
  getting better visibility into revenue
      cycle, 198–199, *199,* 224
  making selling channels more
      effective, 198, 205–207
  sharing marketing insights
      with frontline sellers, 198,
      201–202, 204
  simplifying selling workflow, 198,
      200–201, *201*
  spanning of functions with, 223–224
  streamlining/personalizing selling
      content supply chain, 198,
      208–210, *209*

Smith, Christian, 63, 76, 104
Smith, Michael, xviii, 30, 114,
    169, 170, 181
Snowflake, 126, 144, 145, 147
Spatial, 173
Spears, Stephen, 63
Splunk, 42, 43, 63, 70, 75, 83, 104
Sports teams, business transformation
    lessons of, 134–135
Spotify, 176
Sprinklr, 124, 126
Standard Oil, 23
Stewart, David, 139
Subscription models, xvi
Sullivan, Stephanie, 160
Systems, definition of, 5

Talent Development:
    developing skills and capabilities, *98,*
        157, 159, 160, 161, 162, 164
    finding new talent, *98,* 157, 158, 160
    ramping new sellers, *98,* 157, 158,
        160, 161, 164
    retaining top talent, *98,* 157, 158
    within Revenue Operating System,
        92, 93, *98,* 157–164
Tangible assets, firm value and, 14
TD Ameritrade, 141
Tealium, 144
    Teamwork facilitating, 63–64
Technology assets, 57–58, *59, 236, 242*
Technology ecosystems, changed
    growth formula and, *16,* 18
TechTarget, 150, 166
Teleweb channels, 117
Tengram Partners, 8
Terminus, 127
Territory and Quota Planning (TQP)
    process, 179–180
Territory definitions, boundaries, and
    assignments, 50, 133, 184, 192
Territory design, 166
Territory planning, 165, 168–170
Third-party data, 144
Thoma Bravo, 9

3D content creation platforms, 173
Tipping, Cam, xviii, 53, 170,
    181, 186, 190
Top-down quota planning, 184
Torrence, Corey, xviii, 45, 47, 57, 61, 62,
    64, 71, 112, 117
Total Billed Revenue (TBR), 45
Total Quality Management, 89, 196
Totango, 159
Toyota, 89
TPx Communications, 65–67, 83
    Training, for sales reps, 155, 156, 158,
        159, 160, 161, 162, 164
Treasure Data, 145
Trichon, Patrice, 153

Uber, 70
United Airlines, 13, 143
United Rentals, xviii, 114
Unity, 173
USIC Genome Project, 174
US Joint Special Operations Task
    Force, 113

Valuation, growth and, xi. *See also* Firm
        value; Growth; Revenue growth
    Value drivers, description of, 91
Value engineering, *98,* 171
Varicent, 96, 166, 169, 186
Vendavo, 172
Virtual sales reps, 116
Virtual assistants, 112
Virtual Reality (VR) content, 173
Virtual selling, *98,* 110, 111, 112, 113
Visibility:
    into the revenue cycle,
        198–199, 199, 224
    into revenue team performance,
        improving, 159
Vista Equity Partners, 8, 9
VMware, 130, 140

Wahbe, Robert, 96
WalkMe, 42, 55, 58, 96, 97, 161,
    162, 167

"War game" scenarios, AI-driven
  simulation-based tools
  and, 189–191
War on terror, 113
Websites and e-commerce, 123
West, Stacy, 77, 78
Westlake, Stian, 13
Wharton Business School:
  "Customer Analytics for Growth
    Using Machine Learning, AI,
    and Big Data" course at, 188
  "Leading the Effective Sales Force"
    at, 167, 185–186
  pricing optimization
    research, 171–172

Sports Analytics and Business
  Initiative at, 134
Wong, Scott, 174, 175, 176
Workload estimates, 185, 187
Wyner, Adi, 134, 135

Xactly, 137, 166
Xant.ai, 116, 126, 144, 145, 149, 166
XiQ, 144, 149

Zhang, John, 30, 171
Zilliant, 172
Zoom, 22, 116, 118, 145
ZRG Associates, 68
Zylotech, 144, 145